M000307528

THE RISE AND DECLINE
of AMERICAN RELIGIOUS
FREEDOM

The Rise and Decline of American Religious Freedom

Steven D. Smith

Harvard University Press

Cambridge, Massachusetts
London, England
2014

Copyright © 2014 by the President and Fellows of Harvard College

All rights reserved

Printed in the United States of America

Library of Congress Cataloging-in-Publication Data

Smith, Steven D. (Steven Douglas), 1952-

The rise and decline of American religious freedom / Steven D. Smith.

pages   cm

Includes bibliographical references and index.

ISBN 978-0-674-72475-4 (alk. paper)

1. Freedom of religion—United States.   2. Church and state—United States.   I. Title.

KF4783.S645 2014

342.7308'52—dc23   2013021352

To Merina

Still, always

Contents

This work bears the title of an essay in the strictest sense of the word. No one is more conscious than the writer with what limited means and strength he has addressed himself to a task so arduous. . . . In the wide ocean upon which we venture, the possible ways and directions are many; and the same studies which have served for this work might easily, in other hands, not only receive a wholly different treatment and application, but lead also to essentially different conclusions. Such indeed is the importance of the subject that it still calls for fresh investigation, and may be studied with advantage from the most varied points of view. Meanwhile we are content if a patient hearing is granted us, and if this book be taken and judged as a whole.

—JACOB BURCKHARDT, *The Civilization of the Renaissance in Italy*

The Rise and Decline
of American Religious
Freedom

The Standard Story
and the Revised Version

In good conscience I can concede, cheerfully, this much: the oft-told, much beloved story of religious freedom in America is not wholly false. In fact, the story contains a number of partial truths. And yet a collection of partial truths can combine, as we know, to make up a tale that is, in the aggregate, profoundly misleading. As in this instance.

The Standard Story

The story of American religious freedom has been told in many places and many ways. But most of the venerable tellings include several or all of the following themes:

1. *Americans as Enlightened innovators.* When Americans committed themselves in their new Constitution to church-state separation and the free exercise of religion, they were initiating a novel and even radical "lively experiment." Or so it is typically supposed.

For centuries, under the pattern and practices of what we sometimes describe as "Christendom," political and religious authorities had imposed religious orthodoxies on their subjects and had repressed dissent through laws punishing heresy, blasphemy, and apostasy. This orientation was on macabre display in the Inquisition and in the execution of presumed heretics, such as the defiant English Protestants burned at the stake under Bloody Mary and celebrated in John Foxe's legendary *Book of Martyrs*. The American founders, freed up by the Enlightenment, boldly broke from this centuries-old pattern. They thereby achieved what the eminent historian of religion Sidney Mead described as "one of the two most profound revolutions that had occurred in the history of the church."[1] (The first revolution, Mead thought, was the Constantinian revolution that had initiated Christendom fourteen centuries earlier. So the second revolution—the American one—in effect overthrew the first, Christian revolution.)

By now, of course, the American innovation has come to be accepted in much of the world, if not in its particulars at least in its basic commitment to religious freedom, and has been adopted in international law. But at the time Americans adopted the commitment, it represented an audacious new vision and a bold break with the past.

2. *The monumental, meaning-full First Amendment.* The Americans' daring departure was accomplished by their adoption of the First Amendment—in particular, of that amendment's religion clauses, which provided that "Congress shall make no law respecting an establishment of religion, or prohibiting the free exercise thereof." That tersely momentous declaration reflected a deliberate decision by the Founders to strike out on a fresh path in the relations between government and religion.

More specifically, the First Amendment's religion clauses embraced sweeping commitments to preventing government from sponsoring or intruding in religion, to ensuring that citizens of all faiths (or of none) would be treated equally, and to keeping government religiously neutral and secular. Even though these commitments were not fully honored and perhaps not fully comprehended at the time, they were in some sense contained or implicit in the First Amendment from the outset. So more recent American history in this area has consisted of the (admittedly imperfect) recovery and implementation of the content of that celebrated provision.

Consistent with this theme, judges, lawyers, scholars, politicians, pundits, and citizens in general often refer back, approvingly and even reverently, to commitments or principles presumed to have been embraced by the Founders and embodied in the First Amendment. The converse is also true: if the First Amendment can arouse reverence, perceived departures from the provision's presumed meaning can provoke indignation. Judges, presidents, and other officials seen as deviating in these matters are censured for misunderstanding, subverting, or betraying the Constitution's (supposedly) long-standing commitments.

3. The long, dark interlude. Alas, the bold and Enlightened principles embodied in the First Amendment were not realized overnight. On the contrary, even as Americans were undertaking momentous new commitments and deliberately building these commitments into their Constitution, they were simultaneously reverting to older, unenlightened ways. So the new nation persisted for generations in practices that were fundamentally incompatible with constitutional principles.

Some states—most prominently Massachusetts and Connecticut—maintained state-supported churches for decades after the Constitution was adopted. There and elsewhere, dissenters who defied the religious consensus of their communities were occasionally prosecuted for blasphemy, and far from standing up in defense of the dissenters, judges tended to support and even applaud the prosecutions. From the founding period through the middle of the twentieth century, governmental institutions at all levels, from Congress on down to local public schools, sponsored and supported Protestant Christianity in a variety of ways. And Americans persecuted, or discriminated against, or at best ignored and marginalized the adherents of minority faiths—Native Americans, Catholics, Jews, Mormons, Jehovah's Witnesses, and others—not to mention agnostics and atheists.

During this long relapse, the founding generation's commitments to religious freedom and equality remained mostly on hold, as the Supreme Court did little or nothing to honor those commitments. Worse yet, the Court itself sometimes flagrantly traversed constitutional principles: an embarrassing instance was the Court's notoriously sectarian declaration in *Holy Trinity Church v. United States* that "this is a Christian nation."[2]

4. The modern (court-led) realization. Beginning in the 1940s, however, and especially from the 1960s on, a now more courageously committed Supreme Court acted to redeem the constitutional promise of religious freedom. Sometimes in the face of powerful popular and political resistance, the Court moved to end school prayer and Bible reading in the nation's public schools and to terminate the public subsidization of religious schools. Especially since the 1980s, the courts have struggled, albeit in vacillating fashion, to eliminate sectarian public displays and expressions—publicly sponsored nativity scenes, crosses, Ten Commandments displays, and the like—that symbolically treat people outside the mainstream faiths as second-class citizens.

All these themes are familiar features in the standard story of American religious freedom. They are typically presented and accepted as well-established facts or obvious truisms. A fifth theme is more recent and contested and thus perhaps is not as securely part of the standard story, but the idea is nonetheless taken as pretty plainly true in some circles.

5. *The conservative religious retreat from constitutional principles.* In recent decades, the so-called Religious Right has become active and politically influential, and the American political system has accordingly experienced a retreat from or even a degradation of the constitutional principles of religious freedom.[3] Religion has become more conspicuous in public life and in politics, and the courts have sometimes been loath to honor constitutional commitments. In an article tellingly titled "Life after the Establishment Clause," the late Steven Gey, a respected constitutional scholar, worried that "the new majority on the Supreme Court is about to embark on a wholesale reinterpretation" that "would abandon any pretense of church/state separation."[4]

As a result of these developments, the distinctive American experiment in religious freedom and equality—and in Enlightened governance generally—has been placed in jeopardy. Writers of an apocalyptic bent foretell an imminent "theocracy."[5] The late Ronald Dworkin reported that "[m]any Americans are horrified"—it is not wholly clear whether Dworkin counted himself among the company of the horror-stricken—"by the prospect of a new dark age imposed by militant superstition; they fear a black, know-nothing night of ignorance in which America becomes an intellectually backward and stagnant theocracy."[6] (Dworkin was speaking in the Bush era; it may be that the election and reelection of Barack Obama have calmed these fears to some extent.)

These four and often five themes run through a good deal of writing and speaking about religious freedom in America. Not every speaker or author tells the story in the same way, of course. Scholars may offer more sophisticated and hedged versions of the story; politicians, pundits, and preachers may put forth bolder but more simplistic versions. And not everyone gives equal emphasis to each theme. More patriotic or celebratory renderings may omit or quickly pass over the embarrassing third theme—what I have called the "long, dark interlude" in which commitments to religious freedom and equality ostensibly were suppressed or ignored and religious minorities were discriminated against or oppressed. Conversely, more lachrymose treatments may dwell on (and sometimes, it seems, even revel in) these unfortunate episodes,[7] and they may play up the persistence of American intolerance and hypocrisy even in more recent times. Despite such differences, these recurring themes are sufficiently common and connected that I think it is fair to talk about a "standard story" of American religious freedom.

And, truth be told, the standard story is a pretty compelling one with a number of winsome features. For one thing, the story is by now reassuringly familiar; in some circles, at least, it has taken on a commonsensical "as we all know" quality. For another, the story is by and large flattering to Americans (except those Americans associated with earlier or contemporary retrenchments) and especially to judges and their self-appointed advisers, that is, lawyers and legal scholars. In the typical renderings, Americans (and especially the modern judiciary and legal profession) come across, by and large, as courageous, principled, visionary, and enlightened. Religious freedom is sometimes depicted as America's gift to the world.[8]

The standard story also has the formidable rhetorical advantage that it makes the history of the legal treatment of religion run closely parallel to the well-known, oft-recited history of the legal treatment of race. In each story, the American Republic begins with a commitment to new and noble and essentially egalitarian ideals. "All men are created equal": that fundamental "proposition" to which the new nation was "dedicated" (as Abraham Lincoln later put it) contains radical implications for both race and religion. Having made these commitments, the nation lapses back into old patterns, maintaining slavery and then Jim Crow segregation and promoting Protestant Christianity and discriminating against religious minorities. Then, in the middle of the twentieth century, a more enlightened Supreme Court rededicates itself to the founding-era ideals in visionary and controversial landmark decisions—*Brown v. Board of Education*, the school-prayer decisions— and then, in the face of recalcitrant public opinion and political opposition, courageously goes on in later cases to insist that Americans honor those ideals. And yet . . . resistance persists, judicial commitment eventually wanes, and practice continues to fall short of full compliance. With the end of the progressive Warren Court and the advent of the less visionary Burger, Rehnquist, and now Roberts Courts, judicial resolve has slackened or even reversed, thereby jeopardizing the distinctive American commitments to racial and religious equality. So Americans today may need to recommit themselves to revered ideals lest these be lost or abandoned.

In sum, the standard story is an appealing, edifying, usefully orienting one—a story that is mostly reassuring but is also possessed of critical bite that can arouse to action. Still, it is perhaps permissible to ask: for all its endearing features and its rhetorical power, is the story actually, well, . . . true?

As I have already indicated, all the ideas that make up the story contain a measure of truth—sometimes, as with the idea of "Americans as enlightened innovators," a generous measure. And yet, taken individually, each of these themes is deceptively incomplete, or worse. Aggregated, the standard themes add up to a story that is, if not flatly false, at least fundamentally misleading. Or so I shall argue in this book.

Some of the themes are misleading because they state partial truths that, separated from essential companion or complementary truths, give a distorted picture of the American experience. The idea of "Americans as enlightened innovators" falls into this category, I believe: while properly stressing the ways in which Americans departed from immediately preceding practice, this theme typically overlooks or understates the even more important ways in which the American approach was a recovery and consolidation of earlier Christian precedents, arguments, and campaigns—with a little paganism thrown in for good measure. Other themes are misleading because mislabeled or mischaracterized: although the standard tellings are based on elementary facts, they convey those facts under descriptions or assessments that are fundamentally wrong and even backwards. The idea of "the modern (court-led) realization" is an instance of this sort of mistake. To be sure, the courts did begin in the mid-twentieth century to intervene aggressively in matters of religion. But in reality those interventions have done more to undermine and undo the distinctive American approach to religious freedom than to realize it. Or so I will argue.

Still other ideas are inaccurate, for the most part, on the level of basic fact. I will argue that the familiar idea of the "monumental First Amendment" is an instance of an assumption, taken by many as an obvious truth, that is for the most part simply mistaken. In reality, the enactors of the First Amendment's religion clauses did not intend by them to do anything radically novel, or indeed anything much at all. On the contrary, the purpose of the clauses was to preserve the then-existing political situation with respect to religion.

These are impertinent and uncouth claims, perhaps—hardly claims that I can expect anyone to accept lightly. The rest of the book will be devoted to explaining and supporting them. It may be helpful, though, to preview very briefly the revised version of American religious freedom that I will be presenting.

The Revised Version

For each of the themes that make up the standard story, the revised version will develop a different idea that will sometimes complement and sometimes contradict the counterpart theme in the standard story.

1. *American religious freedom as a (mostly Christian, marginally pagan) retrieval and consolidation.* The standard story is correct to note that in embracing church-state separation and freedom of conscience, Americans departed from the pattern of the immediately preceding period in Europe—a pattern repeated in diverse ways in the American colonies—in which the church was viewed basically as a subordinate department of the state and religious uniformity was legally enforced. Even so, the American constitutional commitments were hardly concocted ex nihilo. They reflected a recovery, adaptation, and consolidation, under the fresh circumstances of the New World, of themes that went back centuries—of the medieval theme of *libertas ecclesiae* (freedom of the church) and of the more recently evolved corollary theme of freedom of the "inner church" of conscience. These were distinctively Christian notions. And the Enlightenment, far from repudiating Christianity wholesale, actually served as a conduit by which these Christian notions were imported into the creation of the new Republic. The overall American approach to religious pluralism also incorporated recognizably pagan attitudes that had been taken up in the Enlightenment, although these were less central and distinctive.

Thus the dimension of continuity in the American approach was at least as important as the dimension of innovation. And the Christian element was more essential than any Enlightenment-inspired revolt against Christianity.

2. *The unpretentious, unpremeditated First Amendment.* Far from embracing grand and novel principles of religious freedom, the religion clauses of the First Amendment were understood at the time as doing nothing especially noteworthy—which is why (to the occasional consternation of modern historians) they were enacted with almost no discussion or controversy either in Congress or in the state ratifying conventions. The central purpose of the clauses was simply to reaffirm the jurisdictional status quo—to acknowledge in writing that even under the new Constitution, matters involving the establishment and exercise of religion would remain the business of the states, as nearly everyone agreed they should be. The clauses did not reflect the acceptance by Americans of any commitment to religious equality, secular government, or governmental neutrality in matters of religion.

Insofar as the clauses turned out to have momentous consequences (contrary to what their enactors contemplated), these consequences were more backed into, so to speak, than knowingly embraced. In keeping the most essential matters of religion within the jurisdiction of the states, the religion clauses stipulated that these matters would not be within the province of the national government. Consequently, there could be no national church, and no interference by the national government with the exercise of religion—not because the enactors had deliberately constitutionalized commitments to church-state separation or religious freedom, but because these matters were not within the jurisdiction of the national government. Over time, though, this jurisdictional purpose came to be largely forgotten, leaving the nation with what seemed to be more substantive constitutional commitments. But in reading these commitments back into the First Amendment, we do not implement but rather overrule the intentions of that amendment's enactors.

3. *The golden age of American religious freedom.* The standard story depicts the period from the adoption of the First Amendment to the mid-twentieth century as a time of backsliding in which, in contravention of constitutional principles, Americans promoted Protestant Christianity and ignored or discriminated against minority religions. Meanwhile, a complicit Supreme Court looked on with complacency or even approval. The revised story turns this assessment on its head. Without denying the episodes of intolerance and bigotry to which Americans (like other human beings

throughout history) sometimes have succumbed, the revised story sees the Republic's first century and a half as the period in which the country's distinctive and distinctively promising approach to religious pluralism—what we might call "the American settlement"—was worked out and progressively realized.

And what was the American settlement? Basically, it consisted of two specific constitutional commitments and also one more general principle that, whether or not comprehendingly embraced, came to be embodied and expressed in American practice. The specific commitments, entrenched in the Constitution as it came to be understood, were to separation—separation of *church from state*, mind you, not of *religion from government*—and to freedom of conscience. The more general principle, not expressly articulated in the formal Constitution but entrenched in the nation's "constitution," or its constitutive practices and self-understandings, was one not of secularism or neutrality but rather of open contestation. From the Republic's beginning, Americans have generally agreed on the importance of religious freedom, but they have strenuously disagreed about what religious freedom means, or what it entails. And far from settling such disagreements, the American approach preserved and protected them.

More specifically, understandings of religious freedom have reflected broader, competing interpretations of the American Republic. Thus from the outset some prominent and patriotic Americans (including Washington, Adams, Lincoln) have acted on providentialist interpretations of the nation; other equally prominent and patriotic Americans (Jefferson, Madison, Jackson) have embraced more secularist interpretations. And the distinctive genius of the American approach, in the period of its formation and mature vigor, was that it left this disagreement resolutely unresolved. The American settlement operated to ensure that both the providentialist and secularist interpretations would have a continuing place at the constitutional table.

By embracing a commitment to religious freedom while leaving open to contestation the particular conception of that commitment, the American settlement managed to do what for centuries had seemed impossible. It managed to take a mass of individuals and groups embracing a multitude of different faiths and, without suppressing their differences, to hold them together as a single community constituted around a shared and yet contestable commitment. Out of a turbulent *pluribus* emerged a (still-turbulent) *unum*, without thereby negating or suppressing the *pluribus*.

4. *Dissolution and denial.* Unfortunately, the modern Supreme Court rejected this settlement—or simply failed to understand it. Consequently, when the Court decided to intervene aggressively in the nation's religious affairs in the second half of the twentieth century, it in essence dissolved the principle of open contestation that had been central to the American settlement, elevated one of the perennially competing interpretations (namely, the secularist interpretation) to the status of hard constitutional law, and proceeded to impose that interpretation on the nation.

Or at least sometimes the Court did this. In fact, enforcement of the secularist interpretation has been erratic. It has been erratic in part because the Court has never been wholly clear about what it has been trying to do, and in part because religious motivations and expressions have permeated American public life from the beginning (from the Declaration of Independence to Washington's First Inaugural Address to Lincoln's majestic Second Inaugural to Obama's inauguration ceremony). The courts could not possibly (and probably never wanted to) eliminate all such religiosity from American governance. Which is fortunate: insofar as it has managed not to negate the American version of religious freedom, the Court has done so not so much through its doctrines and deliberate decisions as through its failures, inconsistencies, and omissions.

The result, to be sure, has been a constitutional jurisprudence widely regarded as incoherent, together with an increasing polarization of Americans sometimes described as the "culture wars." Citizens who hold to providentialist views of the nation are alienated because these views have been officially declared heretical. Citizens who favor more secularist interpretations of the nation are often embittered as well because of what they understandably perceive as a failure to live up to secularist commitments that the Court professes but does not (and cannot) consistently implement. How can it be, these citizens ask, that government is constitutionally forbidden to send messages endorsing religion and yet Americans pledge allegiance to "one nation, under God," and every dollar bill declares, "In God We Trust"?

In attempting to realize the promise of religious freedom, in short, the modern Supreme Court unwittingly undermined the distinctive American settlement and initiated a divisive dynamic of resentment, alienation, and bewilderment that affects citizens both religious and secular.

5. Religious freedom in jeopardy. One effect of the modern Court's elevation of public secularism to the status of hard constitutional law is that the classic rationales for religious freedom, because they were and are theological in nature, are thought by many theorists and jurists to be inadmissible for purposes of public justification. Secular substitutes are proposed, but these are of doubtful efficacy. Increasingly, therefore, theorists gravitate to the conclusion that there is no justification for giving special protection to religious freedom. Churches and devout individuals should have the same rights of speech, assembly, and so forth that other citizens have—no more and no less. Indeed, to grant special protection to religious freedom seems to some theorists to discriminate in favor of religion and religious believers, and thus to violate fundamental commitments to equality. A similar stance is discernible in some recent policies of the Obama administration.

As a result, the status of religious freedom is currently in jeopardy, as the standard story says. But the threat comes not so much from religious conservatives who reject constitutional commitments as, perhaps paradoxically, from secular egalitarians who purport to be carrying out the commands of the Constitution's (self-subverting) commitment to religious freedom.

Stories, Counterstories, and Metanarratives

In sum, for each of the standard themes, my account will offer a complement or countertheme, and these will work together to form a different overall account of the nature and course of American religious freedom. A revised version.

Although the overall presentation may seem a bit audacious, or perhaps perverse, it is far from being wholly original: indeed, from an academic perspective, it might seem that the standard story—or at least some of its features—have already been subjected to severe criticism, and that the story has long been less than fully credible. And yet the story remains powerful in American law, politics, and culture. Its power may derive in part from its resonance with a larger account, or metanarrative, that many find compelling. I have presented the standard story in terms of four or five recurring themes, but those themes might be consolidated into a single, larger story whose basic plotline recounts the triumph (not without ongoing struggle and intermittent setbacks) of reason over prejudice and superstition. In this understanding, America is the scion of the Enlightenment, itself understood as a sort of rationalist revolution in which reason—or, better, Reason[9]—began to push aside the darkness of centuries of credulity and ignorance (which were nurtured by and closely associated with religion). And yet Reason must remain vigilant because the darkness of unreason is always lurking in the shadows, ready to rush back in if it is not stoutly restrained.

We live by stories and metanarratives,[10] and the metanarrative of Enlightenment Reason has surely been central to the American self-understanding (as well as to the individual self-understandings of countless scholars, thinkers, and jurists). This centrality helps account for the continuing appeal of the standard story of American religious freedom despite its vulnerabilities on a purely historical level. But the revised version of religious freedom also resonates with a metanarrative, albeit one that is perhaps not as familiar or comfortable, at least to twentieth- and twenty-first-century Americans. That alternative metanarrative recounts how Christian or Judeo-Christian commitments came to be (imperfectly) realized under the conditions of American political life. Borrowing a title, we might say that the revised story is about "the Kingdom of God in America."[11] And if the hero of the metanarrative supporting the standard story prefers to go by the name of Reason, the surprising protagonist of the revised account would probably be called . . . Religion. Thus in one story, religious freedom is the product of Reason. In the revised story, it is the ripe fruit of Religion.

That last sentence is, of course, a greatly simplified summary of a story that itself is greatly simplified (as any story about complex developments encompassing millions of people and unfolding over centuries will be). Stories, we are told, are a distinctively human form of understanding the world. But no single, unitary story carries all the truth. I offer the revised story of religious freedom here as a needed complement to and corrective of the standard story. But I hasten to add that these contrasting stories are not wholly hostile, just as Reason and Religion are not invariably antagonistic.

And indeed, there are important similarities in the stories. Each presents American religious freedom as a distinctive and distinctively valuable achievement—as something Americans might justly celebrate and value and seek to maintain. Each version also sees that distinctive achievement as presently embattled—indeed, as in real jeopardy of being forgotten or forsaken (although the stories offer drastically different accounts of whence the threat to religious freedom comes and what it consists of). A fully adequate account, if such were possible, would no doubt draw on both stories—and on others as well.

Finding ourselves afflicted (or perhaps blessed) with finite minds, though, we cannot entertain too many stories at once. And forced to choose between the standard and revised stories, I would favor the revised story as more illuminating, more perspicacious, ultimately more true. This book will attempt to explain and defend that judgment.

1

American Religious Freedom as Christian-Pagan Retrieval

Instead of dividing up time into BC and AD (or BCE and CE), in thinking about religious freedom and perhaps even about religion itself, we might more aptly mark the years and centuries as BFA and AFA—before and after the First Amendment. Or so it may seem from standard accounts.

BFA, the domain of religion was a dark and turbulent one, perpetually troubled by persecution, oppression, strife, torture, and death. That statement simplifies, obviously, and selects. Christopher Hitchens notwithstanding,[1] religion wasn't always and in all respects poisonous: surely it sometimes inspired acts of courage, charity, or mercy. Who would not admit as much? Even so, at least for our purposes, the aforementioned features—persecution, oppression, strife, torture, and death—were pretty much the salient ones.

Or so it may seem from standard accounts. Consider this official statement from Justice Hugo Black's majority opinion in the seminal case of *Everson v. Board of Education*:

> The centuries immediately before and contemporaneous with the colonization of America had been filled with turmoil, civil strife, and persecutions. . . . With the power of government supporting them, at various times and places, Catholics had persecuted Protestants, Protestants had persecuted Catholics, Protestant sects had persecuted other Protestant sects, Catholics of one shade of belief had persecuted Catholics of another shade of belief, and all of these had from time to time persecuted Jews. In efforts to force loyalty to whatever religious groups happened to be on top and in league with the government of a particular

time and place, men and women had been fined, cast in jail, cruelly tortured, and killed. Among the offenses for which these punishments had been inflicted were such things as speaking disrespectfully of the views of ministers of government-established churches, nonattendance at those churches, expressions of non-belief in their doctrines, and failure to pay taxes and tithes to support them.[2]

Conspicuous in this presentation, of course, are Christians—Catholics and Protestants in their various "sects" and "shade[s]"—who were driven, it seems, by an insatiable urge to persecute. Justice Black went on to explain that it was against this pattern of persecution—of Catholic and Protestant persecution—that Americans (and in particular the Americans most prominently associated with the Enlightenment, i.e., Thomas Jefferson and James Madison) eventually rebelled, thereby putting the new nation on a more sensible and peaceable path. This more irenic course was marked, as *Everson* and other modern decisions and descriptions explain, by two new, Enlightenment-inspired, distinctively American legal commitments: to separation of church and state and to freedom of conscience.

This depiction of American religious freedom as an Enlightened departure from a dark and dogmatic Christian past is common in writings about religious freedom. Often it provides a sort of backdrop, not so much asserted or argued for as taken more or less for granted, against which discussions of religion and religious freedom take place. That backdrop has been with us for a long time. Thus summary presentations like Justice Black's reprise a theme that some thinkers of the "Age of Reason" (as Thomas Paine unhumbly christened his time)[3] had developed in a more sustained and scholarly way, and had traced further back in history.

In this vein, the historian Edward Gibbon in his epic *The Decline and Fall of the Roman Empire*—the first volume was published in the same year as the Declaration of Independence (and as Adam Smith's *Wealth of Nations*)—related how a narrow and dogmatic Christianity arose in, and subverted, a Roman world of religious paganism characterized by the genial acceptance of a profuse diversity of deities and faiths. Upon achieving ascendancy under the emperor Constantine, the new religion pushed aside pagan tolerance—the "mild spirit of antiquity"—and substituted for it "the intolerant zeal of the Christians."[4]

A few years earlier, David Hume had sounded similar themes in more universal terms. Polytheism is intrinsically "sociable," Hume argued. Conversely, monotheistic religions such as Judaism and Christianity are inherently dogmatic and intolerant: this censorious spirit inspires "the continued efforts of priests and bigots" as institutionalized in "the inquisition and persecutions of ROME and MADRID." The inquisitors take "fatal vengeance" on "virtue, knowledge, love of liberty" and thereby "leave the society in the most shameful ignorance, corruption, and bondage."[5] In Voltaire the same motifs recurred; even more so in thinkers like Diderot and d'Holbach.[6]

More contemporary scholars often tell a similar story. For example, the distinguished Yale historian Ramsay MacMullen describes, with barely contained outrage even after all these many centuries, the brutal transition from the congenial, vibrant "spongy mass of tolerance and tradition" that was classical paganism to "the murderous intolerance of the now dominant religion" after Constantine came to power.[7] Robin Lane Fox's lengthy and scholarly *Pagans and Christians*[8] is in a similar vein. Likewise Jonathan Kirsch's more popular *God against the Gods*.[9]

In this version of history (and for its proponents this is not a "version of history" but simply the way things were), the repressive Christian rulers of an aging and embattled empire—Constantine and his successors—served as a segue into a Christendom whose salient features were inquisitions, crusades, the auto-da-fé, and, after the Protestant Reformation, the "wars of religion." Only with the Enlightenment's rejection of Christianity—or if not exactly of Christianity in its entirety, then at least of Christendom—did the American break with this dogma-dominated past become possible.

I have already indicated in the Prologue that this familiar narrative contains a measure of truth: how else could it enlist the support of so many eminent thinkers and historians? But the reality was considerably more complicated and, I am afraid, less conveniently composed of clearly marked good guys and bad guys. Unless the crucial complications are acknowledged, we will be burdened with a grossly distorted understanding of what the American achievement actually was. And we will badly underestimate the extent to which American religious freedom was not so much a repudiation of and departure from the Christian past as a retrieval and consolidation of that past.

Christianity among the Pagans

So although this is a book about religious freedom in America, to understand what happened in America, we need first to look backward and begin where the more elaborate accounts do—with the rise of Christianity in the Roman Empire. What follows does not purport to be anything like a history of church-state relations in the West from the Roman Empire to the American founding: I have neither the need nor the competence to offer any such history. But it is important to recall some of the major pertinent developments and events that preceded the American Republic, with its commitments to church-state separation and freedom of conscience.

In Rome's republican period, which collapsed with Julius Caesar, and in the early empire, which began with Augustus, a polytheistic paganism saturated Roman life. Indeed, Romans prided themselves on being the most religious people in the world, and they sometimes attributed their military and political success to this overarching piety.[10] As the empire came to replace the republic, Augustus and his successors actively reaffirmed worship of the traditional gods, restoring old temples and erecting new ones. They also supplemented that worship with the practice of deifying the emperors themselves.[11]

Roman paganism could be conducive, as Gibbon and Hume and company have told us, to an inclusive tolerance and freedom, for more than one reason.[12] For one thing, polytheism by its nature gives people choices in religion. If you find it hard to feel much reverence for Jove (a pompous and philandering fellow, by all accounts), you can pay your devotions to the sprightly Diana instead, or to the serene and comely Venus, or to the magisterial Apollo, or. . . . And of course there were the exalted emperors. As deities proliferated with an infusion into the empire of Eastern cults and sects devoted to Mithra, Isis, Serapis, et al., devotees were offered a prodigious pantheon of divinities and rites from which to choose. Gibbon waxed rhapsodic on the subject: "The deities of a thousand groves and a thousand streams possessed, in peace, their local and respective influence; nor could the Roman who deprecated the wrath of the Tiber, deride the Egyptian who presented his offering to the beneficent genius of the Nile."[13]

A vast variety of eligible deities meant options for the devotees. "One would only worship the gods one wished to," the French historian Paul Veyne observes, "and when one wished to."[14] Jonathan Kirsch concurs: "[T]he fundamental theology of polytheism honors the worshiper's freedom to choose among the many gods and goddesses who are believed to exist."[15]

In one respect, to be sure, the appearance of a capacious menu of divinities may be deceptive: that is because the various deities could be regarded as essentially just different faces of the same cozy company of gods. Charles Freeman explains that "local gods would be merged into the Roman pantheon—a provincial god of thunder could simply be seen as Zeus or Jupiter in a different guise."[16] The possibility of consolidating deities, however, was still conducive to tolerance. If all the various divinities are just different personifications of the same contained set of familiar gods, or possibly even of a single ultimate One or divine reality, then there seems little reason to quarrel, or perhaps to care, if your neighbor appears to be worshipping a different deity than you do. It all comes down to much the same thing. Gibbon thus explained that "[t]he Greek, the Roman, and the Barbarian, as they met before their respective altars, easily persuaded themselves, that under various names, and with various ceremonies, they adored the same deities."[17]

Religious tolerance in the Roman Empire was also a natural by-product of the Romans' pragmatic, hands-off attitude toward governance of conquered lands. Given Rome's remarkably rapid expansion in the later centuries of the republic and the lack of a well-developed governmental bureaucracy or police force, the Romans preferred to rule acquired territories indirectly, often maintaining the preexisting governments in a now-subordinate condition.[18] Just as Rome could enter into a range of political arrangements with conquered peoples, it could cheerfully put up with a spectrum of devotions—especially if those devotions conduced to good civic behavior. Gibbon captured the idea, perhaps a bit too cynically: "The various modes of worship, which prevailed in the Roman world, were all considered by the people, as equally true; by the philosopher, as equally false; and by the magistrate, as equally useful."[19]

This sort of pragmatic tolerance—the point is crucial—was essentially a tolerance of indifference. It did not reflect what modern theorists might call a "principled" commitment to religious toleration, freedom of conscience, human rights, or human dignity. Religions were left free to flourish because, and to the extent that, they were not perceived as disruptive of the Roman order or ethos. J. A. North explains:

> [I]f there was tolerance it was not tolerance born of principle. So far as we know, there was no fixed belief that a state or individual ought to tolerate different forms of religion; that is the idea of far later periods of history. The truth seems to be that the Romans tolerated what seemed to them harmless and drew the line whenever there seemed to be a threat of possible harm; only, they saw no great harm in many of the cults of their contemporary world.[20]

Not always, though: sometimes the Romans did perceive possible harm in a religion, and then their reaction could be savage.[21] Ruthless repression was thus the fate, from time to time, of Jews, Druids, Chaldeans, Manichees, and the devotees of Bacchus and Isis.[22]

And, of course, of Christians. The Roman historian Tacitus described how, under the emperor Nero, Christians were "[d]ressed in wild animals' skins" to be "torn to pieces by dogs" or "made into torches to be ignited after dark as substitutes for daylight."[23] The two greatest early church leaders, Peter and Paul, may have perished in that Neronian outburst of repressive violence. In a later era, the Christian bishop and historian Eusebius chronicled the Diocletianic persecution that he himself lived through.[24] Eusebius described one instance:

> [A] certain man [named Peter] was brought into a public place and ordered to sacrifice. When he refused, he was hoisted up naked and lashed with whips until he should give in. Since even this failed to bend him, they mixed salt with vinegar and poured it over the lacerations of his body where the bones were already protruding. When he scorned these agonies too, a lit brazier was applied, and the rest of his body was roasted by the fire as if meat for eating—not all at once, lest he find too quick a release, but little by little. Still he clung immovably to his purpose and expired triumphantly in the middle of his tortures.[25]

Modern celebrants of "the mild spirit of antiquity," as Gibbon affectionately put it,[26] tend not to linger over these episodic explosions of pagan ferocity. Why let such unseemly lapses disturb the pleasant picture of a broad-minded, humane pagan toleration in a cosmopolitan and religiously diverse society?

Let us be amiable and acquiesce in this happy depiction. For the first three centuries of their existence, Christians did nothing to disturb or challenge this regime of (selectively) genial religious pluralism. They couldn't; they had no power. They were occupied in trying to defend themselves, with mixed results, against often suspicious or hostile authorities and fellow subjects. Nonetheless, Christianity did introduce two potent ideas, or clusters of ideas and practices, that contrasted markedly with paganism, and that carried portentous implications for the distant future, including the American future.

Over time, and depending on their context and on how they were interpreted and used, these new ideas and practices would prove to be transformative—but transformative, paradoxically, in conflicting ways. The distinctive Christian contributions could (and did) inspire a more principled and aggressive intolerance. That is the dimension of Christianity picked out for emphasis by Gibbon, Hume, MacMullen, and company. But those contributions also could (and did) support a more earnest and principled commitment to religious freedom. That is the dimension of Christianity that would eventually come to (imperfect, and fragile) fruition in the American Republic.

The two jurisdictions. One crucial new idea asserted the existence of independent jurisdictions or authorities—a temporal jurisdiction and a spiritual jurisdiction—each of which exerts a legitimate claim on human beings. This idea was first offered almost offhandedly—or so it may seem—by the religion's founder in fending off a potentially deadly question. Opponents had asked Jesus whether it was permissible to pay taxes to Caesar. The question may seem innocuous enough, but it was calculated to catch Jesus in a dilemma. If he answered that, yes, it was permissible to pay taxes to Caesar, he would likely forfeit the loyalty of his more zealous Jewish followers, who chafed under what they viewed as illegitimate and oppressive Roman rule. But if he said no, he would be guilty of stirring up rebellion against Rome—and the Romans did not deal gently with rebels.

More quick-witted than his interrogators, Jesus requested a coin and asked whose image appeared on it. "Caesar's," he was told, and he then famously instructed, "Render therefore unto Caesar the things which be Caesar's, and unto God the things which be God's."[27]

The statement might easily be passed off as nothing more than a deft deflection of a cunning question. But taken seriously (and the statement was taken *very* seriously by later Christians),[28] Jesus's instruction implied not just the existence of two types of concerns, temporal and spiritual, but of two different and independent authorities, or jurisdictions, each of which imposes legitimate obligations on us. In ensuing centuries, this dualistic theme would be sounded over and over again—by Augustine with the metaphor of the "two cities"[29] and by Luther and Calvin with the imagery of the "two kingdoms."[30]

Under the exotic (to us) hermeneutics of medieval interpretation, other scriptural passages would be taken as supporting the same idea. For example, the New Testament records that as Jesus faced increasing opposition that would culminate in his crucifixion, he warned his followers of impending violence; someone responded with "Lord, here are two swords," and Jesus said, "It is enough."[31] In the coming centuries, this seemingly insignificant and opaque passage would be interpreted symbolically, so that the two swords would come to signify the distinct temporal and spiritual powers.[32]

The idea of two separate and independent jurisdictions, temporal and spiritual, had at least ambiguous antecedents in Judaism,[33] but it contrasted sharply with Roman views and practices. In the Roman Republic and later in the Roman Empire, the dominant idea was just the opposite: political authority and religious authority were deliberately melded together. Thus political leaders were simultaneously the holders of the various Roman priesthoods—"a lifelong priesthood," Hans-Joseph Klauck observes, "was an indispensable part of every political career"[34]—and Augustus and his imperial successors held the highest religious office, that of *pontifex maximus*.[35] Cicero explained:

> Among the many institutions . . . created and established by our forbears under the inspiration of the gods, nothing is more famous than their decision to commit to the same men both the worship of the gods and the care of state interests; the result was that the most illustrious citizens might assure the upholding of religion by the proper administration of

the state and the upholding of the state by the careful interpretation of religion.[36]

Nor did the next major power to conquer large parts of what had been the Roman Empire embrace the concept of dual jurisdictions. Bernard Lewis explains that "[c]lassical Islam recognized a distinction between things of this world and things of the next, between pious and worldly considerations."[37] But "[t]he dichotomy of *regnum* and *sacerdotium,* so crucial in the history of Western Christendom, had no equivalent in Islam."[38]

The Christian notion of dual jurisdictions did not have any immediate impact on governance in the Roman Empire. For their first three centuries Christians were a suspect and persecuted minority without political power. Even after Christianity became the favored religion of the realm in the fourth century, emperors continued (as their imperial predecessors had done) to exercise religious authority, calling councils to settle theological controversies and claiming the right to confirm the selection of church officials.[39]

Moreover, the conception of dual jurisdictions could be pushed in an authoritarian direction. Bishops could contend that just as the eternal transcended the temporal, so the spiritual authority should have preeminence over the temporal authority. Centuries later, in the fullness of the Middle Ages, ambitious popes would on this premise claim authority to make and unmake emperors and kings.[40] But the conception of dual jurisdictions also had the potential to support what Americans would later call a "separation of church and state." In the waning Roman Empire, Western bishops (especially including the bishops of Rome) repeatedly asserted that idea.[41] And beginning in the eleventh century, that potential began, haltingly and in the face of powerful resistance, to be realized.

Before considering this development, however, we should take account of the other major transformative idea, or cluster of ideas and practices, that Christianity introduced.

A new religiosity. The term "religion" is apt to mislead. Paganism and Christianity were both religions, perhaps,[42] but they were very different kinds of religions. "Nothing could have been more different," Paul Veyne asserts, "from, on the one hand, the relationship between the pagans and their gods and, on the other, that between the Christians and their God."[43] We can consider the pertinent differences in terms of four contrasts.[44]

First, and most obviously, Christianity was monotheistic. To be sure, it was not the only monotheistic religion; indeed, Christianity with its "three in one" deity was less uncomplicatedly monotheistic than Judaism, which preceded it, or Islam, which would follow. Even so, compared with a sprawling, capaciously polytheistic paganism (Gibbons's "deities of a thousand groves and a thousand streams"), Christianity was conspicuously a faith focused on the "one true God."

This feature of the faith had political implications. We have already noticed how polytheism could be conducive to an easygoing freedom and tolerance. You can worship your deity in your way; I will worship my deity in mine; and both forms of worship are presumptively valid and authentic. Conversely, if there is only one God, then it may seem to follow that other supposed deities must be either illusions or impostors—demons, maybe.[45] And it is hard to treat the worshippers of either illusions or demons with genuine respect. As noted, these differences led thinkers like Hume to argue that monotheistic religion is inherently intolerant.

A second difference was Christianity's earnest emphasis on—some might say obsession with—truth. Pagan religion, as Hume said, rested "easy and light on men's minds";[46] it supported a relaxed attitude toward truth. In late antiquity and ever since, observers have often asked, "Did the pagans really believe in their gods?"—in that fractious family of willful and often whimsical divinities that Jupiter, Juno, Cupid, and company composed? And the answer that historians have sometimes come to is "Sort of." There is no warrant for saying that most Romans flatly did not believe, or that they regarded the gods as nothing more than pious fictions. (Although a few probably did hold this view, as Gibbon contended, "conceal[ing] the sentiments of an Atheist under the sacerdotal robes.")[47] But neither does it seem quite accurate to say that the Romans actually and fully believed in their deities in the same straightforward sense in which we believe in unseen but real entities like, say, germs, or genes, or molecules, or in the same strong sense in which Christians would believe in their God.

Attempting to capture the cognitive posture of pagan religion, Paul Veyne argues that although for us "[t]his question of truth [in religion] may seem natural," for the pagans the question generally did not directly present itself.[48]

"A pagan . . . professed nothing, did not declare his belief in the gods: given that he addressed a cult to them, it went without saying that he believed in them!"[49] Believed in some sense, anyway: Veyne goes on to suggest that "paganism was crammed with too many fables and naiveties," so that "a pious and educated pagan no longer knew what he should or could believe."[50] Elsewhere, Veyne deploys the phrase "modalities of belief"[51] to suggest that the nature of pagan belief was not quite what the term might connote for us.

The overall idea is that pagans performed their rituals, they implicitly believed insofar as belief is implied by practice, and they refrained from asking too closely about truth. J. A. North argues that belief in the gods was virtually universal among Romans, but then he qualifies this claim: "[I]t is a mistake to overemphasize any question of the participants' belief or disbelief in the efficacy of ritual actions. . . . These rituals are not saying things, but doing things."[52] In a similar vein, Robert Wilken observes that "[i]n the cities of the ancient world, . . . [o]ne did not speak of 'believing in the gods' but of 'having gods.'"[53]

The Christian attitude was strikingly different. Believing took on a more rigorous cast, corresponding to a more exacting emphasis on truth (and a more strenuous rejection of error, or heresy). The Jewish and later Christian "requirement of truth in religion," Guy Strousma explains, was "found nowhere else in the ancient world"; it amounted to "a new status for truth."[54]

This emphasis on truth may have been related to monotheism. If there is only one God, then belief in others must be false, and it accordingly becomes important—imperative, even—to figure out which is the true God and, more generally, what the truth in religion is. The determination to state the truth accurately was evident in the Christians' seeming obsession with formulating creeds and doctrines,[55] often through councils that wrangled over distinctions and verbal formulations that today glaze the minds even of the devout, but that believers were nonetheless enjoined to accept under threat of damnation.[56]

Once again, the Christian earnestness about truth had implications for the possibilities of religious freedom and tolerance. A relaxed stance toward truth supports a complacent attitude toward other people's religious beliefs: the question "Are those religious beliefs true or false?" may come to seem at least impertinent, maybe even a kind of category mistake. As Robin Lane Fox remarks, "There was . . . no pagan concept of heresy."[57] Conversely, if it is "the truth [that] will make you free," then it becomes imperative to follow the preceding injunction to "know the truth."[58] And so the flourishing of false belief becomes something to be deplored and, if possible, eliminated— first, because false beliefs might sow error among the faithful, but also because if you follow the commandment to "love your neighbor as yourself," you can hardly just look on complacently while your neighbor sinks under the damning burden of false belief.

The importance of pursuing and embracing truth was the greater because in the Christian view, religion was not just about maintaining civic unity or propitiating the gods with the hope of good harvests or success in battle. Here is a third major difference: for Christians the stakes posed by religion were infinitely higher. Pagan religiosity was for the most part about human welfare in this world; the honor paid to the gods reflected "their power over crops or forces of the weather."[59] By contrast, as Veyne explains, "the new religion prompted questions and hopes far greater than those of paganism. . . . Our existence on earth was no longer an absurdly brief transition from one nothingness to another." On the contrary, Christianity invited all to participate in "a vast divine project designed for human beings."[60] Indeed, nothing less than your eternal salvation turned on getting religion right: finding and adhering to the true faith might determine whether you spent eternity in unutterable bliss or unquenchable brimstone.

These distinctive features of Christianity—its monotheism, its concern with truth, its emphasis on eternal salvation over this-worldly peace and prosperity—could provide powerful motives for religious intolerance. But a fourth feature altered the whole equation, at least potentially. The Romans were pervasively religious, as we have noted—but not exactly, it seems, profoundly religious. Pagan religion was largely an outward affair; it was, as Robert Wilken observes, "civic and communal and public" in character.[61] What a person actually *believed,* or what she *desired* or *felt*: these were private matters that pagan religion largely left alone. "Among pagans," Fox observes, "there was no question of punishment for a passing evil thought in everyday life."[62] Christian religion, by contrast, was more comprehensive (or, if you prefer, more aggressively intrusive) in its concerns and claims. Unlike paganism, Christianity was an internal religion: it was intensely concerned about the state of a person's soul—about what was in his heart or in her mind.[63] On these internal features a person's salvation depended. Guy Strousma observes that "the idea of the transformation of the internal life remained unknown to the official religion of the ancient city, as well as to the mystery cults." And he suggests that "[i]f one has to specify in a single word the nature of this change [from paganism to Christianity], I would accept the Hegelian analysis that stresses the *interiorization* of religion."[64]

Thus Jesus seemed to teach that hatred was as sinful as physical violence, lust as deplorable as actual adultery.[65] The kingdom of God was not to be perceived outwardly; rather, the kingdom of God was *within* the faithful.[66] Jesus's most influential follower, Paul, preached that a person is saved by faith, not by outward works.[67]

The point should not be pushed too far. To say that Christianity cared about the inner person is not to imply that it was indifferent to life in the world. Christians placed great emphasis not only on faith but also on moral conduct; in this respect as well, Christianity contrasted with the typical pagan orientation.[68] For every Paul who stressed salvation by faith there was a James who insisted that "faith without works is dead."[69] Faith and works: just how these themes might be reconciled was and remained a subject of intense, sometimes agonized Christian reflection. Centuries after Paul and James (and, in a later round, Augustine and the priest Pelagius) had given up the debate and passed on to whatever rewards awaited them, the issue could rend the soul of an earnest, tortured believer like Martin Luther, leading to religious and political revolutions. Yet even Luther, with all his contempt for "works righteousness," insisted on the importance of good works and service to the world.[70]

In addition, although for their first three centuries Christians were more subjects and sometimes victims than wielders of political power, they were not indifferent to politics and governance. They prayed for the emperor, sometimes served in the Roman armies, and insisted that they were loyal subjects and citizens of the empire.[71] Against charges that Christians were unpatriotic, the Christian apologist Tertullian protested that "[w]e are forever making intercession for the emperors. We pray for them a long life, a secure rule, a safe home, brave armies, a faithful senate, an honest people, a quiet world, and everything for which a man and a Caesar may pray."[72]

Through all this, however, the central and distinctive Christian concern was for the disciple's inner life. And this emphasis on inner righteousness had practical political consequences. It could inspire a more intrusive intolerance. But it could also culminate in a more principled dedication to religious freedom.

Thus if a person's eternal salvation turned on what was transpiring inside his head and heart, then religious leaders, entrusted with caring for their followers' spiritual welfare, could hardly be indifferent to these vital matters. There was no private domain beyond God's watchful eye—or the eyes of his vigilant earthly representatives. And if political rulers were working in cooperation with those representatives, then they might naturally take an interest in that inner domain as well. That interest might manifest itself in, for example, . . . an inquisition.

At the same time, there was a sense in which the emphasis on inner righteousness rendered external meddling in matters of faith pointless, or even counterproductive. Maybe, sometimes, the magistrate could force his subjects to confess the true creed with their lips, but if they did not sincerely believe what they were being made to recite, what was the point? So Christian innerness could support a powerful argument for freedom from coercion in matters of religion. This argument would be insistently urged centuries later by the likes of Roger Williams, John Locke, and James Madison. But it was clearly articulated by early Christians as well. The fourth-century Christian author Lactantius, adviser to Constantine and tutor of his children, spoke eloquently on the theme: "Liberty has chosen to dwell in religion. For nothing is so much a matter of free will as religion, and no one can be required to worship what he does not will to worship."[73]

The argument that saving faith must be sincere and voluntary had the potential to gather in and reorient the other distinctive features of Christian religion—potentially, as we have seen, sources of religious intolerance—into a powerful rationale for freedom in matters of faith. The most important thing a person can do in this life is to maintain a faithful relation with the one true God. In comparison, all other goods are of little consequence. And in the allocation of jurisdictions, God (and not the emperor) is sovereign over the domain of faith. God (and not the world) is also the source of eternal life, and of blessings beyond mortal imagining. And a relationship with the one true God can be achieved only by a freely held faith.

From this perspective, not only is freedom in matters of religion indicated: freedom carries a vast eternal significance beside which mere earthly goods—material prosperity, bodily health, political peace—pale in comparison. The willingness (and even perverse eagerness) of many early Christians to accept martyrdom gave eloquent testimony to this ordering of priorities. It was an ordering that favored (or potentially could favor) freedom in matters of faith—or, as it later came to be called, freedom of conscience.

In short, Christian religion was distinctively different from the paganism that prevailed in the late Roman Empire. Its distinctive differences—a commitment to dual jurisdictions, an earnest emphasis on the one true God and on inner, saving religion as a means of attaining goods beyond reckoning in the next life—had the potential to inspire an intrusive religious intolerance in ways that a less ambitious and externally oriented paganism did not. But those differences also contained incipient commitments to what would later come to be described as "separation of church and state" and "freedom of conscience."

The Intolerance of Early Christendom

At least from our standpoint, and measured against modern liberal commitments, it was the religion's intolerant tendencies that became conspicuous upon acceptance of Christianity by the Roman authorities. The details of the developments are excruciatingly complicated, and almost every one of them is disputed by historians. Fortunately, we need not review the history extensively here, or take sides in the historians' debates. It will be enough to note the decisive transition and to describe the general pattern that came to prevail as the Roman Empire declined or evolved into the kingdoms and empires that composed Christendom.

Beginning in 303 under the emperor Diocletian and continuing for about a decade, Christians were subjected to the most savage and sustained persecution they had yet endured.[74] Robert Markus observes that "[i]n the Great Persecution at the beginning of the fourth century, the forces of Roman conservatism rallied in a last attempt to eliminate a dangerous threat to the traditional consensus."[75] But in 305, uncharacteristically for an emperor, Diocletian retired to tend to his beloved cabbages, and from the power struggle that ensued, Constantine eventually emerged as the supreme ruler of the empire. His success was a welcome one for Christians. That is because, after a vision that he experienced (or at least later reported that he had experienced) at the Milvian Bridge outside Rome immediately before a decisive battle in 312, Constantine embraced Christianity as a faith that would be first tolerated and later favored in the empire.

Constantine was, and is, a huge and immensely controversial figure. Some historians have viewed him as a "cynical opportunist"[76] who turned to Christianity for crass political purposes. To the noted Swiss historian Jacob Burckhardt, he was an "essentially unreligious" man who was "driven without surcease by ambition and lust for power."[77] The dominant view among historians today, by contrast, seems to be that Constantine was a sincere and zealous (though far from virtuous) convert who embraced Christianity even though it offered him no political advantage.[78] Either way, within less than a generation Christianity had passed from being a persecuted to a preferred faith.

While favoring Christianity with influence and lavish endowments, Constantine himself maintained a policy of toleration toward pagan religion. Paul Veyne asserts that "[d]espite his deep desire to see all his subjects become Christians, . . . [Constantine] never persecuted pagans or denied them the right to express themselves; nor did he disadvantage them in their careers: if superstitious people wished to damn themselves, they were free to do so."[79] Later rulers were less accommodating, and within less than a century the emperor Theodosius was proscribing pagan sacrifices, and Christian mobs were on occasion rampaging, destroying pagan shrines, and murdering prominent pagans.[80] (To be fair, in those tumultuous times, the rampaging often ran both ways, and it was not always perfectly clear "who started it.")[81]

Just how and why this shift to intolerance happened is, once again, a matter of debate among historians. H. A. Drake contends that imperial policy under Constantine and his son Constantius was broadly tolerant and inclusive. However, the effort of the emperor Julian ("the Apostate") in the mid-fourth century to restore paganism by legally marginalizing Christianity[82] revived Christian memories and fears of the persecutions under Diocletian earlier in the century, thereby provoking a repressive backlash after Julian's early death.[83]

Whatever the exact course and causes of the development may have been, by the fifth and sixth centuries a new pattern had emerged that would prevail for centuries. Two features are important for our purposes.

First, political rulers claimed and often, if intermittently, exercised power to suppress nonconforming religion (both pagan and heretically Christian). Although pagan rulers had exercised a similar power on occasion toward religions deemed subversive, the Christian concern with the inner life and with heresy gave greater scope to this power. In this vein, Jonathan Kirsch describes Constantine as having instituted "the first totalitarian state in history."[84]

This description seems a bit excessive in light of Constantine's policy of toleration and the lax repressive efforts even of more severe successors like Theodosius. Thus Rodney Stark observes that the proscriptions against paganism were deliberately underenforced,[85] and he points out that "Theodosius, the emperor who, according to Gibbon, extirpated paganism, appointed nearly as many men who were openly pagans as he did Christians to the positions of consuls and prefects."[86] Peter Brown describes "polytheists firmly established in small cities all over the eastern empire . . . up to and beyond the end of the sixth century,"[87] and he recalls that "even a century and a half after the battle for the public faith of the empire was lost to Christianity, the philosopher Proclus would be writing, in the mood of a still evening after thunder, intimate hymns to the gods and a totally pagan *Elements of Theology*."[88] Still, if the official repression of paganism was uneven, it was nonetheless real and, over time, effective. Under the weight of this repression (and also, of course, through efforts at conversion), paganism receded from public life and gradually dwindled.

Second, although political rulers now no longer formally held religious offices, they continued to assume considerable responsibility for overseeing and intervening in the church. Not that the temporal and spiritual jurisdictions were entirely consolidated: the church was not the state. In this respect, the Christianized empire departed from the pattern of the pagan empire. A slightly more complete account would need to relate episodes such as the Catholic bishops' resistance to Constantius's efforts to impose the Arian creed on the empire,[89] Bishop Ambrose's (partially) successful chastising and disciplining of the emperor Theodosius in the late fourth century[90] or Pope Gelasius's feisty assertion of independence from the emperor Anastasius a century later.[91] Still, emperors convened, presided over, and bullied church councils regarding matters of doctrine and theology—Constantine set the leading precedent with the famous Council of Nicaea in 325—and they demanded a say in the selection of church leaders.[92] When Pope Liberius resisted the anti-Nicene conclusion of a synod supervised by the heretically Arian emperor Constantius, the emperor had Liberius arrested and exiled. The humiliated pope was permitted to return to Rome only after signing a statement hedging on the Nicene doctrine.[93] When Popes Vigilius and Martin resisted imperial efforts to promote what they viewed as the Monophysite heresy, they were arrested, dragged to Constantinople, imprisoned, tried, and humiliated.[94] For his similar resistance, Maximus the Confessor was likewise tried and exiled after having his tongue and right hand cut off.[95]

In the centuries after the conversion of Constantine, in sum, Christian and imperial tendencies toward intolerance and official interference with religion were conspicuously on display. (As Gibbon, MacMullen, and company have been at pains to remind us.) The potential for a more principled tolerance remained largely latent. And the intolerant tendencies within Christendom persisted throughout late antiquity, the Middle Ages, and the early modern period. The medieval inquisitions were vivid and infamous manifestations of these tendencies; the persecution of Jews and their expulsion from the various kingdoms of Europe were another.

And yet Christian intolerance was only part of the picture. Compared with classical paganism, as we have seen, Christianity had the potential for a more aggressive intolerance but also for a more principled tolerance. Although the former tendency was perhaps more conspicuous, over time the more benign potential began to be realized as well.

The Campaign for Freedom of the Church

One momentous development began late in the eleventh century with what is called the "investiture controversy," or sometimes the "papal revolution."[96] As we have seen, emperors and kings had long demanded a role in the selection of bishops and popes; given the position of bishops as major landowners and political leaders, this demand is perfectly understandable.[97] In some periods, moreover, royal superintendence had been a force for ecclesiastical integrity. For example, the ninth century was for the papacy a "dark century" of assassinations and sordid politics, perhaps most gruesomely exhibited in the macabre "cadaver synod" of 897 in which Pope Stephen VI ordered the mummified corpse of a predecessor exhumed, dressed in pontifical vestments and propped up on a throne, put on trial for perjury and other crimes, and then hacked up and flung into the Tiber.[98] Determined to purify the church from such scandals, German emperors such as Otto I and Henry III intervened in an effort to restore a measure of sanctity to the papal office.[99]

Partly as a result of these imperial interventions, by the mid-eleventh century a series of more reform-minded popes assumed the office and undertook to restore the church to its ideals. This was not a single-issue campaign—it included efforts to eliminate simony (the buying and selling of ecclesiastical office) and clerical marriage—but a central goal of the reform agenda was to free the church from outside political interference. Thus the popes began to resist the claims of kings to a role in the selection and appointment of bishops. Conflict ensued and came to a head in the celebrated controversy between Pope Gregory VII and King Henry IV of Germany.[100]

In 1075, Gregory forbade "lay investiture," as it was called—basically, the appointment of bishops by secular rulers. That same year, a dispute over the election of a bishop in Milan brought king and pope into conflict. As relations deteriorated, Gregory accused Henry of conduct that was not "becoming"; Henry responded by calling the pope a "false monk" and a usurper who should step down from office.[101] Gregory declined the suggestion; instead, he excommunicated the king, "releas[ing] all Christian men from the allegiance which they have sworn or may swear to him, and . . . forbid[ding] anyone to serve him as king."[102] Some of the excommunicated king's nobles took advantage of the papal decree by refusing to support him and throwing their support instead to a rival, Rudolf of Swabia.

In an effort to break the impasse, a conference between king and pope was arranged. In the winter of 1077, though, before the conference could convene, an impatient Henry took the pope by surprise by showing up outside a castle at Canossa, in the Italian Alps, where Gregory was staying on his trip to the scheduled meeting. For three days Henry waited abjectly outside the castle in the snow, ragged and barefoot, imploring the pope's pardon "with many tears."[103]

"[M]oved by pity and compassion," Gregory eventually consented to absolve the penitent sinner and to "[r]eceive him into the grace of Holy Mother Church."[104] Henry thereupon returned to Germany and consolidated his power. He then led an army that drove the pope from Rome and installed a new pope, or antipope, who reciprocated by elevating Henry from king to emperor. The fugitive Gregory was eventually rescued by an army of Normans. But, alas, the unruly rescuers in turn proceeded to sack Rome, provoking the wrath of city residents against the pope, who fled once again and died in exile.

Although the story did not end happily for Gregory or the church, the controversy signaled the beginning of a campaign for *libertas ecclesiae*— freedom of the church from secular control—that continued over the next several centuries. Extravagant assertions of authority were advanced on each side, and kings and popes and their allies drew on every available argument and analogy to advance their jurisdictional claims. The scriptural tidbits about rendering unto God and Caesar and about the "two swords" were now served up for all they were worth.[105]

Nor was the struggle limited to polemics. Resources differed, of course: while kings commanded soldiers with swords and shields, popes could threaten and sometimes impose the spiritual sanctions of excommunication (as Gregory had done with Henry) or interdict (thereby prohibiting the administration of all sacraments, including communion and marriage, in a ruler's realm). Perhaps the most famous episode, commemorated centuries later in an Oscar-winning movie, was the conflict between Henry II of England (Peter O'Toole) and Thomas Becket (Richard Burton), archbishop of Canterbury, in the twelfth century. Formerly friends, king and archbishop quarreled over issues of royal versus ecclesiastical jurisdiction. Becket was forced to flee to the Continent; after returning, he was murdered by four of Henry's nobles in Canterbury Cathedral (which thereupon became the preferred pilgrimage site in Britain).[106]

As Gregory's and Becket's fates suggest, the campaign for freedom of the church was far from an unmitigated success. The church's standing in the struggle reached a high point in the thirteenth century; a series of conflicts and royal defeats led to the downfall of the Hohenstaufen imperial dynasty.[107] In the same century, after another disputed episcopal appointment, Pope Innocent III forced King John of England to cede England and Ireland to the pope and receive them back as feudal fiefs.[108] But fortunes flipped at century's end with Pope Boniface VIII's disastrous confrontation with the French king Philip the Fair over the king's taxation of the church. Philip defied the pope's orders, preempted a pending excommunication by temporarily taking the pope captive and forcing him to capitulate,[109] then showed off his strength by bullying the pope's successors into repudiating the Knights Templar.[110]

Through the ups and downs of the struggle, the partisans of both the church and the royal power came to accept the basic idea of dual jurisdictions even as they quarreled incessantly over how and where the jurisdictional boundaries should be drawn. "There were through the mediaeval centuries great overlap and great conflict between Church and state," Charles Taylor explains, "but in all versions, and on all sides, it was axiomatic that there had to be a separation of spheres."[111]

As a component of this separation, rulers and bishops accepted a system of ecclesiastical courts with exclusive jurisdiction over some persons (especially clerics) and some matters (such as marriage).[112] Likewise, medieval thought and practice embraced "the right of sanctuary," under which a fugitive taking refuge in a church could claim to be beyond the reach of secular authorities. Robert Rodes observes that "[i]n some cases, [churches] became ultimately not a refuge but a center from which [the felon] could sally forth for further depredations or a hostel in which he could live in comfort on his ill-gotten gains."[113]

A decisive turning point in the Anglo-American theater of the struggle was Henry VIII's takeover of the English church in the 1530s. Resisted by a few Catholic faithful, including Thomas More (the "man for all seasons" of another Academy Award–winning film) and Bishop John Fisher, both of whom went to the scaffold rather than accept Henry's unsanctioned divorce and effective seizure of the English church, Henry's measures were a major defeat for the public campaign for freedom of the church. The consolidation of those measures under Henry's daughter Elizabeth,[114] the so-called Virgin Queen, after whom the commonwealth of Virginia was named (perhaps ironically, at least from the standpoint of this story, because Virginia departed most dramatically from the Elizabethan church-state settlement), effectively brought the public campaign for freedom of the church to an end—for a couple of centuries, anyway.

And so a project begun by Gregory VII and his colleagues gave way to an Erastian arrangement in which the church was effectively reduced to a department of the government. Similar developments occurred in other European countries. José Casanova observes that after the Reformation, "[t]he churches attempted to reproduce the model of Christendom at the national level, but all the territorial national churches, Anglican as well as Lutheran, Catholic as well as Orthodox, fell under caesaropapist control of the absolutist state."[115]

Even so, the ideal of a church free of state control did not so much die as go underground. The ideal was carried on by dissenting and nonconforming sects, some of which ended up escaping to the New World—to wild, fearsome places like Massachusetts, Connecticut, Rhode Island, and Pennsylvania.[116] Upon settling in Massachusetts, the Puritans set up a governmental system self-consciously committed to a separation of church and state.[117] Thomas Curry explains that "[b]y divesting religious bodies of temporal power and confining them to spiritual matters, Puritan New England began rearranging the components of Church-State relations into their future American pattern."[118]

To be sure, the Puritan conception of church-state separation was drastically different from the conceptions that Americans later came to embrace. Nor were Puritans averse to persecuting dissenters (or, in one notorious and aberrant episode, executing supposed witches); it is for that proclivity, probably, that they are chiefly remembered today. And yet in certain respects Puritan separation was actually stricter than modern separationist notions. Thus ministers were legally prohibited from serving in public office; the Puritans believed that such dual service would be an impermissible mixing of the spiritual and the temporal.[119]

The upshot is that the notion of "separation of church and state" was far from being a Jeffersonian invention. On the contrary, the idea had its roots in the earliest Christian teaching. As Christendom evolved, the idea had been expounded, debated, and defended by churchmen and scholars, by lawyers and kings' counselors, in innumerable treatises and tracts over a period of centuries. It had been vividly and physically memorialized, as we have seen, in epic political struggles and in legendary martyrdoms. And it had been accepted in practice and embodied in institutions that had endured for generations prior to the Erastian intermission initiated by rulers like Henry VIII.

Even then, the idea had been fervently preserved and maintained by Christian dissenters. Indeed, the metaphor of the "wall of separation," today most often associated with Jefferson, had been deployed almost two centuries earlier by Roger Williams, that deviant and fanatical (and fanatically separationist) Puritan.[120]

Thus in embracing the "separation of church and state," Americans were in effect recovering and implementing (in a distinctively American way, to be sure) an ancient Christian ideal. Before considering how they did this, though, we need to consider another Christian theme that Americans also and even more emphatically and explicitly embraced—namely, the commitment to freedom of conscience.

Conscience, the "Inner Church"

At about the same time that the visible, official church was being subjected to the domination of rulers like Henry VIII and his more overtly Protestant successors, the Protestant understanding of the church was itself changing. Catholic teaching had emphasized the indispensable role of the church as an intermediary between God and humans; Protestants, by contrast, favored a more direct relation between the individual and God. In the "priesthood of all believers," people could read scripture for themselves—Protestants were thus enthusiastic supporters of vernacular translations of the Bible[121]—and could commune with God directly without the intercession of priests, saints, or sacraments. This more independent and individualistic attitude was evident in Luther's legendary defiance of church teachings that happened to conflict with his own judgments: Luther deemed himself compelled to follow his own interpretations of God's will as revealed in scripture. "Here I stand; I can do no other."[122]

It was not that Protestants wanted to get rid of the institutional church. Nor was there a single, monolithic Protestant conception of the church: the Reformers differed significantly among themselves, and Luther's own ecclesiology changed over time.[123] The sacraments of baptism and communion were typically retained (although even these were interpreted by many Protestants in more symbolic and less metaphysically realist terms). In general, though, for Protestants the church remained important principally as a community of believers and as a conduit through which the word of God is conveyed. The central place of encounter between God and humans had shifted from the external, visible church to the individual conscience.

Thus in Protestant thinking, John Witte explains, "[e]ach individual stands directly before God, seeks God's gracious forgiveness of sin, and conducts life in accordance with the Bible and Christian conscience."[124] The change can be expressed with the help of an instructive exaggeration: in Protestant thinking, the individual conscience *became* the church—the "inner church," so to speak.

But if the conscience in a sense became the church, then the medieval ideal of "freedom of the church" might naturally develop into an ideal of "freedom of conscience." In this way, the campaign to keep the church independent of secular jurisdiction was partially reconfigured as a commitment to keeping the conscience free from secular regulation. Brian Tierney explains that "[t]he old claim that the church ought not to be controlled by secular rulers was now taken to mean that the civil magistrate had no right to interfere with any person's choice of religion."[125]

This deployment of the ancient Christian theme of dual jurisdictions in favor of conscience converged with the modern emphasis on the other distinctive and ancient Christian theme—namely, the emphasis on sincere inner faith as the essential path to eternal salvation. Because outward coercion could not produce a sincere inner faith, such coercion was pointless and perverse.

Early modern and modern advocates of religious toleration like Roger Williams, John Locke, and, later, James Madison, insisted on this point. "Forced worship stinks in God's nostrils," Williams fulminated; it is a form of "soul-rape."[126] In more measured tones, Locke made a similar point: "All the life and power of religion consist in the inward and full persuasion of the mind; and faith is not faith without believing." Consequently, compelled but insincere professions of faith, "far from being any furtherance, are indeed great obstacles to our salvation, . . . add[ing] unto the number of our other sins those also of hypocrisy, and contempt of his Divine Majesty."[127] James Madison's renowned *Memorial and Remonstrance* asserted that religious coercion is futile because "the duty which we owe to our Creator and the Manner of discharging it, can be directed only by reason and conviction, not by force or violence."[128] Or, as Jefferson's seminal Virginia Statute for Religious Liberty put it, "Almighty God hath created the mind free," and governmental coercion in matters of religion is thus "a departure from the plan of the Holy Author of our religion, who being Lord both of body and mind, yet chose not to propagate it by coercions on either, as was in his Almighty power to do."[129]

Of course, one need hardly be Protestant, or Christian, or even religious to see that coercion is unlikely to produce sincere conviction; a skeptic or agnostic could cheerfully acknowledge as much. But that conclusion, though cogent as far as it goes, hardly does justice to the commitment to freedom of conscience that developed in early modern Christian thought. The claim about the futility of coercion was conjoined to two other distinctively Christian ideas. First, a sincere faith is necessary for the attainment of the transcendent good of eternal salvation—a blessing that vastly surpasses all earthly goods—so that to intrude into the inner domain of faith is to interfere in the most sacred aspect of human life. Second, the domain of conscience is not merely something into which it would be futile or imprudent or even unjust for government to intrude; rather, that domain is outside government's *jurisdiction*.

This powerful conjunction of ideas was apparent in the declaration of the eighteenth-century Connecticut legislator and Yale rector Elisha Williams in an essay cumbersomely but revealingly titled "The essential Rights and Liberties of Protestants: A Seasonable Plea for the Liberty of Conscience, and the Right of private Judgment, In Matters of RELIGION, Without any Controul from human Authority." "If CHRIST be the Lord of Conscience," Williams contended, "the sole King in his own Kingdom; then it will follow, that all such as in any Manner or Degree assume the Power of directing and governing the Consciences of Men, are justly chargeable with invading his rightful Dominion; He alone having the Right they claim."[130] Less passionate but equally categorical was James Madison's conclusion: "Religion is wholly exempt from [the] cognizance" of society and government.[131]

In short, it was not merely that government ought to leave religion alone. Government had *no jurisdiction* in the realm of religion.

What about the Enlightenment?

We should pause to take stock. As we have seen, the standard story as conveyed in official accounts like that of *Everson v. Board of Education* depicts

American religious freedom as the happy result of an Enlightenment-inspired revolt against the perverse patterns of centuries of Christendom. Thus far in this chapter, by contrast, we have been observing the themes most often associated with religious freedom in the United States today—namely, separation of church and state and freedom of conscience—as the product of the distinctive teachings of Christianity. So, is the Enlightenment to be stripped of all the credit it has heretofore claimed and enjoyed?

Not at all. As with the other major terms we have been using—Christianity, paganism—the Enlightenment was in fact a multifaceted development, with various themes and emphases that not only differed but sometimes contradicted one another. Some thinkers and themes that we associate with "the Enlightenment" were overtly anti-Christian and indeed antitheistic; others were much more comfortable with Christianity.[132] Consequently, it is misleading to attribute any particular developments in this area simply to "the Enlightenment." Nonetheless, we can credit aspects of the Enlightenment with contributing to the development of American religious freedom in at least two quite distinct ways.

First, as we have seen, Christianity was a complex body of ideas, traditions, and practices, some of which could (and did) support repressive policies, while others could (and did) counsel in favor of toleration and freedom. Some Enlightenment thinkers worked within a generally Christian framework to articulate and underscore those aspects of Christianity—the division of spiritual and temporal jurisdictions, the necessity of freedom for genuine faith and virtue—that pointed to church-state separation and freedom of conscience. Indeed, we have already noted this contribution. We have already seen, in other words, that some of the major figures who argued for these freedom-oriented themes were thinkers typically associated with the Enlightenment: John Locke, James Madison, Thomas Jefferson.

Consider Locke, often regarded as the thinker who most influenced the American framers.[133] In his writings on religious toleration, Locke explicitly developed the Christian rationales for religious freedom. In the first sentence of his "Letter Concerning Toleration," Locke explicitly stated that his treatment of the subject grew out of a conviction that "toleration [is] the chief characteristic mark of the true church." The second sentence identified this church with "the church of Christ."[134] Locke then explained the centrality of the dual-jurisdiction conception to his project: "I esteem it above all things necessary to distinguish exactly the business of civil government from that of religion, and to settle the just bounds that lie between the one and the other."[135] And in denying coercive jurisdiction over religion to the state, Locke prominently featured the same "voluntariness" rationale—the claim that saving faith must be sincere and hence uncoerced—that predecessors in the Christian tradition from Constantine's adviser Lactantius to Roger Williams had insisted on. We know that "the care of souls is not committed to the civil magistrate" because "true and saving religion consists in the inward persuasion of the mind, without which nothing can be acceptable to God. And such is the nature of the understanding that it cannot be compelled to the belief of anything by outward force."[136]

Or take Jefferson. Although hardly an orthodox Christian, in his seminal Virginia Statute for Religious Freedom, as noted, Jefferson contended for the end of state-imposed religion on the premise that religious coercion was "a departure from the plan of the Holy Author of our religion."[137] Although Jefferson deliberately avoided any more specific or sectarian reference, in eighteenth-century Virginia, to whom could "the Holy Author of our religion" have referred except the biblical God?

In short, insofar as it fed into American religious freedom, the Enlightenment was not an antagonist to Christianity but rather a conduit for it—for Christianity under a benign and freedom-favoring interpretation. Hence it is not surprising that American figures associated with the Enlightenment—Jefferson and Madison in particular—could in this respect join forces with evangelicals like Isaac Backus and John Leland. Henry May describes the period in which state and national governments moved to disestablish religion and adopt legal protections for freedom of conscience as the "Jeffersonian moment" in which "a temporary alliance [was formed] between the Enlightenment and Protestant Christianity."[138]

There was also, however, another and quite different way in which the Enlightenment contributed to American religious freedom. To appreciate this contribution, we need to notice a phenomenon that has recurred repeatedly since the late Middle Ages: figures whom we think of (and who thought of themselves) as forward looking or progressive have often harked back to antiquity and have admired classical paganism as a refreshing alternative to current conditions that have seemed to them unattractive or oppressive. To be sure, opinions have differed widely about what those unacceptable conditions were, or are. Renaissance thinkers and artists might look back to classical times—and to paganism—as an alternative to what they experienced as the suffocating aridity of late medieval Scholasticism:[139] it is easy to feel this sense of freedom in, say, Botticelli's *Birth of Venus* or *Mars and Venus*. Describing the "pagan tendencies" of Renaissance humanists, Jacob Burckhardt offered this interpretation:

> But now, as competitor with the whole culture of the Middle Ages, which was essentially clerical and was fostered by the Church, there appeared a new civilization, founding itself on that which lay on the other side of the Middle Ages. Its active representatives became influential because they knew what the ancients knew, because they tried to write as the ancients wrote, because they began to think, and soon to feel as the ancients thought and felt.[140]

Later, a sensitive and romantic soul like William Wordsworth, feeling "forlorn" in a world of rationalism and commercialism, might find solace or at least "glimpses" in remembering the more enchanted world of paganism: "Great God! I'd rather be a pagan, suckled in a creed outworn."[141] A more hard-edged and defiant thinker like Friedrich Nietzsche might look back to paganism for a vision of a life not yet crushed by the slavish, sniveling mediocrity that he ascribed to Christianity and the world it had constructed.[142]

This admiration of and even yearning for paganism was evident in the Enlightenment as well. Indeed, we have already observed the phenomenon; we have seen how the Enlightenment historian Edward Gibbon depicted paganism in wistful and affectionate terms, contrasting the cosmopolitan and humane pagan world with the harsher, less congenial Christian civilization that succeeded it. Gibbon famously opined that "[i]f a man were called to fix the period in the history of the world, during which the condition of the human race was most happy and prosperous, he would, without hesitation, name that which elapsed" between the emperors Domitian and Marcus Aurelius.[143] We have seen as well how David Hume praised polytheism and excoriated monotheism—Christianity in particular. More generally, in his noted history of the Enlightenment, Peter Gay picks out this fondness for paganism as the central animating theme. Gay's subtitle makes the point: *The Rise of Modern Paganism.*[144]

This recurring fondness for paganism and the pagan world naturally has sometimes led to a specific wish to restore the "mild spirit of antiquity" (as Gibbon put it) in place of the perceived dogmatism of Christianity. Or, in other words, to embrace religious toleration in place of the practice of imposing Christian orthodoxy. This theme is prominent in Gibbon, Hume, and other Enlightenment thinkers. As a nice succinct expression of this idea, consider Thomas Jefferson's oft-quoted plea for religious toleration: "It does me no injury for my neighbor to say there are twenty gods, or no god. It neither picks my pocket nor breaks my leg."[145] This statement, quite different from the explicitly theistic rationale offered in Jefferson's Virginia Statute for Religious Freedom ("Almighty God hath created the mind free"), exhibits none of the distinctively Christian features: a commitment to monotheism, or an earnest concern for truth or for the salvation achieved through inner faith. Rather, Jefferson's statement resonates nicely with the easygoing pagan toleration fondly recalled (or constructed) by Enlightenment thinkers like Gibbon.

If Jefferson's pithy declaration looked backward to pagan attitudes, his statement ("It does me no harm") also looked forward to the idea most influentially articulated by John Stuart Mill and often referred to as "the harm principle." Mill would propose that "the sole end for which mankind are warranted, individually or collectively, in interfering with the liberty of action of any of their number, is . . . to prevent harm to others."[146] And on the basis of this supposedly "very simple principle," Mill would go on to argue for a wide scope for individual freedom in thought, expression, and conduct.

The intuitive appeal of Mill's harm principle has made it a powerful, if often *sub silentio,* force in American constitutional thinking, including the protection of religious freedom. Courts sometimes treat the principle as if it were part of the Constitution.[147] Law students often suppose the same thing: Andrew Koppelman, a law professor at Northwestern, notes that "each year at least one of my students recites the [harm] principle as if it were part of the Constitution, and everyone else in the room nods with approval."[148] In my own seminars on Religion and the Constitution, students often seem to regard the "free exercise of religion" as essentially a derivative corollary of "the harm principle," if they make any distinction between the two at all.

And it seems likely, if impossible to demonstrate or quantify, that the harm principle has done useful work in preserving a space for the practice of a variety of religions in the United States. We look out at the world and observe people believing and worshipping in a prodigious variety of ways. Most of this believing and worshipping will strike any one of us, if we are candid, as peculiar or absurd or at least implausible: if it were otherwise, we ourselves might feel impelled to join in the believing and worshipping. But we have learned to let people believe and worship as they choose. And we reflect (along with Jefferson) that however exotic or bizarre some of these religions may seem, they "neither pick [our] pocket nor break [our] leg." We behave, in other words, as good civilized pagans would behave. And we, and our society, are the better for it. Or at least so most of us have come to suppose.

The Perils of (Mere) Paganism

Even so, two points need to be stressed. First, this attitude of leaving alone what does not harm us hardly captures the distinctive American achievements in the realm of religious freedom. Indeed, like the harm principle itself, this pagan or, if you prefer Enlightenment, or if you prefer libertarian attitude has nothing distinctive to do with religion or faith; it applies equally to any form of belief or practice that does not inflict "harm" on others. But the celebrated American achievements in the realm of religion have been, first, an insistence on a "separation of church and state" and, second, a principled commitment to freedom of conscience. These distinctive and revered constitutional commitments are not at all equivalent to—and can hardly be dissolved without loss into—Mill's more generic "very simple principle." And, as we have seen, neither commitment was embraced in classical paganism. On the contrary.

Second, it would be reckless to suppose that the harm principle can assure anything like the sort of freedom that the American commitments to church-state separation and the free exercise of religion have (sometimes, imperfectly) afforded. For one thing, upon even moderately close inspection, the idea of "harm" turns out to be almost infinitely malleable.[149] In actual human experience untutored by liberal or libertarian instruction, not only bodily injury and economic loss but also psychic injury—including feelings of subordination or alienation or indignation—are harms. The harm principle might easily be invoked, therefore, to justify governmental regulation of all manner of activities; proponents of the harm principle manage to contain its antilibertarian potential only by twisting and gerrymandering the concept of "harm" in labyrinthine and often openly conclusory ways. Closely scrutinized, the real underlying argument ends up being, *not* that government cannot regulate *x* because *x* causes no harm, but rather that the very real and directly experienced evils associated with *x* must not be classified as "harms"—the term is now being used in a highly specialized and artificial sense—because we do not think government ought to regulate *x*.

Perhaps the most sophisticated proponent of the harm principle, the political philosopher Joel Feinberg (who elaborated the principle in a much-admired four-volume opus),[150] was endearingly candid about this necessary shaping and gerrymandering. The notion of "harm" must be carefully refined and limited, Feinberg explained, because otherwise the harm principle "might be taken to invite state interference without limit, for virtually every kind of human conduct can affect the interests of others to *some* degree, and thus would properly be the state's business."[151]

Moreover, to say that religious faiths and practices inflict no "harm" on others is, if we are candid, wildly implausible. Forget about "spiritual" harms, or harms to the soul, that the devout may attribute to religious beliefs they consider false: begging central questions, perhaps, let us stipulate that those types of harms cannot count. Even so, in the view of critics of particular religions, or of religion in general, religious beliefs and practices lead directly to a host of very real and wholly this-worldly evils. If you doubt the point, just read . . . well, any number of recent vehemently antireligious books or tracts by widely (though not universally)[152] respected authors such as Christopher Hitchens or Sam Harris.[153] Or consider the following assertion from a recent scholarly review by a professor at an Ivy League university: "[O]n a macro level," Professor Ross Koppel maintains, the "net effects of religion and faith are . . . a few thousand years of horrible wars, genocide, slavery's ideology, sexual exploitation, torture, devaluing others as not human, terrorism, and organized hatred."[154] So now, imagine a legislature composed of Hitchenses or Harrises or Koppels, or any of a host of like-minded thinkers, whose respect for freedom is shaped and limited mainly or exclusively by the harm principle. Under these conditions, how much protection or respect would the freedom to practice religion receive?

It may be that when religious freedom has flourished in America, that condition has been a result of the happy blending of Christian commitments with pagan or Enlightenment attitudes—of the distinctive American commitments to church-state separation and the free exercise of religion reinforced by a Jeffersonian or libertarian assumption that it does no harm if our neighbors believe in twenty gods or none. Conversely, it could be that religion and religious freedom are most vulnerable under conditions in which the darker, intolerant dimensions of Christianity and paganism converge.

Thus Christianity teaches, as we have seen, that the inner life matters— that it is important not only what people do, but what is in their hearts and minds. But this concern for the inner life is hardly a unique possession of Christians: as the history of the last century testifies, many secular thinkers and secular regimes have cared intensely that people have the proper thoughts and attitudes. Combine this concern for the inner life with the pagan assumption—one that Jews and Christians and Druids and others experienced firsthand—that although religion should be left alone when harmless, it can be properly and even savagely repressed when it threatens to cause harm. The conclusion of such a convergence of modern secular variants of the Christian and pagan attitudes is hardly a happy one for freedom of religion (or, for that matter, for other freedoms, such as freedom of thought or freedom of expression). Largely in disregard of the historical facts, critics like Jonathan Kirsch may suggest that Constantine's governance was "totalitarian,"[155] but the secular totalitarianisms of modern times[156] make Constantine and even his sterner successors like Theodosius look like paragons of restraint and civility. And we need not go so far as to consider such horrific examples as the Third Reich or the Communist regimes described by Solzhenitsyn or the reign of Pol Pot. Less extreme but closer to home, secular and even "liberal" puritans are far from being a mere abstract possibility.

If freedom of religion is a valuable feature of American life, therefore (and as we will see in Chapter 5, this is today far from being an uncontested or merely rhetorical "if"), we would do well to recall its sources and rationales (as we have done in this chapter), and to observe just how these rationales have played out in the American experience. In this respect, the standard story has not served us well. We will try to correct or compensate for its deficiencies in the ensuing chapters.

The American Retrieval

Let us retrace our steps to this point. Standard tellings of the story of American religious freedom depict the American position as a radical break with the past—as an Enlightenment-inspired break with and from a Christian past. And there is truth in this depiction. America's embrace of church-state separation was a break from the immediately preceding Erastian pattern in which the state controlled the church and operated it more or less as a department of the government. And the embrace of freedom of conscience was a repudiation of practices that had been common during the period of Christendom—the Inquisition being the most vivid example.

And yet this depiction is incomplete in central respects that cause it to be badly misleading. What the standard tellings (such as the Supreme Court's official account in *Everson v. Board of Education*) fail to acknowledge is that the major components of the American position were not new ideas; rather, they represented a retrieval and consolidation, under the circumstances of the new American Republic, of distinctively Christian themes that had been defended and sometimes practiced for centuries. The commitment to separation of church and state manifests the family features of a descendant of the ancient Christian ideal of dual jurisdictions—an ideal that had driven the centuries-long medieval struggle for "freedom of the church" from secular control. And the American commitment to freedom of conscience was a modern embodiment of another long-standing Christian commitment; this commitment was grounded in the convergence of the idea of inner, sincere religion as the prerequisite for salvation with the more Protestant development in which "freedom of the church" came to be extended to the "inner church" of conscience.[157]

The Enlightenment figured in forming the American approach in important part because it served as a conduit for these Christian themes. To be sure, the Enlightenment was a carrier of classical paganism as well. And the retrieval of paganism—or at least of the easygoing cosmopolitan toleration that thinkers like Hume and Gibbon perceived in paganism—was another important feature, even if a secondary and less distinctive one, of the American approach to religion and religious pluralism.

This convergence of Christian and pagan themes created the possibility of a political and cultural environment conducive to the practice of a diversity of religious faiths. At the same time, each strand—the Christian and the pagan—had, and has, a darker, more oppressive side. The convergence thus created as well the possibility of a politics and law that would be intrinsically unfriendly to the practice of religion. We will see indications of both possibilities in the ensuing chapters.

2

※

The Accidental First Amendment

Freedom of the church. Freedom of conscience. Chapter 1 suggested that these notions were the contributions, derived from centuries-old Christian themes and doctrines that, when accepted and adapted in American constitutional law, helped shape the distinctively American approach to freedom of religion.

But aren't we getting ahead of ourselves? And did Chapter 1 assume too much at the end of its survey? Did these classical commitments—to freedom of the church and freedom of conscience—actually make it into the American constitution? And if so, how exactly did they get there, and where are they located? Those will be the questions for this chapter.

Is a whole chapter really necessary, though? Shouldn't a paragraph, or at most a couple of pages, be sufficient? There is, after all, a quick and easy and already intimately familiar answer to the questions: The standard story of American religious freedom tells how visionary and courageous founders embraced principles of church-state separation and freedom of conscience and then wrote those principles into the First Amendment's religion clauses. The founders incorporated the principle of church-state separation—which, we can now see, is an American variant on or at least a descendant of the classical freedom of the church—into what is usually called the establishment clause ("Congress shall make no law respecting an establishment of religion"). And they incorporated the principle of freedom of conscience into the free exercise clause ("Congress shall make no law . . . prohibiting the free exercise [of religion]"). The story thus supposes that these principles were put into, and thus somehow contained in, the First Amendment from the outset, even if it took decades for Americans and their judges to realize and fully accept what the religion clauses actually meant.

We cannot simply recite this familiar story and move on, though, for one simple reason: as it happens, the story isn't true. (Although, it will turn out, the story isn't exactly and flatly false either.) In reality, the Americans who wrote and adopted the religion clauses did not imagine that they were enacting novel principles for churches or conscience or religion, or that they were doing anything especially visionary or courageous or even controversial. On the contrary: far from innovating, the framers' intention in enacting the religion clauses was basically to keep things as they were. Insofar as standard accounts treat the clauses as full of premeditated and momentous or transformative meaning, therefore, the accounts mislead us.

And yet . . . the First Amendment did somehow function to import commitments to church-state separation and religious freedom into our constitutional law. How did this happen? Not, I will argue, by human design, but rather by indirection, and as a result of later alterations and adjustments that occurred not according to anybody's conscious or deliberate plan. We might put it this way: the founders themselves didn't actually mean to constitutionalize church-state separation or freedom of conscience, and the later Americans who in fact did the constitutionalizing didn't know they were doing it; they supposed it had already been done.

If all of this seems confusing, and confused, that is because it *was* confused. To penetrate the confusion, we need to examine the clauses more closely in their historical context. We need to look at what the First Amendment religion clauses did deliberately (which was not very much), and at what they *didn't do* (which was a lot, measured by modern expectations anyway). And we need to observe how, without anyone directing or even quite realizing what was happening, those clauses came to mean something that the people who wrote and enacted them never exactly contemplated.

Holding on to the Status Quo: The Original First Amendment

A familiar counsel warns people who love sausage not to look too closely at how the stuff is made. Similarly, people who reverence the religion clauses of the First Amendment as something majestically transformative—perhaps as "one of the two most profound revolutions that had occurred in the history of the church," to quote the historian Sidney Mead[1]—would be prudent not to study close-up the actual process by which those provisions came into existence.

That is because the framers were utterly casual—indifferent, it almost seems—as they went about the business of drafting and enacting those provisions. Unless you are a very slow reader, you should be able to read in under fifteen minutes, aloud, the entire recorded discussion in the House of Representatives of what would become the religion clauses.[2] And the little that *was* said was hardly incisive or sagacious, or even very serious. Several of the remarks, reflecting still-fresh antagonisms concerning the Constitution itself, quibbled over whether the new government should be described as "national" or "federal." In this respect, perhaps the high point (or would it be the low point?) of the discussion was Elbridge Gerry's curmudgeonly comment that instead of using the terms "federalists" and "anti-federalists," it would be more accurate to refer to people who had favored and opposed ratification of the Constitution as, respectively, "rats and anti-rats." (Did anyone laugh? The record doesn't say.) Possibly the Senate was more serious about the measure, but no evidence supports that conjecture: there is no record of what the senators said or thought. The Senate changed the House's wording slightly, but the basic substance remained unaltered.

In short, if the framers were the prime movers at a historically momentous event, their attitude was shockingly inappropriate. It is as if Neil Armstrong had stepped out of *Apollo 11* onto the moon and, instead of talking grandly about a "giant leap for mankind," had instead muttered, "Yuck! What a wasteland! When do we get to go home?"

One prominent scholar, Leonard Levy, expressed his consternation:

> The debate [in Congress over the First Amendment religion clauses] was sometimes irrelevant, usually apathetic and unclear. Ambiguity, brevity, and imprecision in thought and expression characterize the comments of the few members who spoke. That the House understood the debate, cared deeply about its outcome, or shared a common understanding of the finished amendment seems doubtful.
>
> Not even Madison himself, dutifully carrying out his pledge to secure amendments, seems to have troubled to do more than was necessary to get something adopted in order to satisfy the popular clamor for a bill of rights.[3]

Instead of waxing indignant over this complacency, though, we ought instead to learn from it. What people don't care much about can be revealing. After all, politicians in the early Republic were as prone to prolixity as politicians today are—maybe more so. And religion stirred up profoundly divergent views then, as it does now; so questions of religious freedom or church-state relations could provoke as much political passion then as, say, a major health-care bill can generate today. If the First Congress was doing something momentous about religion—if it was adopting a constitutional provision or principle that would establish a fresh new relationship between government and religion for generations to come—we would expect that members of Congress would have reflected and negotiated and postured and pontificated at length before making such a transformative decision. The fact that they had very little to say, and that what they did say exuded apathy rather than engagement, suggests that . . . they didn't think that they were doing anything much. Their nonchalance is itself probative evidence; it is a case of the dog that didn't bark—or, more literally, of the politicians who didn't talk.

But how could it be that the religion clauses of the First Amendment were of small importance? To answer that question, we need to step back from the 1789 Congress in which the First Amendment was drafted and recall the Philadelphia Convention that had met two years earlier to draft the Constitution itself. As most people who have taken high-school civics know, the original Constitution contained no bill of rights. It wasn't that the delegates to the Philadelphia Convention didn't consider the issue, or that they didn't care about rights; they did, and they did. But they decided against including a bill of rights mostly because they believed (or at least they said they believed, although in the case of people like Alexander Hamilton there may be cause for suspicion) that because the national government would have only those delegated or enumerated powers given to it in the Constitution, there was no need to set out a list of rights. Why list rights qualifying powers that had never been given to the national government in the first place?[4]

So there was initially no bill of rights—and hence no provision recognizing any right to religious freedom or declaring a "separation of church and state." The Constitution did contain a provision forbidding the imposition of religious qualifications for holding federal offices.[5] That provision would have seemed apt, because of course national offices would be created and qualifications for those offices would be imposed. (The president had to be at least thirty-five, a resident for fourteen years, etc.) Political offices in this country had often carried religious qualifications of one sort or another to prevent Catholics or non-Trinitarians or non-Christians from gaining political power.[6] So if the delegates didn't want offices in the new national government to be restricted to the religiously orthodox, it would be prudent for them to say so; and they did. But because the delegates assumed that the national government's powers did not extend to actual regulation of religion, there seemed to be no need to adopt any right or principle of religious freedom.

When the delegates were sufficiently satisfied with the Constitution they had drafted, they sent it on to state conventions for ratification, and there the issues of a bill of rights, and of religious freedom in particular, came up again. And the supporters of the proposed Constitution—the federalists (or, as Elbridge Gerry would have it, the "rats")—took the same position they had taken in the Philadelphia Convention. No bill of rights and no explicit protection for religious freedom were necessary, they insisted, because the national government had no jurisdiction over religion anyway, and hence no jurisdiction to infringe on or regulate religion. In this spirit, James Madison assured a skeptical Virginia ratifying convention that "[t]here is not a shadow of a right in the general government to intermeddle with religion. Its least interference with it would be a most flagrant usurpation."[7] In the same vein, Richard Dobbs Spaight told the North Carolina convention that "[a]s to the subject of religion . . . [n]o power is given to the general government to interfere with it at all. Any act of Congress on this subject would be a usurpation."[8]

Opponents of the Constitution weren't persuaded. They feared (presciently, as it soon turned out) that under the logic of implied powers, or perhaps under the "necessary and proper" clause, the national government would be able to do all manner of things for which no explicit textual authorization could be cited. Partly in response to this concern, and to forestall the efforts of dissenters to convene a second constitutional convention, and perhaps also as a concession to secure the support of back-state Baptists whose votes he needed to beat out James Monroe for a seat in the House of Representatives, Madison was eventually persuaded to switch sides and support the addition of a bill of rights to the Constitution.[9]

His congressional colleagues remained unconvinced. And given the formidable task they faced of setting up a whole new government more or less from scratch, they grumbled when Madison, fulfilling a campaign promise, introduced such a measure in the House of Representatives in June 1789. One congressman whined about "the inexpediency of taking up the subject [of a bill of rights] at the present moment . . . while matters of the greatest importance and of immediate consequence were lying unfinished."[10] (The matter "of greatest importance" on the floor at that moment, as it happens, was a bill for establishing a land office.)[11] Madison's response was conciliatory, almost apologetic. Perhaps the critics were right in thinking that a bill of rights was superfluous. But some citizens and some states had demanded one, and he had become persuaded that adding a bill of rights could do no harm and might do some good. Madison assured his congressional colleagues that his proposal contained nothing in any way controversial—specific provisions would be limited to those that would "meet with universal approbation"—so that the whole business of a bill of rights might be disposed of "if congress will devote but one day to this subject."[12]

The prediction proved to be overly optimistic, but not by much. So various rights and protections that have since generated libraries of analysis and interpretation were proposed and passed with just a few minutes of lackluster discussion. Congress's ho-hum attitude is almost palpable in the record. Consider the cruel and unusual punishment clause, about which scholars and judges and death-penalty opponents and proponents have since written countless books, articles, opinions, and legal briefs. After the provision was read to the House on August 17, 1789, two representatives spoke. William Smith of South Carolina thought the words were "too indefinite." Samuel Livermore of New Hampshire agreed: the provision sounded humane, he conceded, but who could tell whether it might preclude punishments that are "sometimes necessary," such as whipping culprits or cutting off their ears? No one so much as bothered to answer these objections. The record merely reports that after Livermore's remarks, "[t]he question was put on the clause, and it was agreed to by a considerable majority."[13] You can almost hear Livermore's congressional colleagues complaining: "Sit down, Sam! Let's get on with it. Please, would somebody just call the question?"

Although representatives may have taken little interest in provisions like the cruel and unusual punishment clause, we might have expected them to engage more carefully with provisions dealing with religion. In the preceding centuries, after all, religious differences had been associated with long and bloody wars throughout much of Europe. In the English civil war, a king, Charles I, had been parted from his head. In addition, religion had been severely regulated by European governments: many American settlers had come to this country precisely to escape such impediments to the practice of their various faiths. But in due course religion had been regulated and subsidized here as well, and such measures had been the source of recurring controversies on these shores.

Within the decade just before the adoption of the Bill of Rights, for example, the leading states of Virginia and Massachusetts had adopted or modified (in opposite directions) state constitutional provisions dealing with the subject—Virginia had terminated and Massachusetts had reaffirmed their religious establishments, respectively—and in both cases these measures had provoked wide-ranging and sometimes passionate argument.[14] The subject was thus very much on people's diversely oriented minds. So it might seem that religion would be one matter that Congress would be unable to deal with casually. And yet that is just what Congress did.

Looked at in its political context, though, this complacency becomes less of a puzzle. Remember that virtually everyone in the country—supporters and opponents of the Constitution alike, as well as backers and detractors of state-supported religion—had agreed from the outset that matters of religion had been and should continue to be within the domain of the states: these matters should not be transferred to the jurisdiction of the national government. If Massachusetts wanted to have an established religion, it could; if Virginia wanted to disestablish religion, it could do that too. The Constitution's supporters had argued that the unamended Constitution already left this jurisdictional arrangement intact by not including religion among the powers delegated to Congress. Opponents were skeptical, because they doubted that the strategy of enumerating powers could limit national authority as effectively as supporters sanguinely promised. So the Constitution's supporters basically agreed to put the limitation in writing: they added a provision expressly declaring that "Congress shall make no law."

In this respect, the religion clauses (and the First Amendment generally) were importantly different from the provisions in Amendments II through VIII. Those provisions appear to set forth restrictions on powers that Con-

gress *did* have (or at least might turn out to have); often they did this by list-
ing substantive rights that the national government was not supposed to
infringe—the right to bear arms, the right to counsel, the right to jury trial,
and so forth. The First Amendment worked differently, as its distinctive wording suggests: it reinforced the strategy of limiting governmental power by
explicitly declaring that Congress lacked power in the area of religion. *Not*
"the right of religious freedom shall not be infringed," but rather "Congress
shall make no law."

Yale law professor Akhil Amar, a leading scholar of the Bill of Rights,
observes that the First Amendment's distinctive wording seems to have been
crafted as an explicit qualification of the "necessary and proper clause,"
which was the clause that opponents of the Constitution feared as a source
of implied national powers over various subjects, including religion. "The
First Amendment," Amar explains,

> intentionally inverted the language of the Necessary and Proper Clause,
> which stated that *"Congress shall* have Power To . . . *make all Laws* which
> shall be necessary and proper. . . ."* Note how the First Amendment, which
> read unlike any other, tracked and reversed this language: *"Congress shall
> make no law . . . ,"* meaning that Congress simply had no enumerated
> power over either speech or religion.[15]

Moreover, if Congress could make no law on the subject, then there would
be no law for the executive to execute and no law (or at least no federal law)
for the judiciary to adjudicate. In those youthful days of innocent or at least
professed faith in the efficacy of separation of powers, therefore, it could
seem to follow that denying jurisdiction to Congress meant denying jurisdiction to the national government as a whole. As president, Thomas Jefferson
expressed this understanding in his famous letter to the Danbury Baptists.
"Congress thus inhibited from acts respecting religion," Jefferson wrote, "and
the Executive authorised only to execute their acts, I have refrained from
prescribing even occasional performances of devotion."[16]

The reason that the nation's representatives and senators showed almost
no interest in the religion clauses of the First Amendment, in short, was that
they did not believe that those clauses were doing anything, or at least that
they were changing anything. The clauses were merely reaffirming—probably
gratuitously, but just to be safe—the jurisdictional status quo; they were not

adopting any particular principle or theory of the relation between government and religion.

In reality, it would have been difficult or impossible for Congress to settle on any such principle or theory, because views in the country on that subject diverged widely. Some citizens (like Jefferson and Madison) thought an established religion was unnecessary, and bad for both government and religion; others (like soon-to-be Yale president Timothy Dwight) believed society would fall apart without a state-supported religion.[17] Jefferson's position had recently prevailed in Virginia after a fierce political struggle and over the opposition of Patrick Henry. (Despairing of Henry's powerful influence, Jefferson had written to Madison that "[w]hat we have to do I think is devoutly pray for his death.")[18] Conversely, Dwight's view tended to come out on top in New England states. Michael McConnell explains: "The establishment of religion . . . commanded considerable support among Americans at the time of the founding. It had solid historical roots, it was linked in political theory to republicanism, and it was justified in terms of social utility."[19]

Congress would have found it next to impossible to resolve those deep disagreements.[20] Fortunately, Congress didn't have to settle such conflicts. All that the occasion called for was to confirm in writing what virtually everyone did agree on—namely, that religion was within the jurisdiction of the states, and that the institution of a new national government was not calculated to change that situation. Thus states would continue to be free to maintain established churches or eliminate them, as they had been before the Constitution was adopted.[21]

This interpretation raises questions of detail over which we need not linger here. For example, did the denial of national jurisdiction over religion mean that Congress could not legislate on the subject of religion in domains where it had essentially the same plenary powers that the states had within their own jurisdictions—in the territories or (later) the District of Columbia, for example? For present purposes it is enough to say that the historical record does not furnish confident answers to such questions, in all probability because the enactors simply were not thinking about them.[22]

In sum, members of Congress didn't talk much about what the religion clauses meant because they didn't intend those clauses to do much, or to do anything novel. The clauses primarily confirmed that jurisdiction over essential matters of religion would remain where it was, and where virtually everyone wanted it to remain.[23]

The Substantive Content of "No Jurisdiction"

So the religion clauses were primarily jurisdictional in nature. But of necessity they had a substantive component as well—one that derived directly from their jurisdiction-allocating purpose. A jurisdictional measure, after all, can hardly be without substance: it will necessarily confer or deny jurisdiction over *something*, and it will need to say what that something is.

In this instance, the something encompassed "an establishment of religion" and "the free exercise [of religion]." (Or at least the prohibition of that exercise.) Congress had no jurisdiction to make laws respecting those matters. One thing that followed from this denial of jurisdiction was that the national government was precluded from setting up a national church of the kind that European nations and some states had maintained. This was the immediate practical payoff of the jurisdictional division—no national church—and it may well have been foremost in the minds of Americans who supported the provisions. In this vein, at the conclusion of a recent study, Donald Drakeman explains that

> it is important to appreciate that [the establishment clause] was not the statement of a principle of secularism, separation, disestablishment, or anything else. It was the answer to a very specific question: Would the new national government countenance a move by the larger Protestant denominations to join together and form a national church? The answer was no. . . .
>
> At the time it was adopted, the establishment clause addressed one simple noncontroversial issue, and the list of those who supported it demonstrates that it cannot reasonably be seen as encompassing a philosophy about church and state.[24]

Drakeman reports this conclusion with some disappointment. He had expected and hoped to find a more ambitious meaning and purpose; but it turns out, he thinks, that the enactors were only concerned to prevent the creation of a national church.[25]

It is no small support to Drakeman's interpretation that a very similar interpretation was given at the time by James Madison himself. As noted, congressional discussion of the provision was sparse. But a few questions and concerns were raised, and so Madison explained what the provision was intended to do. "Mr. Madison," the record reports,

> Said he apprehended the meaning of the words to be, that congress should not establish a religion, and enforce the legal observation of it by law, nor compel men to worship God in any manner contrary to their conscience; whether the words were necessary or not he did not mean to say, but they had been required by some of the state conventions, who seemed to entertain an opinion that under the clause of the constitution, which gave power to make all laws necessary and proper to carry into execution the constitution . . . enabled them to make laws of such a nature as might infringe the rights of conscience, or establish a national religion, to prevent these effects he presumed the amendment was intended, and he thought it as well expressed as the nature of the language would admit.[26]

Although Drakeman's conclusion is persuasive in the main, it calls for qualifications. In the first place, in addition to preventing Congress from setting up a national church, the religion clauses explicitly forbade Congress to "prohibit[] the free exercise [of religion]." Drakeman presumably would not quarrel with this assertion; he does not discuss the denial of power to prohibit free exercise, probably, because he is discussing the First Amendment's establishment clause, not its free exercise clause. And in this respect he follows virtually universal contemporary practice, which nearly always treats the clauses separately. The practice is useful and convenient; I am likewise following it, for the most part, in this chapter. Even so, grammatical purists point out that strictly speaking, what we call the religion clauses (plural) are actually a single clause.[27] More important, the enactors' own thinking seems to have tracked the grammar. As the preceding quotation from Madison reflects, the enactors did not typically treat the words as presenting two independent clauses or provisions.[28] Thus the religion clause (singular) as contemplated by the framers clearly did more than merely prevent the creation of a national church: it also denied national jurisdiction over "the free exercise of religion."

In addition, even if we focus on the portion of the First Amendment that we call the establishment clause, the provision did not say that Congress should make no law "establishing a church"—that might have been the clearest and most economical way to convey the meaning discerned by Drakeman—or even "establishing a religion." Rather, the provision says that "Congress shall make no law *respecting* an establishment of religion." Why this more convoluted wording?

The phrase "establishment of religion" need not make trouble for Drakeman's interpretation. An "establishment of religion" might plausibly be read to mean, basically, an "institution of religion." Just as the term "business establishment" is often used to describe a going or operating business enterprise, not necessarily one enjoying any sort of state-conferred monopoly or special privilege, a "religious establishment" might simply refer to an operating, institutionalized religion. In short, to a church. (Or, insofar as "church" is mostly a Christian term, to the institutional equivalent of a church in non-Christian religions.)

The First Amendment, to be sure, says, "establishment of religion," not "religious establishment." But word order may not matter here, and indeed, years later, when Madison as president vetoed a bill to incorporate the Episcopal Church in Alexandria, he quoted the First Amendment, incorrectly but presumably in good faith, as if it contained the reordered wording. The First Amendment, he asserted in his veto message, says that "Congress shall make no law respecting a *religious establishment*."[29] Moreover, Madison evidently believed that this prohibition applied even though the bill adopted by Congress did not propose to set up the Episcopal Church as the exclusive or official church of Alexandria. In short, Madison seems to have interpreted the establishment clause, at least in this instance, to mean, basically, that Congress should make no law respecting an institution of religion or, in other words, a church. In this vein, Douglas Smith makes a strong case, based in part on late eighteenth-century corporation law, that the establishment clause meant that "[j]ust as the federal government lacked the general authority to issue regulations regarding corporations, so too it lacked the specific authority to either create or regulate religious corporations."[30]

So far, so good. But there is another difficulty for Drakeman's restrictive interpretation. Let us accept that the phrase "establishment of religion" was equivalent to "religious establishment," which in turn could mean, basically, "church." Even so, the establishment clause still does not merely prohibit Congress from "establishing [a church]." Rather, it forbids Congress to make laws "*respecting* [a church]." What does that wording add?[31]

Although the legislative history does not answer this question, the wording itself suggests some obvious possibilities. Some states, such as Massachusetts and Connecticut, continued to maintain established churches for decades after the Constitution and the First Amendment were adopted. So suppose, for example, that Congress had passed a law regulating—or perhaps taxing—these churches. Such a law would not be one "establishing" a church. But it would be a law "respecting" churches. At least a couple of comments in the House of Representatives (by Benjamin Huntington of Connecticut and Peter Silvester of New York) suggest, albeit obscurely, that some members of Congress may have been concerned about this sort of possibility—namely, about federal or constitutional interference with state establishments of religion.[32] But any such law would be one "respecting" churches, and hence would be precluded by the First Amendment as it came to be worded.[33]

Or suppose that in some area over which Congress has plenary legislative authority, such as the District of Columbia, Congress were to pass a law requiring all ordained and practicing ministers of the Gospel to be licensed in order to preach or minister, in the way in which doctors or electricians have to be licensed. Once again, this would not be a law creating a church or designating it as the official church. But the law would be one *respecting*—or, if you prefer, *with respect to*—churches. Such a law would thus run afoul of the "respecting" language of the establishment clause.

In sum, even on the entirely plausible assumption that "establishment of religion" meant something like "institution of religion," which basically meant "church," the language of the First Amendment did more than forbid Congress to create or designate an official church. Rather, the language denied the power to make laws "respecting" a church. The provision thus effectively deprived the national government of authority over churches. And, as noted, the second part of the clause also denied the national government power to prohibit "the free exercise [of religion]."

Let us retrace our steps. The purpose of the religion clauses, as we have seen, was not to embrace any particular philosophy or principle of church-state relations or religious freedom, but rather to confirm in writing that

jurisdiction over such matters would remain with the states, where virtually all Americans wanted it to remain. In confirming this jurisdictional allocation, however, the clauses necessarily had a substantive component; they
specified the substance of what the national government was being denied
jurisdiction over. And that denial covered, basically, churches and the free
exercise of religion (which at that time was conceived as virtually synony-
mous with freedom of conscience).[34]

So, if we return to the questions with which this chapter began—namely,
did the classical commitments to freedom of the church and to freedom of
conscience get into the Constitution, and if they did, how did they do so?—
does it turn out that the quick, peremptory answer is basically correct after
all? Does our analysis now allow us to conclude, albeit after some meandering, that the First Amendment's religion clauses adopted the classical commitments to separation of church and state (which, if not identical to the
freedom of the church, at least resembled it) and to freedom of conscience?

Not quite. The First Amendment may have imposed substantive constraints
on the national government, but it did so, once again, merely as part of a
division of jurisdiction, not because the enactors (or Americans generally)
were embracing church-state separation or freedom of conscience as affirmative constitutional principles or commitments. In some practical respects,
perhaps, this distinction would not have mattered much: on either interpretation the government would lack authority to, for example, create a national church. And yet there is an important difference between a limitation
that derives from a jurisdictional allocation and a limitation that derives
from an affirmative substantive prohibition. (Just as there is a difference
between, on the one hand, being told that you can't do x—sell the house,
buy the car, choose the movie—because x is not to be done and, on the
other hand, being forbidden to do x because the decision properly belongs to
someone else.) In the same way, lawyers understand that having a case dismissed "on the merits" is quite different from having the case dismissed "for
lack of jurisdiction." Both decisions have the consequence that the case is
thrown out of court. But the logic and meaning of the decisions are different, and so are the legal implications—some of them, anyway.

In fact, the idea of freedom of conscience probably enjoyed the support of
nearly all Americans at the time;[35] the idea of church-state separation, not so
much. But even with respect to freedom of conscience, when Madison tried

to secure an amendment protecting it against the states, the effort failed.[36] Americans and their representatives were prepared to confirm the existing jurisdictional division, and, as a corollary of that division, to preclude the national government from interfering in religion or religious institutions. They were not prepared, it seems, to embrace church-state separation or freedom of conscience as affirmative constitutional commitments in their own right.

But this conclusion seemingly brings us back to the questions we started with. How exactly did the classical commitments to freedom of the church and freedom of conscience get into constitutional law? Or did they?

Unexpressed Principles?

The quick answer, which I offer with some trepidation and which will require explaining, is that over time the meaning of the words of the religion clauses subtly changed, and expanded. But this is a risky answer, because there is a version of this answer that is by now comfortably familiar, almost platitudinous, but that will lead us astray.

The familiar but misconceived version suggests that beyond (or would it be beneath, or maybe within?) what they actually *said*, the religion clauses also implicitly constitutionalized some "principle" (whatever that is),[37] or perhaps several principles,[38] that were thereby imported into the Constitution and imposed on the nation even without being explicitly articulated. Constitutional principles, in turn, are thought to be capable of expanding or adapting to changing circumstances or improved understandings. The usual conclusion is that in interpreting and applying a constitutional provision such as the First Amendment, judges are obligated not so much to study and implement either what the enactors consciously intended or what the provision expressly said as to extract the principle implicit in it, and then to elaborate and enforce that principle. Indeed, a good deal of modern constitutional law proceeds on the assumption that not just the First Amendment but the Constitution generally should be viewed not as a mundane legal instrument but rather as a sort of repository of lofty principles.[39] In this spirit, dismissing contemptuously those who think of the Constitution as akin to "a document with the texture and tone of an insurance policy or a standard form of commercial lease," Ronald Dworkin insists that the Constitution is an expression of "broad and abstract principles of political morality" whose "scope is breathtaking."[40]

So, what exactly were the "principles" implicit in the First Amendment's religion clauses? Let us focus first on the establishment clause. Answers differ, but today the leading views hold that the establishment clause contained a principle of secular government, or a principle that government must be neutral toward religion. Or both: the "secular government" and "neutrality" principles are typically thought to be at least compatible with each other and probably mutually entailing or reinforcing. As we will see in Chapter 4, nearly all modern constitutional adjudication and scholarship in this area proceeds on some such assumption.

Such attributions of principle to the establishment clause are embarrassed, however, by the historical evidence (or lack thereof). There is little or no evidence that the enactors believed they were constitutionalizing any such principle. So the argumentation consists mostly of wishful thinking—of contemporary values and agendas projected backward onto the past. ("If *we* were adopting religious freedom provisions today, we would embrace principle *x*; therefore, *the framers* must have enacted principle *x*.") This practice of attributing to provisions adopted two centuries ago currently popular principles is fully in accord with Ronald Dworkin's influential prescription that when the meaning of a constitutional provision is uncertain (and what constitutional provision cannot be rendered uncertain by sophisticated interpreters?), the interpreter should assign it the meaning that will make it "the best it can be."[41]

In the case of the establishment clause, though, it is not just that historical evidence of the adoption of currently favored principles is lacking. In fact, the same people who wrote and voted for the establishment clause promptly proceeded to behave in ways inconsistent with the principles ostensibly contained in it by supporting and endorsing and being distinctly nonneutral toward religion in a whole variety of ways. They appointed chaplains to begin congressional sessions with prayer. They authorized President Washington to proclaim a national day of prayer and thanksgiving, and Washington enthusiastically did just that.[42] Government officials of the period used religious language routinely in their official acts and statements.[43] Laura Underkuffler explains that at the time of the founding governmental papers were replete with mention of "God," "Nature's God," "Providence," and other religious references. Religious references on the Great Seal of the United States were apparently deemed desirable by conservatives and reformers alike. When proposed designs were solicited, Franklin suggested an image of Moses lifting up his wand and dividing the Red Sea, with the motto "Rebellion to tyrants in obedience to God," and Jefferson proposed the children of Israel in the wilderness "led by cloud by day and a pillar of fire by night." Reformers tolerated such references, apparently, because they were not believed to implicate core concerns.[44]

Proponents of the "neutrality" and "secular government" principles typically attempt to explain away such disappointing and seemingly deviant behavior by saying that the favored principles were novel, so that even people who liked and voted for the principles did not fully grasp their implications. Thus Steven Green, a strong proponent of a secularist construction of the First Amendment, acknowledges the frequent religious expressions by early governmental bodies and officials but offers the curious dismissive rejoinder that "[t]he ubiquity of religious discourse cautions against reading too much into such statements."[45] Green is confident that "[a]pparent inconsistencies in rhetoric aside, the founders knew they were creating a nation based on secular principles."[46] The argument seems to be that we should not take the founding generation's religious expressions too seriously as evidence of what they were thinking and doing because that was just the way everyone always talked (and thought?) in those days. The logic of this dismissal is not easy to discern. Or the modern supporters sometimes say, as Justice David Souter suggested, that the enactors of the establishment clause were politicians who, when it was opportune to do so, conveniently forgot (as politicians will) to follow unpopular principles.[47] Exactly why these politicians would have enacted an unpopular principle in the first place so that they could then promptly and routinely forget to follow it is a puzzle that is typically not explained.

In this vein, Douglas Laycock, a leading scholar and litigator of religious liberty, argues that the establishment clause embodied a principle of "substantive neutrality"[48] that entails, among other things, a prohibition on any governmental endorsement of religion (such as those conveyed by currently controversial Ten Commandments monuments,[49] or crosses placed alongside highways to commemorate fallen police officers,[50] or the National Day of Prayer[51]). So, what are we to make of the fact that the same members of Congress who wrote and approved the establishment clause endorsed religion—and did so officially and repeatedly and unapologetically in their legislative prayers and national days of prayer and thanksgiving and such? Didn't these actions and expressions endorse religion?

Well, yes, they did, Laycock concedes. But these actions are not probative of the original meaning, he insists, because in these instances members of Congress were not acting on the principle of "substantive neutrality" that they had recently adopted. Rather, they were acting from "unreflective bigotry" in disregard of that principle.[52]

If they could be revived and given a chance to defend themselves, though, the enactors might protest that such charges are grossly unfair. Isn't it harsh to attribute to them a principle—of "substantive neutrality" or public secularism or whatever—that they themselves never articulated or pretended to accept, and then to accuse them of hypocrisy or "unreflective bigotry" for repeatedly and routinely violating an ostensible principle they never signed onto? "If you want a constitutional principle of 'substantive neutrality,'" they might retort, "enact it yourselves. We gave you a method of doing that, in Article V of the Constitution. And if you can't get your principle enacted (maybe because Americans generally don't want it in your day any more than they wanted it in ours), that's your problem: don't go accusing us of being hypocrites for not following a principle we never pretended to favor in the first place."

Of course, there is nothing to prevent us from projecting our preferred principles onto the Constitution if we want to do that. Such projection is not only possible; we've seen it done—on a massive scale. (More on that in Chapter 4.) So if we like the principles of secularism or neutrality, we can easily enough read those principles back into the religion clauses: rewriting history to suit our needs is common enough in constitutional law. But there is little to support the claim that the people who enacted the religion clauses in the first place were thereby consciously embracing (but somehow, oddly, failing to articulate) these principles as affirmative constitutional commitments.

So, if the original purpose of the First Amendment religion clauses was merely to confirm a jurisdictional arrangement (albeit one that admittedly deprived the national government of authority to interfere with institutions of religion or with the free exercise of religion), and if the clauses were not intended to constitutionalize "principles" that were not actually articulated, then it seems our stubborn initial question remains. Once again, how, if at all, did the affirmative commitments to freedom of the church (or its more modern iteration or offspring, "separation of church and state") and freedom of conscience get into our Constitution?

The Meandering Amendment of Constitutional Meaning

The cumbersome and inelegant answer, it seems, is that the clauses came to reflect and express acceptance of these commitments as a result of two complicated changes that have taken place over the course of American history. The first change was in the realm of opinion, and of linguistic meaning. The second was in the structure of constitutional law as interpreted by the Supreme Court.

In tracing the meandering course of these changes, it will again be helpful to treat the establishment clause and the free exercise clause separately. Start with the establishment clause. We have seen that Americans of the founding era were divided about the idea of separating church and state: some favored state-supported religion, and some didn't. Over the next few decades, though, opinion shifted: a consensus developed in support of church-state separation, or at least of religious disestablishment.[53] Thus in 1833, the last holdout, Massachusetts, abandoned its established religion. Proponents of the standard story sometimes try to project this later consensus back onto the enactors of the religion clauses themselves.[54] But although that sort of anachronism is untenable, the consensus did eventually develop, and this shift of opinion was accompanied by a subtle but important linguistic change. As Kurt Lash has argued, the words of the First Amendment, which had originally carried a jurisdictional meaning, came to be widely understood in a more affirmative and nonjurisdictional sense.[55] Lash explains:

> The Founders had been anything but unanimous about the dangers of a union between church and state and had not intended to express any such

nonestablishment value. However, by Reconstruction, northern state courts had translated the prohibition of the original Establishment Clause to be an expression of a fundamental religious liberty. So complete was the re-interpretation of the Establishment Clause that its language—sui generis at the Founding—now began to appear in the organic law of states.[56]

This shift in meaning is strikingly evident in the Iowa Constitution, adopted in 1857. Iowans wanted to forbid an established church—and not just because they thought this question should be left to the states: after all, they *were* a state. And in order to achieve their end, they used language that precisely tracked the wording of the First Amendment: "The General Assembly shall make no law respecting an establishment of religion, or prohibiting the free exercise thereof."[57] Those words, originally jurisdictional, had come to convey a more unqualified and affirmative commitment to church-state separation.[58]

Professor Lash describes this change in meaning as a "second adoption" of these clauses, and we can imagine a fantasy world of hyperaware linguistic purists and nitpickers in which such a shift would actually lead, formally, to a "second adoption" of the provision.[59] "Decades ago," the purists might explain, "when we adopted the First Amendment, the words 'Congress shall make no law respecting an establishment of religion' merely described a jurisdictional arrangement. At that time we did not agree about whether church-state separation was a good idea; we could agree only that this was no proper concern of the national government. Today, though, most of us have come to support an affirmative commitment to church-state separation. This is a weighty commitment, and it ought to be reflected in our Constitution. So we ought to enact a new constitutional amendment for that purpose. But actually, come to think of it, the existing wording already expresses our present intention. So we may as well just adopt that wording again. In place of the old First Amendment, which read 'Congress shall make no law respecting an establishment of religion,' we will therefore ask the states to ratify a new First Amendment, which will read 'Congress shall make no law respecting an establishment of religion.'"

But of course this sort of thinking would be bizarre. So nothing of this kind happened, or could have happened. For one thing, the change in opinion had been gradual, and the change in linguistic meaning had been barely perceptible, as such changes usually are. So there was no reason for anyone even to notice what had happened. And even if people had noticed, the existing constitutional language was perfectly adequate to convey what was desired, so what would be the point of reenacting the same constitutional language that was already in place?

Consequently, no formal amendment was made. And yet, as a result of evolving opinion and linguistic understanding, the national government, previously limited by a jurisdictional restriction that entailed church-state separation at the national level, came to be limited by an affirmative commitment to church-state separation. Nor was this commitment contained merely in some ghostly "principle" that somehow lurked in or emanated from the words. It was what the words themselves actually *said,* and actually meant.

Even so, the restriction still applied only at the national level. That limitation was eventually lifted as well as a result of a second major change. This change, which was extraordinarily convoluted, occurred not so much in the general culture as in the legal profession and the courts, and it has engaged lawyers and judges and legal scholars for almost a century and a half by now. A summary overview will be sufficient for our purposes. In 1868, in the aftermath of the Civil War, the nation adopted the Fourteenth Amendment. This amendment applied to *the states,* not just to the national government, as the Bill of Rights had done, and it required states to respect the "due process of law," to provide "equal protection of the law," and to honor the "privileges and immunities of citizens."

Whether these provisions "incorporated" (as lawyers say) the provisions of the Bill of Rights and thereby extended those provisions to the states is a question that has generated countless volumes of learned discussion. It seems that most scholars and judges today have concluded that the Fourteenth Amendment *did* extend the original rights (including those contained in the First Amendment's religion clauses) to the states.[60] That is a convenient and congenial conclusion, obviously, but even so it may be correct. Initially, however, the Supreme Court took a stingier view.[61] And in the 1870s, when Congress was contemplating a different constitutional amendment on the subject of religion (the so-called Blaine Amendment), members of Congress, many of whom had been in the 1868 Congress that had drafted and approved the Fourteenth Amendment, did not seem to suppose that the earlier amendment had already made the religion clauses effective against the states.[62]

So it was not until the twentieth century that the Supreme Court ruled that various rights contained in the Bill of Rights were incorporated into the Fourteenth Amendment. (Even then, according to prevailing scholarly opinion, the Court picked the wrong clause as the locus of incorporation: the Court said the rights were "incorporated" into the due process clause—which seems an inapt receptacle for that purpose—when a much better choice would have been the privileges and immunities clause.)[63] And it was not until the 1940s that the religion clauses were extended to the states in this way.[64]

From a detached perspective, this whole process may look impressively (or perhaps comically) convoluted. The nation adopts a provision limiting the jurisdiction of the national government; the provision's purpose is to keep things as they are. As the provision's jurisdictional purpose recedes from active memory, however, it comes to be understood as expressing more affirmative substantive commitments. And these affirmative commitments are then extended to the states by a new constitutional amendment—except that decades pass before the Supreme Court realizes that the new amendment had this purpose or this implication.

Be that as it may, through a decades-long development of shifting opinion, evolving linguistic meanings, and flip-flopping legal interpretations, a provision casually adopted in order to confirm the jurisdictional status quo came to express major and more affirmative constitutional commitments. In particular, it came to express an affirmative commitment to "separation of church and state." In this meandering fashion, something like the classical commitment to freedom of the church wove its way into American constitutional law.

Freedom of the Church and Church-State Separation

I say that "something like" the classical commitment came into the law advisedly, though, because the relation between the classical "freedom of the church" and the American "separation of church and state" is not perfectly clear. Are these merely different labels for the same essential idea, or at least closely related ideas? Or is there no very close connection?

What we can say with confidence is that both notions—freedom of the church and separation of church and state—resonate with the classical and Christian idea of dual jurisdictions, or of the independence of spiritual and secular authorities, that we examined in Chapter 1. This was not the position favored in the Roman Republic or the Roman Empire, as we saw: the Romans believed that religious and temporal powers should be united in a single authority. More modern thinkers like Hobbes have embraced the same conclusion.[65] In separating church from state, by contrast, the Americans opted for the dual-jurisdiction approach. In that respect, the classical "freedom of the church" and the American "separation of church and state" are of a piece.

Whether the notions are identical, however, is in a sense an artificial and unanswerable question, for at least two reasons. First, there has never been any canonical statement of the meaning of either notion anyway. On the contrary, their meanings have always been energetically contested. Surveying the sprawling array of conceptions of church-state relations that were put forward during the Middle Ages and early modern period, the legal historian John Witte sorts these conceptions into four "models" that differ significantly among themselves.[66] And of course interpretations of the meaning and implications of church-state separation have diverged significantly in American constitutional discourse as well.

Second, for better or worse, "freedom of the church" has not been the subject of the kind of sustained attention or devotion in the American political tradition that "freedom of conscience" has received. Given the Protestant character of early America and the conspicuous strand of anticlericalism that has often characterized American culture,[67] this lack of emphasis is hardly surprising: even devout Americans have often looked on "the church" with wary suspicion. Thus states in nineteenth-century America often regulated churches in intrusive ways, specifying what their legal structures must be and limiting the amount of property they could hold.[68] Such measures sit uneasily with any robust conception of freedom of the church.

In other cases, however, a commitment to the churches' autonomy from the state has been recognized, and indeed eloquently affirmed by the courts. Such affirmations have been especially conspicuous in cases involving disputes over church property, beginning in the late nineteenth century and continuing to the present.[69] (Although it has often been unclear whether these decisions were based on the establishment clause, the free exercise clause, or some combination thereof, or something else altogether—like "federal common law.") Similar pronouncements have issued from cases limiting the government's ability to regulate religious institutions.[70] The most recent such affirmation, and one of the most emphatic, occurred in a 9–0 decision of the Supreme Court handed down in 2012;[71] we will consider that decision more closely in Chapter 5. And although the Supreme Court has not declared tax exemption of churches constitutionally mandatory, it has warmly approved such exemptions:[72] this stance reinforces the idea that religious institutions are independent of the state. More generally, constitutional doctrine over the last four decades has forbidden "excessive entanglement" between government and religion.[73]

All these decisions and pronouncements affirm a commitment to keeping churches independent of governmental control or regulation. Thus it seems secure to say that American constitutional law contains a commitment to the classical idea of freedom of the church, even though the commitment has received only intermittent attention, and even though the exact content and implications of the commitment remain uncertain.

The Gradual Adoption of Freedom of Conscience

Thus far we have been looking at the path by which the classic commitment to freedom of the church came to be associated with the First Amendment's establishment clause. But what about the other classic commitment (to freedom of conscience) and the other religion clause (namely, the free exercise clause)?

The path by which freedom of conscience came to be accepted in American constitutional law ran roughly parallel to that followed by freedom of the church. In the founding era, "freedom of conscience" and the "free exercise of religion" were essentially interchangeable concepts.[74] Thus the First Amendment's free exercise clause in its original jurisdictional understanding protected freedom of conscience in the limited sense of forbidding the national government to interfere with that freedom. And as with the establishment clause, what was initially a jurisdictional provision over time came to be understood in more unqualifiedly substantive or affirmative terms that amounted to a sort of "second adoption" of the free exercise clause.[75] Decades later, in the 1940s, the Supreme Court then found that this reformed free exercise clause had been "incorporated" into the due process clause of the Fourteenth Amendment and was thus binding on the states, as well as the national government.[76]

In fact, the evolution from "jurisdictional limitation" to "affirmative substantive commitment" was even easier with free exercise than with separation. Unlike separation of church and state, which was controversial in the founding period and only gradually came to command general assent, the idea of freedom of conscience was widely accepted by Americans even at the time of the founding.[77] All that was necessary was for the original jurisdictional meaning of the provision to recede from prominence and memory; support for the more affirmative commitment was already there from the outset.[78]

The fact that the free exercise clause was originally enacted casually as part of a confirmation of the jurisdictional status quo, though, rather than through the deliberate and reflective adoption of an affirmative constitutional commitment, has likely contributed to uncertainty about the meaning and implications of the "right" that almost invisibly evolved. More specifically, two questions have tormented free exercise jurisprudence.

The first question, over the issue of so-called free exercise exemptions, appeared from the outset, at least under state laws. State constitutions recognized a right to freedom of conscience, or free exercise of religion. But did this right merely mean that governments should refrain from telling citizens which churches to belong to or not belong to, what forms of worship to practice or not practice, or what creeds to profess or not profess? That government should refrain, in other words, from punishing people for being Catholic or Protestant or whatever, as rulers in Christendom had traditionally done? Or, conversely and more ambitiously, did free exercise mean that governments must affirmatively accommodate religious believers, exempting them from laws that would require them to violate their faith, even if the laws were not intended to persecute but instead were adopted to serve generally legitimate ends? Should Quakers be exempted from military service, for example, or devout Jews from appearing in court on Saturdays, which was for them the Sabbath?[79]

In short, was the right to free exercise basically a right only to be free from actual religious persecution? Or did it go further and require affirmative accommodation as against generally valid and legitimate laws?

A standard depiction presents the judicial response to this question in three stages.[80] During the nineteenth century and about half of the twentieth, the Supreme Court did not interpret the clause as requiring free exercise exemptions, or affirmative accommodation of conscience. Free exercise meant that a person was free to believe whatever he or she felt drawn to believe, but it did not give any license for conduct that violated generally applicable law.[81] Then, from about the early 1960s until 1990,[82] the Court expanded its protection for religious exercise, ruling that government must exempt religious objectors from generally applicable laws unless there was a compelling reason to require compliance. Finally, in a controversial decision in 1990 (the famous or infamous "peyote case"), the Court declared that although legislatures may choose to exempt religious believers, as long as a law is religiously "neutral" and "generally applicable," the Constitution does not require that religious believers be exempted from compliance.[83] In short, the Court went more or less full circle: it went from not requiring "free exercise exemptions" of conscience to requiring them, and then retreated to something like its initial "no required exemptions" position.

The reality has been less orderly, both in the past and the present. Plausible scholarly arguments contend that nineteenth- and early twentieth-century courts were actually more friendly to free exercise exemptions than the standard depiction allows (even if they were unwilling to go so far as to allow Mormons to marry multiple wives).[84] And the current "no mandatory exemption" position is qualified, first, by exceptions of uncertain and elastic scope that lower-court judges sometimes exploit[85] and, second, by both state and federal statutes that offer more accommodation to religious believers than current constitutional doctrine demands.[86] All these matters are disputed on the levels both of normative prescription and of historical description or interpretation. We will look at two recent Supreme Court cases in Chapter 5, and will see that they point in contrary directions.

What we can safely say, then, is that the Constitution has long been construed to support a commitment to the free exercise of religion. But whether this means merely that government should not deliberately and coercively interfere in religious matters or that government should affirmatively accommodate religious conduct is an issue that has been debated throughout American history, with no decisive resolution in sight.

The other major issue that has troubled free exercise jurisprudence has been what exactly falls within the scope of legal protection. At the founding, as we have seen, "freedom of conscience" essentially meant the same thing as "free exercise of religion." But with the passage of decades, that identity was sundered. So, which deserves protection—"religion" (whatever that is), "conscience" (whatever that is),[87] or both? In recent decades, both judges and scholars have typically tended to expand the scope of what should be protected to include even conventionally nonreligious exercises of conscience:[88] the Vietnam War–era military conscription cases were exemplary in this respect.[89] But then what exactly counts as conscience? Judicial and scholarly opinion on these questions remains profoundly divided.

A Glance Backward—and Forward

We began this chapter by asking whether and how the classical Christian commitments to freedom of the church and freedom of conscience made their way into American constitutional law. It would be convenient if we could answer simply that visionary founders embraced those commitments and wrote them into the establishment and free exercise clauses, respectively. That answer, as we have seen, is too clean. The enactors of the First Amendment were not attempting to do anything new or visionary. On the contrary, they were trying merely to preserve the jurisdictional status quo, leaving religion to the states. In keeping the national government out of questions of religious establishment and free exercise, though, the religion clauses effectively treated the national government as subject to the classical commitments. And as the jurisdictional character of the original settlement receded and was replaced by more affirmative understandings, and as those understandings were later extended through the fact or fiction of "incorporation," the classical commitments gradually slipped into constitutional law—through the back door, so to speak.

This quiet and largely unplanned entrance has had its drawbacks. For one thing, there has never been a single moment and a deliberate or authoritative decision to which we can look back in order to figure out what the constitutional commitments actually mean. Instead, courts have given those commitments meaning through a more unmoored process of constructive interpretation and perhaps invention.

In one way, though, this difficulty has not been especially inconvenient. That is because, at least until recently (as we will see in Chapter 5), some of the central evils that the classical commitments were calculated to avoid or resist have not really been live possibilities, in this country anyway. A few Americans in the founding era may have feared, as Madison acknowledged, that the new government would set up a national church. But given Americans' religious pluralism and their suspicion of ecclesiastical hierarchies, there was never any realistic possibility of that happening, First Amendment or no First Amendment. And although public sentiment has from time to time risen up in hostility to particular religious groups—Catholics, Mormons, Jehovah's Witnesses, perhaps today Muslims—there was never any real temptation to pass laws mandating that everyone embrace some particular faith or forbidding particular forms of worship. Nor was there ever any likelihood on these shores of something systematic like the Spanish Inquisition.

We might exaggerate just slightly and say that by the time the classical commitments had worked their way into American constitutional law, the historical practices and dangers that had generated those commitments were already to a significant extent a thing of the past.[90] What was now politically problematic was not so much the church (or even the "inner church" of conscience) but rather a relative newcomer on the scene—namely, "religion." Consequently, the primary challenge would be not *the church*, as in medieval and early modern times, but rather *religion*, and in particular religious pluralism. It would be that challenge—the challenge of something called "religion"—that would lead to America's distinctive and distinctively valuable (albeit now mostly forgotten or misunderstood) achievement.

We will look in Chapter 3 at what the achievement was. And in Chapter 4 we will consider how this achievement has been forgotten, misunderstood, and undone.

3

The Religion Question and the
American Settlement

Perhaps surprisingly, the main protagonist in our story thus far has been . . . the church. Freedom of the church, or separation of church and state, are on their face church-centered subjects. Freedom of conscience not so much, maybe, or at least not so obviously: still, in the period we have mostly been considering—namely, from the inception of Christianity up through the early American Republic—conscience was connected to the church. As we saw in Chapter 1, the commitment to freedom of conscience descended from a convergence of the idea that the church is a jurisdiction independent of the state with the Protestant extension of that jurisdiction to the "inner church" of conscience. This association of conscience with church was apparent in the early American Republic: people who talked about "freedom of conscience" typically meant something like the freedom to join (or not) a church, or to worship (or not) as one saw fit.[1]

Over the decades and centuries, however, this focus on the church has been subtly displaced by an emphasis on something different and more amorphous—namely, religion. With the benefit of hindsight, we can see that even as the American nation was getting started, the political centrality of churches was already past its high point (even in countries, like England, that continued to maintain at least the vestige of an established church). In the United States, officially established churches were a thing of the past by the 1830s. Religion, by contrast, was a whole other story: contrary to the expectations and predictions of numerous social theorists and secular prognosticators, both the varieties and the demographic reach of religion in American society have, if anything, increased since the founding period.[2]

But religion has been a diverse and sometimes fractious affair. How to deal with religion has thus presented a major and sometimes vexing question. In America, the constitutional commitments to separation of church and state and freedom of conscience have formed an outer framework within which that question—the "religion" question—has been presented and addressed. But those commitments still leave a great deal pertaining to religion—its role in and relation to government—stoutly unresolved. And because people care passionately about religion, those unresolved issues can be divisive and even incendiary.

Beginning in its early years, the American Republic developed a distinctive, and distinctively valuable, approach to the challenge of religion: we can call it "the American settlement." This arrangement had a down-to-earth, blue-collar, somewhat uncouth quality. For all its practical virtues, in terms of sheer philosophical or theoretical elegance the American settlement would not score high marks; indeed, its lack of philosophical contours might cause it (and has caused it) to go mostly unrecognized by theoretically inclined scholars and jurists. Nor does the American settlement fit comfortably into the standard modern story of American religious freedom as sketched in the Prologue—or for that matter, into progressive accounts of the development of Western responses to religious pluralism since the Reformation. The American settlement has accordingly been widely overlooked, misunderstood, and forgotten—especially in recent decades. And the practical consequences of that forgetting have not been happy ones.

In this chapter, therefore, we will attempt two things. First, we will consider the rise of "religion," and the partial displacement of what we might call the "problem of the church" by the more modern "problem of religion." Then we will try to recover and delineate the American response to the problem of religion—or what I am calling "the American settlement."

As in Chapters 1 and 2, we will not be attempting any sort of comprehensive history, but will be selectively examining major pertinent developments and themes. That examination will reveal that the American settlement did not follow the trajectory that progressive secular thought sometimes ascribes to post-Reformation efforts to cope with religious diversity; even so, it constituted a practically effective, if inelegant, strategy for addressing that challenge. This presentation will set the stage for Chapter 4, where we will observe how the American settlement has been largely undone and will consider the unfortunate consequences of that undoing.

The Invention of Religion

In Chapter 1 we talked about religion in the classical and medieval worlds—about the pervasiveness of pagan religion in the Roman Empire and the gradual displacement of paganism by Christian religion. But although this shortcoming may not have been apparent, there was all along something quite anachronistic about this way of talking. *We* often think of "religion" as some discrete thing or category, or some distinct compartment of life. But people in classical and medieval times probably didn't think in this way. We might almost say that to them, there wasn't any such thing as religion.

We might *almost* say this, because to say it outright would be to replace one mistake with a worse one. There was, of course, much in the Roman and medieval worlds that would fit comfortably within our category of religion. The Roman world had its temples and processions and rituals, its auguries and animal sacrifices. Medieval societies had their cathedrals, monks, bishops, holy days, pilgrimages, liturgies, sacred relics. The problem is that there was little or nothing that, to people then, did *not* fall within the province of religion, or that did not have a religious dimension. Thus Ran Hirschl observes that in medieval Europe, "[r]eligion was embedded in the political and social fabric of the community and was integral to, and inseparable from, everything else."[3] In the same vein, William Cavanaugh explains that "*religio* was not a separate sphere of concern and activity, but permeated all the institutions and activities of medieval Christendom."[4]

But in a society in which virtually everything was religious, it was not needful or natural to talk about "religion" as if it were some discrete category of human activity or concern or some separate compartment of life. (Just as it would not be natural for us to talk about a world containing things like people, dogs, cars, computers, and . . . "being.") Thus some scholars have suggested that the concept of "religion" as a distinct category of life or practice or belief is a modern invention.[5] José Casanova describes religion as a "modern secular category."[6] William Cavanaugh declares that "[t]here was a time when religion, as modern people use the term, was not, and then it was invented."[7] More specifically, Cavanaugh argues that "religion" was an invention of Locke and thinkers of his period.[8] In a similar vein, although he places the development slightly earlier, Jonathan Smith describes "the major expansion of the use and understanding of the term 'religion' that began in the sixteenth century."[9]

By now, to be sure, religion seems familiar and natural and unproblematic—unproblematic as a category, that is—even if we have difficulty defining just what "religion" is. But it was not always so. And the modern invention of religion has presented difficult political questions that were previously absent.

We saw in Chapter 1 that in the Middle Ages there were questions, and sometimes serious and violent conflicts, about the role and jurisdiction of the church. And there were also disagreements that we would think of as religious disputes—disputes, for instance, over what was orthodox and what was heretical. But there was not really a conflict over the role of religion in governance. For example, there was no controversy then, as there is now, over whether secular rulers should act on "religious" grounds or for "religious" purposes. If "religion" (as we would call it) was thoroughly intermixed with everything, then *of course* kings and princes would act on "religious" grounds (our description) and for "religious" purposes.[10] To have declared that a king should make and justify his decisions without relying on religious beliefs or considerations would have been approximately as sensible as saying that you should sign your name without using letters or calculate your gross income without using numbers.

Religion, in short, was not a political issue. Or we might put it this way: the controversies that arose were controversies *within* religion, not over or *about* it. Once invented, though, religion quickly became a political issue; indeed, religion came to replace church as the central issue. Think of the leading modern controversies involving the First Amendment's religion clauses—prayer in public schools, conscientious objection to military conscription and to other regulations, public religious symbols such as crosses or Ten Commandments monuments or the words "under God" in the Pledge of Allegiance. All these controversies, we would say, involve religion; most of them do not essentially or inherently involve churches. And even when churches do come into the picture, it is typically because churches are viewed as sources of or sites for the real subject of controversy—namely, religion.

The main reason religion has presented legal and political problems, of course, is that not everyone agrees about religion. Some people embrace one religion, some another, some none at all. And among those who adhere to no religion, some are merely indifferent, while others are vehemently opposed. Consequently, a central problem for modern politics and political thought—some might even say *the* central or at least seminal problem[11]—has been the challenge of religious pluralism.

Coping with Pluralism: Three Phases

Scholars and theorists have often and plausibly understood the modern history of religious freedom, and perhaps even of liberal democracy more generally, as an ongoing effort to address the challenge of pluralism that emerged from the shattering of Christendom by the Protestant Reformation. Not that Western societies were one big, happy, peaceful family before the Reformation. On the contrary, Christianity in the late Middle Ages had been riven by schisms, heretical developments like the Albigensian and Lollard and Hussite movements, the "Babylonian captivity" of the papacy, frequent clashes between popes and kings, and inquisitions. Even so, both clerics and kings accepted the existence of a set of overarching Christian truths, and of institutional mechanisms for figuring out and declaring what those truths were. Thus the historian Brad Gregory explains that on the eve of the Reformation, Western Christendom constituted "an almost riotous diversity held together in an overarching unity by a combination of ingrained customs, myriad institutions, varying degrees of self-conscious dedication, and the threat of punishment." Consequently, "[r]eferences to medieval 'Christianities' that downplay the common beliefs, practices, and institutions of Latin Christendom are as distorting as older, facile exaggerations about the Middle Ages as a homogeneous 'age of faith.'"[12]

The Protestant Reformation disrupted this rather tempestuous unity. Disagreements about Christian truth proliferated and deepened. As the decades and centuries passed, more thinkers, and more influential thinkers, rejected Christian teachings altogether, tacitly or openly. And acceptance of "the church" (in the singular) as an institution with encompassing jurisdiction to resolve such disagreements disappeared, to be replaced by commitments to a variety of more geographically limited churches, or to none.[13] In this vein,

John Rawls explains that the Reformation "fragmented the religious unity of the Middle Ages and led to religious pluralism. . . . This in turn fostered pluralisms of other kinds, which were a permanent feature of culture by the end of the eighteenth century."[14]

As a political matter, proliferating religious diversity presented at least two kinds of closely related challenges. One was the challenge of legitimacy. Lack of agreement about overarching religious truths made it more difficult to accept the ruler's authority as divinely ordained, thus pushing opinion to the view that legitimate government must instead be based, as the Declaration of Independence put it, on "the consent of the governed." But that consent has always been at least in part constructive or fictional— how many of us have ever actually signed some consent form subjecting ourselves to the government?—so if the governed differ radically in their most basic beliefs, how is the requisite consent to be achieved (or plausibly imputed)? Another challenge had to do with deliberation. Especially as governments became or aspired to be more democratic, it was important that citizens be able to reason together about matters of public importance. But the possibility of reasoning together is most real when there are common premises to reason from. If the citizens hold fundamentally different ultimate beliefs, then how is such deliberation achievable?

So the new "hyperpluralism," as Gregory calls it, has posed serious political challenges. Following a familiar narrative, and simplifying a much more convoluted history, we might try to place the modern responses to these challenges into three main phases that our history has followed (or at least *ought* to have followed).[15]

In the first phase, states attempted to reestablish unity by energetically and coercively enforcing a declared orthodoxy. Hence the renewal and intensification of inquisitions in the sixteenth century by the Spanish monarchs and by the Council of Trent.[16] Hence also the "wars of religion" as different rulers attempted to reestablish a Catholic or Protestant orthodoxy for all of Europe.[17] As the possibility of a continentally inclusive orthodoxy receded, states still tried to impose orthodoxies on a more limited geographic basis. Thus the Treaty of Westphalia of 1648 ordained that the religion of each realm would be the religion of its prince, thereby initiating the era of the "confessional state."[18]

Over time, though, it became apparent that the religious differences let loose by the Reformation were too deep-seated to be forcibly suppressed, even within a single nation. Peoples in Europe and America desperately needed to find ways to live together in more pluralistic peace. And so Western societies moved into a second phase that we might call the phase of toleration. The Edict of Nantes, issued by Henry IV in France in 1598, granted limited toleration to Protestants; in England, the Act of Toleration adopted in 1689 granted freedom of worship to some dissenting Protestants (though not to Catholics, Quakers, or unitarians). And a good deal of toleration flourished under less formalized arrangements. Officials would carefully neglect to notice private worship conducted in dissenters' homes, or would permit dissenters to congregate and worship beyond city walls—in fields or in neighboring towns.[19]

These regimes of toleration remained restrictive, however; more fundamentally, they continued to support an established orthodoxy, even if that orthodoxy condescended to tolerate or "put up with" a fair amount of deviation or dissent. This sort of policy was understandably galling to religious minorities and dissenters, who naturally viewed themselves as outsiders or second-class citizens. In this vein, Thomas Paine scoffed that "[t]oleration is not the opposite of intoleration, but is the *counterfeit* of it. Both are despotisms."[20] In a similar spirit, when Virginians convened after independence to adopt a Declaration of Rights for their new state, the young James Madison managed to defeat George Mason's proposal to protect "the fullest *Toleration* in the Exercise of Religion" and instead secured a provision declaring that "all men are *equally* entitled to the full and free exercise of religion."[21] Ralph Ketcham explains that "Madison . . . concluded that mere 'toleration' of other sects was insufficient to protect religious freedom, and that establishments of religion themselves must be dismantled."[22]

The shift from tolerant orthodoxy to religious equality implied that government would refrain from taking any position or siding with any of the competing religious or antireligious views or factions in society. In such matters, government must remain neutral.

But how was government to do that? It seems that if citizens vary widely in their religious beliefs (or lack thereof, or opposition thereto), any religious affirmations by government could not plausibly be described as neutral. Nor would it be neutral for government to engage in antireligious expressions. So what is left? If governments cannot be either religious (as they had been under Christendom, for example) or antireligious (as Communist regimes have often been, for example), then it seems governments must be merely *not religious*. Or, in other words, . . . secular?

We will see more of this logic in Chapters 4 and 5. For now, we can say that on something like this reasoning, Western societies entered into a third phase—one we might call the phase of "secular neutrality." Or so theorists may suppose.

In sum, in addressing the challenge of religious pluralism, Western history since the Reformation, following a kind of evolving progressive logic, may seem to have developed in three rough phases. Efforts to restore unity through a coercively enforced orthodoxy gave way to regimes of more tolerant orthodoxy in which some dissent was permitted, and these regimes in turn matured into governments committed to religious equality interpreted as entailing secular neutrality. This last sort of regime, unsurprisingly, has been lauded and argued for and refined in a seemingly endless stream of political philosophizing typified by the theorizing of John Rawls and like-minded thinkers.[23] Today "there is a broad consensus," Jocelyn Maclure and Charles Taylor approvingly report, "that 'secularism' is an essential component of any liberal democracy composed of citizens who adhere to a plurality of conceptions of the world and of the good."[24]

Recalcitrant America?

So, did America conform to this three-stage depiction? Yes, it did, the standard story suggests—but in a messy and regrettably retarded way.

By the time Americans were writing their Constitution, the first two strategies, coerced orthodoxy and toleration, had already been thoroughly tried. Almost two centuries had passed since the Edict of Nantes, more than a century since the Peace of Westphalia, a century since Locke's "Letter Concerning Toleration" and the English Act of Toleration. One might suppose that the serious shortcomings of phases one and two—of enforced orthodoxy and of orthodoxy-grounded toleration—should already have been apparent, and that Americans would have been ready to move on to phase three, religious equality and secular neutrality.

And, indeed, America's farsighted founders were prepared to do this. Or so relates the standard story. Thus we have already noted how Madison insisted on replacing the theme of toleration in the Virginia Declaration of

Rights with an explicit commitment to equality. More generally, legal historian Steven Green describes in the early Republic "a significant attitudinal shift away from a standard of religious toleration of dissenting sects toward a regime of equality, at least in theory."[25] And partisans of the standard story typically insist (albeit in defiance of the evidence, as we saw in Chapter 2) that the Constitution sought to ensure that the new national government would be secular and neutral toward religion.

But then something went wrong. After signing on to the lofty commitments contained (ostensibly) in the Constitution, American political leaders almost immediately reverted to old bad habits.[26] They appointed legislative chaplains, declared national days of prayer, and subsidized Christian proselytizing among the Indian tribes. As the nineteenth century unfolded, religious revivals swept across the country, and a de facto establishment of generic Protestantism came to infuse society and politics.[27] Under this de facto Protestant orthodoxy, dissenters and atheists were sometimes prosecuted for blasphemy. Catholics, and later Mormons, and (in the next century) Jehovah's Witnesses were persecuted and discriminated against. Jews were marginalized and sometimes officially insulted.[28] The de facto Protestant establishment dominated the developing public school systems: daily religious exercises were conducted, and Catholic students who objected to reciting the Lord's Prayer from the (Protestant) King James Bible were disciplined and intimidated.[29] Sometimes these conflicts led to violence, and rioting. And this dismal picture does not even take account of what was done to Native Americans.

Meanwhile, for the most part, the courts stood idly by, permitting or even assisting in the imposition of a Protestant orthodoxy. Distinguished judges like Joseph Story and James Kent solemnly asserted that Christianity was part of the common law.[30] The Supreme Court itself audaciously declared that "this is a Christian nation."[31] And in this context, "Christian" meant Protestant—Protestant of an evangelical variety. So it was not until more than a century and a half had elapsed after the founding that judges and political thinkers were ready to take the next, long-deferred step into stage three—the era of religious equality and secular neutrality.

So says the standard story, at least in its more hard-edged tellings; more pious or celebratory versions—the versions we might tell to innocent children, or on patriotic occasions—try to look past this bleak century and a half of Protestant hegemony. In registering this lamentation, however, the standard accounts in fact overlook the distinctive American approach to religious pluralism. So I will argue in the balance of this chapter that it was during this middle period spanning the nineteenth century and the first half of the twentieth that the distinctive, and distinctively successful, American achievement in religious freedom—what we can call "the American settlement"—was worked out. Indeed, the later, court-supervised approach (to be considered in Chapter 4) represented not so much a realization or fulfillment of a deferred promise of religious freedom as a dismantling of this distinctive American achievement.

Interpreting the Republic: Providentialist or Secular?

As a point of entry into this middle period, let us jump to the year 1833. In that year, the president of the College of Charleston, Jasper Adams (a scion of the famous Massachusetts family), preached a sermon that he reduced to a lengthy essay titled *The Relation of Christianity to Civil Government in the United States.* Adams then solicited comments on the essay from some eminent national figures. These included James Madison, the revered framer and retired president, as well as two distinguished Supreme Court justices—John Marshall, the great chief justice, and Joseph Story, who was also a Harvard professor and the nation's leading legal scholar. In Adams's essay and the responses it elicited,[32] we can perceive lines of division that have meandered through the nation's history from the beginning to the present.

Adams's sermon and essay were prompted, it seems, by his concern about a view that "is gradually gaining belief among us, that Christianity has no connexion with the law of the land, or with our civil and political institutions." Adams believed this view "to be in contradiction to the whole tenor of our history, to be false in fact, and in the highest degree pernicious."[33] A sounder view, he thought, required a distinction between governmental support for "*one form* of Christianity over *all others*"—Adams opposed this sort of sectarian policy for its unfortunate tendency to "make [Christianity] the odious engine of the State"[34]—and what he regarded as the benign and necessary policy of supporting Christianity in general. On the basis of history, custom, and law, Adams argued that the American form of government was founded on this more ecumenical policy, combined with a commitment to protecting the free exercise of religion for everyone. "Thus, while all others enjoy full protection in the profession of their opinions and practice, Christianity is the established religion of the nation, its institutions and usages are sustained by legal sanctions, and many of them are incorporated with the fundamental law of the country."[35]

In short, the government would not identify with or sponsor any particular Christian denomination. And everyone could follow the religion of his or her choice. Notice here the themes of freedom of the church and freedom of conscience. But government would be based on and associated with Christianity in general.

In his response, Justice Story enthusiastically embraced Adams's interpretation. "My own private judgement has long been," Story explained, "(& every day's experience more & more confirms me in it,)"

> that government can not long exist without an alliance with religion to some extent; & that Christianity is indispensable to the true interests & solid foundations of all free governments. I distinguish, as you do, between the establishment of a particular sect, as the Religion of the State, & the Establishment of Christianity itself, without any preference of any particular form of it.

Story went on to concur in the concern that motivated Adams's essay:

> I look with no small dismay upon the rashness & indifference with which the American People seem in our day to be disposed to cut adrift from old principles, & to trust themselves to the theories of every wild projector in to [?] religion & politics.[36]

John Marshall, the renowned chief justice, likewise expressed approval of Adams's essay, albeit in more guarded terms. Everyone agreed, Marshall said, on "the importance of religion to the happiness of man even during his existence in this world." And given that "[t]he American population is entirely Christian," Marshall thought that "it would be strange, indeed, if with such a people, our institutions did not presuppose Christianity." But Marshall warned that laws involving religion required "great delicacy, because freedom of conscience & respect for our religion both claim our most serious regard."[37]

In marked contrast, the elderly James Madison took issue with Adams's interpretation. Although almost half a century had passed since he had authored his *Memorial and Remonstrance against Religious Assessments*[38] during the legendary struggle for religious disestablishment in Virginia, Madison reprised some themes from that famous manifesto. Experience in America had demonstrated, he observed, that government and religion each flourished better if they remained separate from each other. Conceding that "it may not be easy, in every possible case, to trace the line of separation," Madison nonetheless advocated "an entire abstinence of the Government from interference, in any way whatever, beyond the necessity of preserving public order, & protecting each sect against trespasses on its legal rights by others."[39]

In this revealing exchange we can discern a distillation of two contending views, or families of views, that traced back to the founding and also pointed forward to the twentieth and twenty-first centuries. With misgivings (some of which I will explain shortly), we might call these the "providentialist" and the "secularist" views. These interpretations of the American republic have competed with each other, sometimes cordially and sometimes combatively, from the Republic's inception to the present day.[40]

Thus legal historian John Witte describes a similar rivalry in the positions or "models" advocated by John Adams, the nation's second president, and Thomas Jefferson, the third. The Jeffersonian model, Witte explains, viewed religion as a separable field of knowledge and practice from which government should remain detached.[41] By contrast, although Adams agreed with Jefferson in endorsing religious pluralism and freedom of conscience, he also believed (as Witte puts it) that

> every polity must establish by law some form of public religion, some image and ideal of itself, some common values and beliefs to undergird and support the plurality of protected private religions. The notion that a state could remain neutral and purged of any public religion was, for Adams, . . . a philosophical fiction. . . . It was thus essential for each community to define and defend the basics of a public religion.[42]

Witte thinks these two models have competed with each other throughout the country's history, with Adams's model predominating through the mid-twentieth century and Jefferson's view achieving ascendancy thereafter.[43]

Witte's general diagnosis finds support in other scholarly studies. Fast forward to the present. Writing in the 1990s, the sociologist James Davison Hunter discerned a similar split in American self-understandings. Hunter described the competing positions with the terms "orthodox" and "progressive." The "orthodox" camp, reflecting a "biblical theism" that includes many Catholics, Protestants, and Jews, is defined by "the commitment on the part of adherents to an external, definable, and transcendent authority." This authority "tells us what is good, what is true, how we should live, and *who we are.*"[44] By contrast, the progressive camp is composed both of "secularists" who adhere to no religion and also of persons who, though counting themselves religious, place their trust in "personal experience or scientific rationality" over "the traditional sources of moral authority, whether scripture, papal pronouncements, or Jewish law."[45] The conflict between these contrasting perspectives, Hunter thought, "amounts to a fairly comprehensive and momentous struggle to define *the meaning of America*—of how and on what terms will Americans live together, of what comprises the good society."[46]

Still more recently, Noah Feldman maintains that America today is divided between what he calls "values evangelicals" and "legal secularists."[47] Andrew Koppelman sorts the contending positions on current issues implicating religion into "radical secularists" and "religious traditionalists."[48]

Thus, from the beginning through the present, it seems, Americans have gravitated to two contrasting interpretations of the Republic. Of course, to fit the range of views held by Americans into two broad camps obviously requires a good deal of rounding off and squishing together. And yet these simplifications capture something important in the social and political landscape and thereby aid our understanding. Acknowledging the inevitable simplifications, therefore, we should try to perceive more clearly the essential characteristics of what we are calling the "providentialist" and "secularist" interpretations.

Start with the providentialist view, which, according to Witte, predominated in the early decades of the Republic. In the 1833 exchange, a providentialist perspective was expressed most emphatically by Jasper Adams and Joseph Story. As we have seen, although Adams and Story insisted that government should give no preference to any particular denomination and should protect the free exercise of religion, they believed that some mutually supportive association between government and Christianity in general was not only permissible but prudent and even necessary.

Why necessary? To answer this question, we might turn to another eminent source. In oft-quoted statements, George Washington suggested two reasons that government ought to favor religion in a generic sense. In his famous Farewell Address, Washington asserted that religion is a necessary support for civic virtue.

> Of all the dispositions and habits which lead to political prosperity, Religion and morality are indispensable supports. . . . And let us with caution indulge the supposition, that morality can be maintained without religion. Whatever may be conceded to the influence of refined education on minds of peculiar structure, reason and experience both forbid us to expect that National morality can prevail in exclusion of religious principle.[49]

The notion that religion is necessary for morality and civic virtue is familiar enough, if much disputed, even today. The notion was widely held in the founding period—Daniel Dreisbach explains that "this was a virtually unchallenged assumption of the age"[50]—and it could imply the need for governmental support for religion. (Though this was hardly an inevitable or universally drawn implication: Madison, for example, contended that government support subverted rather than strengthened religion, producing "pride and indolence in the Clergy, ignorance and servility in the laity," and "weaken[ing] in those who profess this Religion a pious confidence in its innate excellence."[51]) But on another occasion Washington expressed a different reason for associating government with religion—one that seems less familiar in some circles today but that is crucial for understanding American political culture. In his first inaugural address, Washington declared that

> it would be peculiarly improper to omit in this first official Act, my fervent supplications to that Almighty Being who rules over the Universe. . . . No People can be bound to acknowledge and adore the invisible hand, which conducts the Affairs of men more than the People of the United States.

Every step, by which they have advanced to the character of an independent nation, seems to have been distinguished by some token of providential agency. . . . These reflections, arising out of the present crisis, have forced themselves too strongly on my mind to be suppressed.[52]

Notice that in this seemingly heartfelt expression, Washington made it explicit that he was engaged in an "official Act"—he was speaking as president and in an official ceremony, not merely as a private individual—and also that the obligation to acknowledge Providence runs to "the People of the United States" as a body or nation, not just to private individuals who happen to be pious. Just as devout individuals often believe, on grounds of gratitude or self-interest or both, that they ought to acknowledge the Almighty, so also the nation itself, or "the People" (as a collective entity), is under a similar obligation.

Notice as well, though, that Washington attempted to make his public supplication as ecumenical as possible. He did not invoke Jehovah, or Jesus, or even God, but rather "that Almighty Being who rules over the Universe" and "the invisible hand, which conducts the Affairs of men." Derek Davis observes that "Washington made every effort to frame his proclamations in language acceptable to all faiths."[53]

In these expressions by Washington, Adams, and Story, we can discern themes that have appeared again and again throughout American history, and that I am calling the providentialist interpretation of the Republic. America's history and institutions, in this view, are subject to an overarching Providence:[54] the nation is, as John Adams put it, part of "a grand scheme and design of Providence."[55] Citizens, and the nation itself, are obligated to acknowledge this dependency on Providence. In addition, public morality and civic virtue rest on a religious foundation. And yet . . . government can and should remain aloof from specific creedal affirmations, which are not important for civic or political purposes. Government and politics should thus be at some level religious, or at least should acknowledge a dependence on deity—but in an inclusive, ecumenical form. The general sense or at least sentiment of the view was nicely expressed in the mid-twentieth century by Dwight D. Eisenhower, who famously insisted that "our form of government has no sense unless it is founded in a deeply felt religious faith[,] and I don't care what it is."[56]

Depending on prevailing demographics, American providentialism has struggled to include Protestants, or Christians, or Christians and Jews, or theists generally.[57] Jasper Adams and Joseph Story talked about general Christianity, as we have seen. And throughout the nineteenth century, proponents of public schools like Horace Mann often urged a curriculum centered on a "nonsectarian" religion that amounted to an ecumenical or generic Protestantism.[58] In the first half of the twentieth century, the fold was expanded to include Catholics and Jews:[59] thus, by the 1950s, as Eisenhower was proclaiming the importance of "a deeply felt religious faith," the sociologist and theologian Will Herberg argued that most Americans had come to embrace "the conception of the three 'communions'—Protestantism, Catholicism, Judaism—as three diverse, but equally legitimate, equally American, expressions of an over-all American religion."[60] More recently, Justice Antonin Scalia has written approvingly in even more expansive or generic terms of an American tradition of "monotheism"[61]—a conception that at least in principle might embrace not only Christians and Jews but also Muslims, and theists and deists generally.[62]

However inclusive it has tried to be, though, the providentialist interpretation has never managed to encompass or enlist all Americans. It most obviously would exclude atheists at one end of the spectrum of belief, and perhaps polytheists at the other end. For some, this lack of complete inclusiveness counts as a disqualifying deficiency. Consequently, the providentialist interpretation has competed from the outset with a different view—one often associated with Thomas Jefferson and advocated by James Madison in the exchange initiated by Jasper Adams—that I am reluctantly calling "secular."

The term is unfortunate, for one reason, because it is our label, not theirs. Noah Feldman explains that

[u]ntil the 1870s, the word "secular" did not even figure in American discussions of church and state. "Secularism" in the contemporary sense was a term unknown to the framers and unmentioned by the Reconstruction Congress that drafted the Fourteenth Amendment. As late as the Scopes trial of 1925, "secularism" was still a term of opprobrium to most Americans, associated as it was with radical atheism and contempt for religion.[63]

In addition, a good case can be made that Jefferson and Madison held a worldview and a conception of American government that were more "providentialist" than "secular" in a modern sense. We have already seen in Chapters 1 and 2 how both men unapologetically justified disestablishment and religious freedom on explicitly theological grounds. Despite his vaunted secularism, Jefferson openly and officially appealed to Americans to join in supplicating the Almighty in prayer for the nation and for himself as the nation's president.[64] In a book aptly titled *The Lost World of Thomas Jefferson,* the historian Daniel Boorstin marshaled abundant evidence showing that Jefferson's views on virtually everything from natural rights to the continued existence of mammoths in North America (as he supposed) rested on providentialist assumptions.[65] Boorstin notes that "Jefferson on more than one occasion declared 'the eternal pre-existence of God, and his creation of the world,' to be the foundation of his philosophy."[66] In a similar vein, Henry May observes that "Jefferson's universe was as purposeful as that of [Yale president and aggressive Protestant] Timothy Dwight and presupposed as completely the existence of a ruler and creator. The world was intelligently planned, benevolently intended, and understandable."[67] Thus it might well be argued that Jefferson and Madison were closer in their worldviews to the providentialists Adams and Story than they were to latter-day thinkers and jurists that we would describe as "secular."

Even so, it seems fair to say that although they were not exactly secular in a contemporary sense, Jefferson and Madison were more secular in their views—in particular, in their views of government—than many of their contemporaries, like John and Jasper Adams or Joseph Story, were. Other early presidents declared national days of prayer. Jefferson didn't, and until the pressures of war persuaded him otherwise, Madison didn't either.[68] Story and other jurists declared that Christianity was part of the common law; Jefferson argued to the contrary.[69] Madison may not have openly objected to legislative chaplains and prayers in the First Congress when they were first instituted, but years later in a private memorandum he indicated his disagreement, describing "the chaplainship to Congs" as "a palpable violation of equal rights, as well as of Constitutional principles."[70] And as we have already seen, Madison opposed the association of government and Christianity favored by Story and Jasper Adams, arguing to the contrary for "an entire abstinence of the Government from interference [in religion] in any way whatever, beyond the necessity of preserving public order, & protecting each sect against trespasses on its legal rights by others."[71] David Sehat argues that "[t]hough he did not say so explicitly, it became apparent in the way Madison talked about rights that his goal was a godless government, sufficiently protected from the encroachments of the religious to ensure individual liberty."[72]

Despite their providentialist premises, these stances justify describing the general position held by Jefferson and Madison as "secular." ("Protosecular" is too cumbersome.) The eminent Virginians represented a resistance to the providentialist view that, in diverse ways, would be taken by "old deists and new freethinkers; Jeffersonian and Jacksonian republicans; Masons; religious liberals; evangelical dissenters; and radicalized working people."[73] And the term "secular" would come to fit more snugly the views of many later Americans, including justices of the Supreme Court, especially in the twentieth century; we will see as much in Chapter 4.

According to the secularist interpretation of the Republic, American government was and is, or should be, "secular" in character—meaning, basically, not religious.[74] As much as possible, government should keep clear of religion, and vice versa. The central contention is that government does not depend on religion and religion does not depend on government, and that both government and religion will flourish better by maintaining their distance from each other. As Justice Hugo Black would later put the point, "[B]oth religion and government can best work to achieve their lofty aims if each is left free from the other within its respective sphere."[75] Stringently applied (as it usually has not been, even by proponents like Madison), this contention seems to imply that government should not give aid to religion, should not act on the basis of religious beliefs, and should not endorse religion or religious faith.

It is important to note that the secularist interpretation need not be—and in its American versions typically has not been—antireligious. Individual secularists may be hostile to religion, of course—think of the recent aggressive advocates of what is sometimes called the New Atheism[76]—but the secularist position itself is not opposed to religion. And in fact, many Americans (starting, arguably, with Roger Williams)[77] have favored secular government on religious grounds.[78] But religion, in this view, should remain in the private domain; it should stay out of the realm of politics and government.

Once again, this description of "secularist" and "providentialist" visions is a simplification. In an intellectual history of American religion and politics (which this chapter emphatically is not), it would be necessary to say a good deal more about how these interpretations or visions of the Republic have been expressed in a variety of ways, and how they have evolved over time. And it would be necessary to observe how the relation between these visions has not been one of simple antagonism: the visions have competed, but they have also collaborated, and blurred into each other. We will say a bit more about this point shortly, but for our immediate purposes, we need not linger over these complexities. It is sufficient to appreciate that in one form or another, both visions have appeared again and again throughout American history, from the founding period to the present. Both have had their eminent representatives: Jefferson and Madison (and, a bit later, Andrew Jackson)[79] on the secularist side; Washington and Adams (and later Lincoln) representing the providentialist position. Indeed, with respect to religion (and much else), the American political tradition might be understood as the product of the ongoing competition and collaboration between the providentialist and secularist interpretations of the Republic.

The Soft Constitution

So the providentialist and secularist interpretations have both been present through American history. But this statement forces on us a question (or so a scrupulous reader might suppose): Which of the interpretations is . . . true? Or, perhaps more pertinently, which interpretation represents the correct reading of the American Constitution?

The question may seem natural enough, even unavoidable, to us. After all, it is obvious—isn't it?—that the different interpretations will have different and often contrary legal implications. On the secularist interpretation, for example, it would seem that religious expressions by government—Ten Commandments monuments on state capitol grounds, congressional and presidential declarations of a "National Day of Prayer"—would be presumptively unconstitutional. Government is supposed to be secular, and these are not secular expressions. A providentialist interpretation would seem to point to a different conclusion: generic religious expressions by government would be permissible and perhaps even obligatory (as Washington suggested in his first inaugural address). We can't have it both ways: there will be a "National Day of Prayer" or there won't be.

So it seems that we would need to choose. Which is the correct interpretation of the Constitution?

In defiance of this "either/or" logic, during the Republic's early and middle years American constitutional law managed not to answer this question. It studiously declined to choose between the competing interpretations: indeed, that deft avoidance of choice informed the distinctive genius of the American approach.

But how was this possible? The question requires us to reflect for a moment on a prior one. When we ask about the meaning of "the Constitution," what sort of thing are we interpreting, and with what consequences or implications? Today there may seem to be a simple answer: we are interpreting a historical legal document—the one that begins with "We the People" and goes on to offer seven articles and twenty-odd amendments, including the First Amendment. And our interpretations are setting forth the supreme law of the land, enforceable by our courts. To be sure, the interpretations may operate at one or two hermeneutical removes; a trained constitutional lawyer or scholar may be needed to make the connection between constitutional texts and current doctrines or decisions. (For example, to connect "due process of law" with a right to abortion.) Still, if we say that some proposition is "constitutional," we are necessarily making reference to the familiar legal document we call "the Constitution." And we are making a claim about the judicially enforceable law that derives from that document.

This is what making a constitutional claim typically means today. In earlier periods, the matter was not so cut and dried. In an illuminating book, Larry Kramer, former dean of the Stanford Law School, describes what he calls the "popular constitutionalism" that Americans inherited from the British and that characterized early American understanding and practice. The Constitution (or perhaps we should say the "constitution," lowercase) referred to "a set of understandings and conventions about rights and liberty that . . . yielded a *framework for argument* rather than a fixed program of identifiable outcomes."[80] Kramer elaborates:

Eighteenth-century constitutionalism was less concerned with quick, clear resolutions. Its notion of legality was less rigid and more diffuse—more willing to tolerate ongoing controversy over competing plausible interpretations of the constitution, more willing to ascribe authority to an idea as unfocused as "the people."[81]

We might try to elaborate Kramer's idea by distinguishing between "the Constitution" and "the constitution." The uppercase term can refer to the formal legal document, presumptively enforceable by courts in the way other legal documents are. The lowercase term—the "constitution"—will refer to the understandings, practices, and commitments that *constitute us* as a people or as a nation.[82] Like the (uppercase) Constitution, these are matters for interpretation and argument, and the interpretations and arguments might well be central to or even determinative of important political decisions. But they will not necessarily be hard "law" in the same positive, formal sense in which "the Constitution" is. And so they will not necessarily be subject to judicial enforcement.

Let us describe the first entity—the formal legal document, enforceable by courts—as the "hard constitution," or simply as the Constitution (uppercase). And we can describe the second, more amorphous but not necessarily less important body of constitutive understandings, practices, and commitments as the "soft constitution," or as the constitution (lowercase).

Kramer argues that today we have largely lost the conception of the soft constitution or, as he calls it, of "popular constitutionalism." "In our world, there is law and there is politics, with nothing much in between. For us, the Constitution is a subset of law, and law is something presumptively and primarily, even if not exclusively, within the province of courts."[83] Maybe. But surely we can still comprehend the notion of central and constitutive understandings and commitments that are not embodied in formal law and hence are not judicially enforceable. And in any case, we need something like this notion in order to understand the "constitutional" framework within which religious freedom unfolded during the years between the founding and the judicial interventions that began in the mid-twentieth century.

Consider again the claims and views exchanged in 1833 in the conversation among Jasper Adams, Joseph Story, John Marshall, and James Madison. (Was it a condition of participation in this conversation that one's name begin with *J?*) We have seen already that in this exchange, Adams and Story and perhaps Marshall adopted a providentialist interpretation of the nation; Madison countered with a more secular construction. But were these interpretations being advanced as propositions of constitutional law? Were they claims about what the Constitution commands and prohibits?

Yes and no. The question is a challenging one, because Madison and Story and others commonly made assertions that look "constitutional" in some ways but not in other ways. Their assertions were surely not just ordinary arguments about what it would be wise or prudent for American governments to do, like "Congress ought to protect American industry by raising the tariffs on the importation of manufactured items from abroad." Rather, the advocates were making claims about *what America is*—about what "constitutes" the country as a distinctive political community worthy of our allegiance and support.

Then and thereafter, such (lowercase) constitutional claims could be supported by invoking not only the text of the Constitution but also early precedents or revered expressions of the American political understanding and traditions. Providentialists could—and do—cite preconstitutional official documents and expressions like the Declaration of Independence, with its appeals to "Nature and Nature's God" and its claim that we are "endowed by our Creator" with rights, for example. They could invoke Jefferson's celebrated Virginia Statute for Religious Freedom, with its references to "Almighty God" and to the "holy author of our religion." A little later they could point to Lincoln's second inaugural address ("With malice toward none, with charity for all"), perhaps the most profound and revered statement ever made by an American official or politician. The address, now engraved on the Lincoln Memorial, was, as one historian observed, a "theological classic, containing within its twenty-five sentences fourteen references to God, many scriptural allusions, and four direct quotations from the Bible."[84]

Proponents of the secular interpretation, by contrast, could—and do— invoke the Constitution's prohibition of religious tests for national office.[85] They could cite a treaty with Tripoli, ratified in 1797, that expressly declared that "the Government of the United States of America is not, in any sense, founded on the Christian religion."[86] And they could—and do—argue that the Constitution itself reflected a secular view of government. That is because unlike its predecessor, the Articles of Confederation, and unlike state constitutions of the time (and since), the Constitution studiously and self-consciously avoided any meaningful acknowledgment of Providence, or the Almighty, or the Supreme Governor of the Universe.[87]

In these ways, Story and Madison and the various advocates of providentialist or secularist interpretations of America throughout the nation's history seem to have been self-consciously engaging "constitutional" questions. At least in the nineteenth century, however, they do not seem to have supposed their arguments to be constitutional, or Constitutional, in the harder or more contemporary sense of the term. They do not seem to have expected, that is, that the Supreme Court should accept one of their positions as *the* correct interpretation of "the Constitution" and then proceed to enforce that position, like it or not, against presidents and legislatures and city councils and school boards.

Take the question of mail delivery on Sundays. During the nineteenth century this was a hotly debated question. Some Americans believed that Sunday mail delivery unacceptably desecrated the Sabbath; others contended that the United States Postal Service ought to deliver mail on every day of the week, and that a refusal to deliver the mail on Sundays would be an improper mixing of government and religion.[88] These were obviously constitutional positions, at least in the soft or lowercase sense. For decades, the more secular view prevailed, and the postman made his rounds, rain or shine, seven days a week. But the secular view prevailed through legislative decision, not because the Supreme Court declared a policy of suspending mail service on Sundays contrary to the Constitution and hence illegal.

This is not to say that questions of religion and government never made it into the courts. They did, often, and in a whole variety of ways. Among other issues, nineteenth-century courts considered challenges to prayer and Bible reading in the public schools, just as twentieth-century courts would do. The nineteenth-century courts reached contrary conclusions on these questions.[89] They *could* reach contrary conclusions because they treated the cases as raising issues of state law (which of course could differ from state to state), not as matters to be definitively decided under "the Constitution."

Indeed, even when the nineteenth-century Supreme Court made pronouncements that today would likely be taken as having a constitutional character, the Court was not exactly declaring what the Constitution required. Consider the intriguing case of *Vidal v. Girard's Executors*.[90] In his will, one Stephen Girard bequeathed property to the city of Philadelphia for the purpose of establishing a school for "poor white male orphan children." Girard was of the aggressively secularist persuasion, it seems, and his bequest prohibited any "ecclesiastic, missionary, or minister of any sect whatsoever" from teaching or even being "admitted for any purpose, or as a visitor, within the premises" of the school. This exclusion of clergy was "antichristian," the famed politician and lawyer Daniel Webster protested, and the will was accordingly invalid. Fortunately for Philadelphia, the Supreme Court disagreed with Webster. But the Court managed to sustain Girard's will only by construing it to permit the teaching of Christianity by lay instructors. The Court seemed to accept Webster's essential premise: if the will had been anti-Christian, then it would have been invalid.[91] (It was apparently acceptable to be anticlerical but not anti-Christian.) The decision thus resonated with a providentialist understanding of American government. Even so (and this is the crucial point for our purposes), the Court located the principle favoring Christianity in the law of Pennsylvania,[92] not in the national Constitution.

Similarly, when in *Holy Trinity Church v. United States* the Supreme Court made its celebrated or notorious declaration that "this is a Christian nation,"[93] the Court's declaration was intended to be constitutional but not Constitutional. The Court invoked a range of laws and "organic utterances" (going all the way back to Columbus) to advance what amounted to a claim about the nation's political character—its "constitution"—for the purpose of discerning Congress's likely or presumed intent in a particular piece of legislation regulating immigration. But the Court did not purport to be declaring the enforceable meaning of the Constitution itself.

True, there were all along citizens who desired a harder, more definitive constitutional commitment one way or the other. Some wanted a hard commitment to the providentialist interpretation. Thus some critics of the original Constitution insisted that it ought to have included some acknowledgment of the Almighty, as the state constitutions did and as the Articles of Confederation had done.[94] David Sehat observes that "[t]o many religious leaders who lined up against the Constitution, the omission of God suggested a depraved sensibility that betokened the downfall of the Christian nation."[95] This position was again widely promoted during the Civil War; many Northerners blamed lost battles on the failure of their Constitution to express due respect to deity (as the Confederate Constitution did).[96] Other citizens took the opposite view, and hence agitated for a more explicit constitutional affirmation of governmental secularism.

In the second half of the nineteenth century, consequently, sustained contrary movements developed in support of constitutional amendments that would have expressly acknowledged Christianity in the Constitution or, conversely, would have explicitly affirmed that the Constitution required governments to be secular. These movements ultimately came to naught: neither the Christianity nor the secularism amendments were adopted.[97] Similarly, Congress rejected a proposed amendment (the so-called Blaine Amendment) that in one of its versions would have addressed the matter of Bible reading in schools, in part because of the view that these matters should be left to the states.[98]

During the nineteenth century, it seems, Americans preferred a soft constitution over a hard Constitution. Under that soft constitution, constitutional questions could be argued, and different states and localities could reach their own conclusions. Thus school prayer or Bible reading might be practiced in some states or school districts and eschewed in others.[99]

The Virtues of Soft Constitutionalism

Americans' apparent preference for a soft constitution governing the relation between religion and government may strike contemporary constitutionalists as odd, maybe even irrational. What sense would it make for school prayer—or financial aid to religious schools, or Ten Commandments monuments—to be constitutionally permissible in Alabama, say, but not in New York? Such a situation, constitutional scholar Rodney Smith asserts, would be an intolerable "mishmash."[100] More generally, Ronald Dworkin, possibly the most influential legal philosopher of recent decades, argued that a legal regime can claim authority only if it reflects a "coherent set of principles." Conversely, a legal regime that adopted a "checkerboard" approach to issues—and the soft constitution surely allowed for what looked like a checkerboard on matters like school prayer—would be illegitimate.[101]

This insistence on principle and coherence undoubtedly animated the less "popular" and more court-centered constitutionalism, including the more aggressive judicial supervision of governmental involvement with religion, that unfolded in the last decades of the twentieth century. In Chapter 4, we will look more closely at that development. Before doing so, though, we should consider defenses that a proponent of the soft constitutional approach might offer against the objections posed by Dworkin, Smith, and others. We will then be in a position to deliver on this chapter's main promise—namely, to describe what the distinctive "American settlement" of the problem of religious pluralism consisted of.

Start with the objection that governance under the soft constitution was "unprincipled." A proponent of the older, softer approach could simply shrug off this objection. "Call it what you like," he might say. "It's how we do things. It works tolerably well. If our approach is 'unprincipled,' so be it: it is what it is."

But a proponent might instead offer a different response. The older approach was no less principled than modern law has become, he might say. Modern critics are simply looking for the wrong kind of principle, and are thereby missing the vital principle that animated the American regime of religious freedom.

Thus the American approach came to embrace basic—and at least somewhat "hard"—commitments to church-state separation and to freedom of conscience. As we saw in Chapter 2, these commitments began as jurisdictional limits on the power of the national government, but they gradually and subtly evolved into more affirmative or substantive commitments that by the mid-twentieth century were treated as constraining both the national government and the states.

More important, though, beyond these particular "hard" commitments the American regime also reflected a more general principle that we can call the "principle of openness," or perhaps the "principle of contestation." The constitutional principle, in other words, was precisely that both secularist and providentialist interpretations of the Republic were, and would continue to be, legitimate contenders. In different times and places one or the other interpretation might dominate as a cultural or political matter. Sometimes the country, or the county, or the city, would lean to providentialism, sometimes to secularism. But neither position would be permitted to establish itself as *the* constitutional principle or, conversely, to banish the other as a legitimate interpretation of the American constitutional order.

The point is not that nineteenth-century Americans consciously thought in terms of a constitutional "principle" of contestation—they were, after all, not yet blessed or burdened with the obsession of twentieth-century constitutional theorists (like Dworkin) with a supposed requirement that constitutional government be "principled"—but rather that American practice as it developed could be seen as embodying such a principle. The embrace of the principle of contestation was more instinctive, if you like, than self-conscious.

This sort of principle—one committed to maintaining an open competition between rival positions rather than to preferring one position and condemning alternatives—should not be difficult to grasp. After all, the free speech clause is often thought to embody a principle of that sort. Free speech, we often say, serves to preserve an open, free marketplace of ideas. In that marketplace, some ideas will inevitably gain acceptance over others, not only among private actors but also by governments: governments will accept, and act on, and thereby indicate their approval of some ideas and not others. But free speech means that the winners are provisional winners only: they are not permitted to banish their rivals from the marketplace. The result might look like a "mishmash"—a riotous, unprincipled anarchy of competing voices and views. Liberal political ideas prevail in this jurisdiction, or at this time, or on this issue; contrary conservative ideas dominate in that other jurisdiction, or at that time, or on that issue. But it is precisely this sonorous cacophony that the principle of free speech serves to preserve.

Similarly, the Constitution reflects a principle of democracy—for some, this is *the* central constitutional principle[102]—that operates to maintain openness in governance. Under the constitutional commitment to democracy, a two-party system has come to constitute the American political system. Typically, both parties—Republican and Democratic—claim to represent or speak for the American people. The role of constitutional law, though, is not to choose between these inconsistent claims, but rather to maintain a system in which both parties (and occasionally others as well) perpetually compete to represent and lead the nation. The principle of democracy might thus support what looks like a "mishmash": in some times and some places Republicans will dominate, to be replaced in other times and places by Democrats, and governance is usually the product of a sort of eclectic mixture of the views and policies of these parties. But it is precisely this competition between parties that the constitutional principle—the principle of "democracy," or "republican government," if you like—is committed to preserving.

In short, if "principle" is a requirement of legitimate government (surely a contestable proposition), the traditional American regime of religious freedom can plausibly be viewed as principled. Its principle, once again, is not a substantive principle either of "providentialism" or of "secularism" (or, anticipating, of "neutrality," or "no aid"), but rather an institutional or procedural principle of openness and contestation regarding the core commitment to religious freedom.

E Pluribus Unum

Beyond articulating the "principle" that animated American disestablishment, a proponent of the old American order might also offer a more pragmatic defense. A soft constitution in matters of religion was legitimate and attractive because . . . it worked. More specifically, the soft constitution worked to do what for centuries many had thought impossible—namely, to take a mass of individuals and groups embracing a multitude of different faiths and, without suppressing their differences, to hold them together as a single community. Citizens by general consensus could join in a shared commitment to religious freedom, and they could also join in a (sometimes tumultuous) debate about what this commitment entailed.

Not everyone would be satisfied with this approach, of course. As we have already seen, some citizens favored a more explicit and hard constitutional commitment to providentialism, or to secularism, but their efforts to amend the Constitution to this effect were unsuccessful. In addition, inevitably, not everyone would be happy with the decisions reached in particular times and places. As we have seen, standard depictions relate how in the nineteenth century, Catholics, Jews, Mormons, Quakers, Unitarians, and later secularists chafed under the generic Protestantism described by its proponents as "nonsectarian."[103] Occasionally these disagreements turned ugly, even violent.[104] Anti-Catholicism was common in the nineteenth century[105] (and later,[106] and perhaps still). So was anti-Semitism.[107] Mormons were subjected to violent persecution.[108]

Even so, during this period the state religious establishments remaining from colonial days were dismantled—without any pressure from the Supreme Court. Religious diversity increased, even exploded, as a variety of new religions sprang up through importation, internal division, or homegrown creation. The country was, as Yale historian John Butler puts it, "awash in a sea of faith," and many of the currents in this sea were innovative and exotic, and thus far from being traditionally Christian.[109] Overall, the Republic supported a measure of religious pluralism, liberty, and toleration on a scale probably not matched in Western history. And out of many, the various peoples became one (diverse and often turbulent) People. *E pluribus unum.*

How did the American (hard) Constitution and (soft) constitution accomplish this result? In the first place, by embracing what nearly all Americans agreed on (namely, religious freedom) while leaving firmly open what Americans did not agree on (namely, exactly what religious freedom in this country meant or entailed),[110] the arrangement was well calculated both to unite citizens around a shared commitment and to bring them together in debating or contesting what was controversial. People of various faiths might find themselves in the minority in different times and places, of course. But by offering assurance that even minorities were still full participants in the constitutional contest, American disestablishment avoided the sort of entrenched sense of alienation or dispossession that might naturally result from having one's view officially ruled a constitutional heresy.

In this respect, modern advocates and scholars who write enthusiastically about the "godless Constitution"[111] notice an important element in the constitutional strategy for maintaining unity amidst pluralism, although they typically mistake the nature of that strategy and thereby draw precisely the wrong conclusion. "Godless" is perhaps overly provocative. But the Constitution—the document itself—was (and is) prudently agnostic: it studiously declines to affirm either secularism or religion, atheism or theism. And this agnosticism serves a valuable function. As constituents of what Will Herberg aptly described as "pre-eminently a land of minorities,"[112] we—all of us—will in different times and circumstances likely find ourselves out of harmony with the expressions and philosophies emanating from national, state, and local governments. (Just as we will find our political party on the losing side of some local or national elections.) That condition of alienation can be painful. And yet we can remind ourselves that the expressions and philosophies (and political parties) that currently prevail are not ultimately *constitutive* of our political community. Above them in the hierarchy of legal and political authority stands the Constitution—the agnostic Constitution that steadfastly declines to align itself with any party, or with either the providentialist or secularist visions of the country.[113] (Or at least we could remind ourselves of this so long as the Constitution itself was not officially identified with either of the major rival interpretations.)

Conversely, by attempting to derive from the Constitution's agnosticism a command that governance at all levels must be rigorously secular, proponents of the "godless Constitution" work to subvert the Constitution's agnosticism and to elevate one of the long-standing interpretations—namely, the secularist interpretation—to the status of constitutional orthodoxy. They thereby subvert a valuable strategy for maintaining unity amid diversity.

A (Secularly) Religious, (Religiously) Secular Republic

But the soft constitution did not merely hold Americans of contrary views together in common contention; it facilitated cooperation between, and even a sort of blending of, these views. How did this happen?

Our discussion thus far has proceeded on the assumption that the secularist and providentialist interpretations of the Republic were simple rivals or antagonists. But is that assumption accurate? Yes and no. Contemplated in their abstract purity, providentialism and secularism do seem to be fundamentally different and even incompatible outlooks.[114] Providentialists declare that God works in history, that it is important *as a people* to acknowledge this providential superintendence, and that the community should actively instill such beliefs in citizens as a basis of civic virtue. Secularists, by contrast, insist that acknowledgments of deity (if there is one) ought to be purely private, and that government acts improperly if it enters into religion or expresses or endorses religious beliefs. What one constituency views as imperative, the other regards as forbidden.

And yet despite this apparent and in some ways actual incompatibility, the different positions have not only coexisted in comparative peace, most of the time, but in some contexts have become blended, or blurred, often producing what Bruce Ledewitz describes as a sort of "hallowed secularism."[115] Thus far, simplifying, we have assigned different historical figures to one or the other side of the divide: Madison and Jefferson and later Jackson were on the secularist side; Washington and Story and Lincoln—and later Eisenhower—were on the providentialist side. But as we have already acknowledged, these depictions oversimplify. In fact, as we have noticed, Jefferson for his part did and said a great deal that might support classifying him as a providentialist. We have already observed his Virginia Statute for Religious Freedom, with its eloquent declaration that "Almighty God hath created the mind free." And in his memorable second inaugural address, he implored fellow citizens to join him in prayer to "that Being in whose hands we are, who led our fathers, as Israel of old, from their native land and planted them in a country flowing with all the necessaries and comforts of life, who has covered our infancy with His providence and our riper years with His wisdom and power."[116]

If "secular" figures like Jefferson had a powerful providentialist streak, it would be easy enough to find a strong secular dimension in the thought and actions of "providentialists" like Joseph Story. Story's judicial opinions generally seem as thoroughly secular as those of other justices. And although Story and other jurists (like Chancellor Kent) maintained that Christianity was part of the common law, a study by legal historian Stuart Banner concludes that this claim operated mostly at the level of metajurisprudence; it did not measurably affect the actual legal reasoning or the results reached by jurists who held this view.[117] In its practical operation, it seems, Story's and Kent's jurisprudence was pretty much secular. The same was true, Steven Green shows, for a later Justice, David Brewer, who was deeply and openly devout. It was Brewer who wrote that "this is a Christian nation" in *Holy Trinity Church*. But he also strongly supported church-state separation, opposed most religiously based legislation, and "apparently had no difficulty with the Court's reliance on secular justifications to resolve church-state disputes."[118]

More generally, the historian Mark Noll observes that "[d]uring and after the war for independence, a wide range of Americans joined together Protestant Christian beliefs and secular political convictions as they were joined nowhere else in the world." This "merger proved exceedingly useful for many projects, both religious and political."[119] In a similar vein, Steven Green observes that in the founding period, "orthodox clergy spoke in contradictory terms, employing both religious and secular themes; in other instances, their language suggested that they viewed the competing theories of government as complementary."[120] A few years later, Alexis de Tocqueville reported that the joinder of religious and secular beliefs was pervasive in

American thought and central to the nation's political achievement: to the Europeans who doubted the possibility, Tocqueville's recommendation was that they visit America and see for themselves.[121] Some did: in the early 1920s, G. K. Chesterton came for a visit and reported back that although the country lacked any established religion, it was nonetheless a "nation with the soul of a church."[122]

Fast forward to the 1950s. A historical survey by legal scholars John Jeffries and James Ryan describes the political atmosphere of mid-twentieth-century America in terms that systematically mix the providentialist and secularist views.[123] Writing in the middle of that period, Will Herberg noted that "[e]very aspect of contemporary religious life reflects this paradox—pervasive secularism amid mounting religiosity."[124] Struck by the fact that "[t]he secularism characteristic of the American mind is implicit and is not felt to be at all inconsistent with the most sincere attachment to religion," Herberg remarked: "So thoroughly secularist has American religion become that the familiar distinction between religion and secularism appears to be losing much of its meaning under present-day conditions."[125]

Conceptual purists might deplore this conflation of distinct and even incompatible views. But as a matter of practical politics, such sloppiness or equivocation, if that is what it is, has arguably been of great value: it has permitted people of fundamentally different views and commitments to live together in relative peace without fully perceiving how different their views actually are. Or, if you prefer, Americans have been enabled to see how, despite fundamental differences, their views are capable of a practical convergence.

The soft constitution was conducive to this sort of mixing and blending and reconciling. Just as legislators of different parties and views typically find ways to deal and cooperate and compromise with each other (at least in times less dysfunctional than the present) and often develop genuine respect and even affection for members of the opposing party, open-ended constitutionalism encouraged the search for common ground. The distinctively American collaboration of the providential and the secular provided the nurturing substance from which arose some of the nation's most visionary political leaders (Jefferson, Lincoln), its most prophetic reformers (Lincoln again, Martin Luther King), and its formative political and social movements from the Revolutionary struggle to abolitionism to the Social Gospel to the Civil Rights movement.

The Practical Genius of the American Settlement

We can now summarize what the American version of religious freedom—or what we have called the American settlement—consisted of. The religion clauses of the First Amendment came to be an anchor for hard constitutional commitments to church-state separation and to freedom of conscience (or "the free exercise of religion"). While providing the encompassing structure within which Americans have dealt with the challenge of religious pluralism, however, those hard commitments did not dictate the entire content of the American approach. As initially understood, the religion clauses were nothing especially grand or ambitious; they were simply a reaffirmation of the jurisdictional arrangement under which religion was within the jurisdiction of the states, not the national government. But this arrangement permitted and implied a more general and "soft" commitment to religious freedom—a commitment that came to be at the core of the American self-understanding.

Although nearly all Americans have embraced that basic commitment, interpretations of the commitment have differed, sometimes dramatically.[126] And an essential feature of the American settlement was that interpretations were *allowed* to differ. One family of interpretations favored secular governance. Government should keep clear of religion in its activities, expressions, and purposes—and vice versa. Another family of interpretations, while striving to be inclusively ecumenical and insisting on protection for the free exercise of religion, interpreted the Republic in more providentialist terms. Both types of interpretations have deep and venerable roots in the American political tradition.[127] And the genius of the American settlement was that instead of officially elevating one or the other of those interpretations to the status of constitutional orthodoxy and condemning the other as constitutional heresy, the American approach left the matter open for We the People to reflect on and debate and negotiate on an ongoing basis.

To have selected one interpretation and rejected the other would have been to commit an American version of the same basic blunder—namely, of officially preferring one among competing faiths or would-be orthodoxies—

that in earlier centuries had produced civil havoc and often war in European societies. The American approach avoided that mistake by embracing a principle not of secularism, or of providentialism, but of Constitutional agnosticism and constitutional contestation among the various interpretations.

The results were not always happy, of course. Religious minorities sometimes suffered estrangement, persecution, even violence. As a gesture to those who prefer a more lachrymose rendering of history and who may accordingly find little satisfaction in the generally positive tone of this chapter,[128] we might pause to acknowledge the real human suffering that religious persecution or conflict sometimes produced on these shores. We can recall with regret ten-year-old Thomas Whall, a Catholic student in Boston, whose principal beat his hands with a stick until they bled because Thomas refused to recite the Ten Commandments out of the King James Bible.[129] We can sympathize with Charles Reynolds, a former Methodist minister and converted freethinker who in 1886 was pelted with rotten fruit and then prosecuted and fined (with the hearty approbation of the *New York Times*) for holding antireligious tent meetings in New Jersey.[130] We can mourn nine-year-old Sardius Smith, whose head was blown off by a rifle at point-blank range, and Thomas McBride, an elderly gentleman who was hacked to pieces with a corn knife, when a Missouri militia attacked a Mormon settlement at Haun's Mill in 1838, killing seventeen and wounding twelve more.[131]

So, yes, America has witnessed its share of cruelties, some committed in the name of religion. Of which societies in history might not the same be said? And yet without belittling this suffering, but also trying to maintain a sense of proportion, we might speculate that to Jews who lived in the time of Antiochus Epiphanes or in the aftermath of the second century Bar Kokhba revolt, or to Christians who endured the Diocletianic persecutions, or to the Jews and Muslims and heterodox Christians who suffered through the Spanish *reconquista* and Inquisition, or to the thousands upon thousands of Huguenots slain in the St. Bartholomew's Day massacre in France, or to the Catholics and then Protestants and then Catholics again who were sent to scaffold or stake or prison in Tudor England, the situation in the American Republic might have looked almost blissfully benign. Intolerance and persecution occurred. Usually, however, they were aberrational, not enduring official policy. And if we focus not on the suffering occasionally incurred by individual dissenters but rather on the political order itself, it seems that the

American arrangement managed for the most part to avoid the religious strife that had periodically convulsed Western societies from the fading days of the Roman Empire through the early modern wars of religion.

In sum, the American settlement fell far short of realizing the millennial condition when lambs shall lie down peaceably with lions. It fell short as well of satisfying the demands of twentieth-century liberal theorists and activists. (Inevitably so, because as we will see in Chapter 4, no regime or policy *could* satisfy those impossible and ultimately incoherent demands.) Under that rough-hewn settlement, nonetheless, religious freedom expanded, the nation grew more religiously inclusive, and the secular and religious perspectives often managed not only to coexist but also to collaborate in supporting a pluralistic but more or less united People.

Throughout this chapter, in describing the distinctively American approach to religious freedom, I have mostly used the past tense. That usage has been deliberate. In Chapter 4, we will see how the modern Supreme Court, while purporting to honor and implement the constitutional commitment to religious freedom, effectively undid the distinctively American achievement.

4

Dissolution and Denial

Up to this point, our narrative has played off of the standard story of American religious freedom, honoring the elements of truth in that story, supplementing and correcting as seemed appropriate. Admittedly, the supplementation and correction in Chapter 3 came close to standing the story on its head: what in its blacker moods the standard story describes as a sort of dark age in which the luminous promise of the First Amendment was dishonored or ignored, I presented as a period in which the American approach to religious pluralism—or what I have called "the American settlement"—achieved its distinctive form and luster. (Subject, naturally, to the frailties and failures of all enterprises carried out by mere mortals.) This narrative inversion will continue in the present chapter, even more starkly. In the standard story, the modern Supreme Court's aggressive incursion into matters of government and religion is typically presented as a long-overdue fulfillment of First Amendment commitments. I will argue, to the contrary, that the Court unwittingly but effectively undermined the distinctive American achievement, with troubling consequences that continue to be felt even today.

We have already noticed two of the developments that set the stage for this unintended subversion. One of those developments was the displacement of what we can call the classical "problem of the church" by the more modern "problem of religion." A natural consequence of this displacement was that modern interpreters came to think—or to assume, without needing to think—that the religion clauses of the First Amendment were mostly calculated to regulate the relation between government and religion.

This change combined with another one—the change briefly noted already in conceptions of "the Constitution" and of constitutional law. As we saw in Chapter 3, the "soft" constitutionalism of the nineteenth century gave way by the mid-twentieth to a harder conception in which to say that a commitment or principle was "constitutional" meant that the courts were obligated to enforce it against unwilling actors who might have a different conception of what the "constitution" meant or required. Under this harder constitutionalism, the courts undertook to supervise governments, national, state, and local, in order to ensure compliance with the newly discovered or devised principles regulating the relation of government to "religion."

These developments, though subtle, were also momentous or even transformative in their constitutional implications. Or at least the developments under the First Amendment's establishment clause turned out to be transformative. The consequences for free exercise jurisprudence were important but more contained. Basically, instead of conceiving of conscience as the "inner church" in which the individual hears and responds to the promptings of the divine, modern interpreters came to think of conscience as something like "religious" convictions, unmoored to any conception of church or even (eventually) to God or the transcendent. But then once the centuries-old moorings have been severed, what should count as a "religious" conviction?[1] In an ever more diverse culture, the category might be construed capaciously to cover something like a person's "ultimate concern" (in a formulation of the theologian Paul Tillich that the Supreme Court once or twice saw fit to borrow),[2] or perhaps as extending to personal commitments that are "sincere," "intense," and "durable," as two leading contemporary scholars would have it.[3] The apparent effect of these reconceivings was to extend the potential reach of the free exercise clause. But as with a river that issues from a narrow gorge into an ample lake, breadth may be inversely correlated with depth. And this is just what happened in free exercise doctrine: as the scope of free exercise coverage expanded, the extent of actual protection contracted. Eventually, the Supreme Court abandoned earlier doctrines that appeared to require actual accommodation of religious exercise in favor of a newer, more frugal doctrine under which as long as government refrains from actually targeting or persecuting religion, no accommodation is constitutionally required.[4]

In establishment clause jurisprudence, the effects of replacing "church" with "religion" were more far-reaching. We observed in Chapter 2 how the establishment clause had come to be seen as standing for "separation of church and state"–an idea at least closely akin to the classical "freedom of the church." But although a long line of Supreme Court decisions affirmed (and continues to affirm) this church-oriented doctrine,[5] in modern establishment clause discourse "freedom of the church" has been a secondary and underdeveloped theme. Judges, scholars, and pundits have supposed that the clause is primarily about something else: it is about keeping government from supporting, promoting, endorsing, or getting mixed up with . . . "religion" (whatever that is). Jefferson's legendary "wall of separation between *church and state* has come to be seen as a judicially patrolled boundary between *religion and government*.[6] The Court's declaration of that boundary amounted to an (unwitting, and thus unevenly honored) repudiation of the distinctive American settlement of the challenge of religious pluralism.

To see how this is so, we need to begin with a succinct survey of the primary movement of modern Supreme Court's establishment clause decisions and doctrines. We will then consider more closely how, in a well-intended but less than prescient effort to realize constitutional commitments, the Court in reality undermined the distinctive American strategy for dealing with the challenges of religious diversity, with cultural consequences that become ever more conspicuous.

A Brief Interpretive Tour of Establishment Clause Jurisprudence

Although the fact is insufficiently recognized, the beginning of modern establishment clause jurisprudence turned out to be, basically, a resounding false start. In 1947, in *Everson v. Board of Education,*[7] the Supreme Court confronted a challenge to a New Jersey program for subsidizing the transportation of students to and from schools, including religious schools. The Court ruled for the first time that the establishment clause applied to the states (via the Fourteenth Amendment) and that it created a "high and impregnable . . . wall of separation" between church and state. *Everson* interpreted this wall not primarily in the classical jurisdictional sense—although some classical motifs are discernible in the decision[8]—but rather as imposing an ostensibly strict prohibition on governmental aid to religion (although the Court approved the particular New Jersey program by a 5–4 vote).

Extensive commentary followed, both pro and con,[9] and it came to be commonly supposed that what happened in establishment clause jurisprudence over the ensuing half century was basically an outgrowth and implementation of *Everson*. In this vein, John Jeffries and James Ryan assert that *"Everson* began the modern edifice of separation of church and state," and that "[f]or half a century, the Supreme Court followed *Everson's* lead."[10] Douglas Laycock reflects the common wisdom in deeming *Everson* "[t]he most important Establishment Clause case."[11]

This common opinion begs for correction. In fact, except for a couple of cases in which the Court invalidated one program and upheld another in which public school students were let out of class to receive "release-time" religious instruction,[12] not much happened with or to the establishment clause for a decade and a half after *Everson*. Then, in the early 1960s, in the controversial school-prayer decisions, the Court tacitly and perhaps inadvertently retreated from the *Everson* doctrine and set the judiciary—and thus the nation—in a different direction. So the real story of modern establishment clause jurisprudence, we might say, begins with the second chapter (although the first chapter has remained in place to distract and confuse people—justices included).[13]

In the prayer cases—*Engel v. Vitale*[14] and *Abington School District v. Schempp*[15]—the Court ruled unconstitutional the long-standing practice in many of the nation's schools of beginning the school day with a brief and perfunctory religious exercise, including a prayer (such as the Lord's Prayer, or the so-called Regents' Prayer in New York) and sometimes a reading of several verses from the Bible. The invalidations might have been supported on various constitutional grounds,[16] but in *Schempp* the Court chose to justify its conclusion by articulating two themes that would dominate establishment clause jurisprudence—and would indirectly but powerfully influence constitutional discourse generally—from that day to this. Those portentous themes were . . . first, neutrality and, second, secularism. Or maybe it was the other way around: first, secularism and, second, neutrality. The themes have been intimately intertwined in the Court's opinions, but the nature of that association is not entirely clear: it is not certain which theme is supposed to be derived from which, or whether the themes are independent and freestanding or, conversely, really just different names for the same basic idea.

The longest and most searching opinion in *Schempp* was a concurrence by Justice William Brennan. After an extended analysis of history and precedent, Brennan concluded that the establishment clause requires "strict adherence to the principle of *neutrality*" in matters of religion.[17] Neutrality, in turn, entails or at least is connected with "a public *secular* education."[18] Justice Tom Clark's more plodding opinion for the Court accepted and even codified this position. Clark agreed that what the establishment clause requires of government is a "wholesome 'neutrality'" toward religion.[19] And neutrality implied that government must remain in the domain of the secular. To that end, Clark announced a constitutional "test." "[T]o withstand the strictures of the Establishment Clause," his opinion for the Court declared, "there must be a secular legislative purpose and a primary effect that neither advances or inhibits religion."[20]

Both themes—neutrality and governmental secularism—were destined to have long and influential constitutional careers (which even today show no signs of having run their course). Five years after *Schempp,* the Court returned to the neutrality theme in *Epperson v. Arkansas,*[21] striking down a statutory relic from the era of the Scopes trial that purported to prohibit the teaching of evolution in Arkansas public schools. "Government in our democracy, state and national, must be neutral in matters of religious theory, doctrine, and practice," the Court solemnly intoned. "[T]he State may not adopt programs or practices in its public schools or colleges which 'aid or oppose' any religion. *This prohibition is absolute.*"[22] That same year, in another case considering aid to religious schools,[23] the Court reiterated *Schempp*'s "secular purpose and effect" requirements. Shortly thereafter, in *Lemon v. Kurtzman,*[24] the Court added a third requirement: a challenged law or program must not foster "excessive entanglement" between government and religion. The result was the three-pronged *Lemon* test (secular purpose—secular effect—no excessive entanglement) that, with two or three brief recesses,[25] has governed establishment clause cases for the past four-plus decades.

Beginning with the school prayer cases, therefore, the doctrinal emphasis shifted from *Everson*'s "no-aid" prohibition to "secular neutrality" as explicated in the *Lemon* test. At least one astute observer, Michigan law professor Paul Kauper, immediately perceived the implicit abandonment of the *Everson* theme. Writing shortly after the decision, Kauper observed that "[t]he new emphasis in *Schempp* is on the neutrality principle." And he argued that "[this] emphasis on neutrality indicates that the no-aid-to-religion test, as a principle of construction, has lost its significance. It is not a viable test."[26]

Kauper was unusual, however, in noticing the significance of this shift. Indeed, the Court itself was slow to grasp the implications of its announced doctrine. (Not for the first time—or the last). Thus, during the decade and a half following the reception of *Schempp*'s "secular purpose and effect" requirements into the *Lemon* test, the Court frequently invalidated but occasionally approved a variety of state and federal programs for giving aid to religious schools through grants or loans of resources or through supplementary teaching.[27] The hairline or perhaps illusory distinctions on which these decisions turned—religious schools could be provided with books but not maps or overhead projectors,[28] for example—subjected those cases (and the Court) to ridicule. Characteristic was Leonard Levy's complaint that the decisions turned on "distinctions that would glaze the minds of medieval scholastics."[29] What disdainful critics (and justices as well) failed to notice was that the various school aid decisions were not so much erratic applications of the explicit *Lemon* doctrine at all, but rather lingering manifestations of a residual commitment to *Everson*'s "no-aid" principle.

Thus the Court uniformly found that the challenged aid satisfied the first *Lemon* requirement: in providing money or books or teachers, the Court thought, governments were acting with the entirely legitimate secular purpose of promoting education. The difficulties most often arose under the second or "effects" prong.[30] At least in its explicit formulation, though, *Lemon*'s second prong prohibits only laws or programs that have a *"principal or primary* effect" of advancing religion: officially, at least, advancement of religion as a secondary or "incidental" effect is not constitutionally problematic.[31] How to tell a "principal" or "primary" effect from an "incidental" one is something the Court has never managed to make clear. Still, if the *purpose* of an aid program was the legitimate secular purpose of promoting education, as the Court repeatedly concluded it was, then why was it not plausible to suppose that the *primary* effect of the program would match its permissible purpose—namely, promoting education—even if religion also received some benefit as a secondary effect?

In the school aid cases, the Court never satisfactorily answered, or even squarely addressed, or perhaps even noticed this question. Its decisions in effect treated the second prong as equivalent to *Everson*'s blunter no aid prohibition.

Eventually, though, the announced shift to secular neutrality began to take hold. Thus, after 1985, the Supreme Court sustained aid to religious education in case after case, repeatedly ruling that as long as religious schools were included in a neutral (or "even-handed") program for aiding education generally, constitutional demands were satisfied.[32] Indeed, in several cases the Court went further, holding that neutrality meant that governments were constitutionally *required* to treat religious recipients as eligible for the same assistance or resources available to comparable secular institutions or programs.[33] (Neutrality meant this, that is, except when it didn't.)[34]

To be sure, dissenting opinions (and concurring opinions by Justice Sandra Day O'Connor) often attempted to preserve the no aid theme left over from *Everson*.[35] And depending on future appointments to the Supreme Court, it is entirely conceivable that the no aid theme might at some point again emerge ascendant. But this theme could gain little traction in a constitutional framework now centrally devoted to *neutrality*, understood as governmental secularism, rather than to separation or "no aid" as independent constitutional commitments.

The relaxation of *Everson*'s "no-aid" principle, however, emphatically did not mean that establishment doctrine had lost its bite. Instead, beginning in the mid-1980s, its principal force came to be directed against a different set of practices—namely, governmental expressions or symbols perceived as endorsing religion—that have been endemic in American political life from the beginning, and that the justices in the *Everson* period seemingly had not perceived as problematic. *Everson* had quoted without apparent embarrassment the declaration in Jefferson's Virginia Statute that "Almighty God hath created the mind free."[36] And it was the Supreme Court itself, speaking through Justice William O. Douglas, that had declared in 1952 that "[w]e are a religious people whose institutions presuppose a Supreme Being"[37]—surely (despite Douglas's later awkward disclaimer)[38] an endorsement of religion. But these official expressions are hard to square with the assumption that government is constitutionally required to be secular (in the dominant contemporary sense in which "secular" means, basically, "not religious").[39] In the years following the school-prayer decisions and the *Lemon* test, therefore, governmental religious expression increasingly came to seem suspect: "no aid" to religion gave way to "no endorsement" of religion as the dominant theme.

Critics of public religious expressions such as the national motto (In God We Trust) had long argued, initially without much success, that such expressions violated *Lemon's* secular purpose and effect requirements.[40] This argument gained force when in 1984, in a concurring opinion, Justice O'Connor proposed that the establishment clause be explicitly reconceived in terms of a prohibition on governmental actions or messages that endorse or disapprove of religion.[41] In O'Connor's concurrence, the abandonment of *Everson's* no-aid prohibition was explicit (although perhaps not deliberate or fully understood, as her approval of the no-aid theme in other opinions may indicate).[42] A measure that does not endorse religion satisfies constitutional requirements, O'Connor asserted, even if "it in fact causes, even as a primary effect, advancement or inhibition of religion."[43]

O'Connor's "no endorsement of religion" proposal resonated nicely with the "secular neutrality" logic of *Schempp* and *Lemon*. After all, how can a government that is "secular" and religiously "neutral" consistently issue statements or sponsor displays endorsing religion? Unsurprisingly, therefore, within a few years a majority of justices had accepted the no-endorsement test.[44] And in the years since that acceptance, controversies involving perceived endorsements of religion—in the Pledge of Allegiance, in Ten Commandments monuments, in crosses on public property, in the National Day of Prayer—seem to have pushed aside the older financial-aid cases to occupy center stage in the public gaze and the Supreme Court's docket.[45]

Rigorously implemented, the no-endorsement doctrine on its face would seem to condemn a great deal of governmental expression that has been practiced and valued in the American political tradition,[46] including the national motto (In God We Trust), the official use of prayer in legislative sessions and presidential inaugurations—even, ironically, Jefferson's celebrated Virginia Statute for Religious Freedom (which *Everson* had read into the First Amendment as the basis for modern establishment jurisprudence).[47] After all, a statute officially declaring that "Almighty God hath created the mind free" and that religious coercion is inconsistent with "the plan of the holy Author of our religion" surely sends a religious message. Faithfully applied, the no-endorsement doctrine would seem to require invalidation of all such expressions.

A few prescient observers had foreseen this consequence as soon as the Court announced the brave new world of secular neutrality in the school-prayer decisions. A *Wall Street Journal* editorial had opined that the doctrine announced in those cases "must logically require the excision of all those other countless official references to God—such as in the Declaration of Independence, the Pledge of Allegiance, the Star-Spangled Banner, the words used to inaugurate the President, open the Congress and convoke the Supreme Court itself."[48] In a concurring opinion in *Engel*, an enthusiastic Justice Douglas had inferred that the opening invocation at Supreme Court sessions ("God save the United States and this honorable Court") was as constitutionally infirm as school prayer, and he hopefully proceeded to list other measures vulnerable to potential invalidation: the national motto, the words "under God" in the Pledge of Allegiance, legislative and military chaplains, presidential religious proclamations, the use of the Bible in administering official oaths—perhaps even, Douglas hinted tantalizingly, official recognition of the Christmas holiday.[49] Learned observers had scoffed, insisting that the decisions were narrow in their implications. But the elaboration of the no-endorsement doctrine gave new credibility to these earlier predictions.

In reality, it seems unlikely that either the justices (possibly with a few exceptions, like Douglas) or most mainstream supporters of the secularist conception have favored or perhaps even contemplated seriously disruptive or draconian consequences. Judicial insouciance with respect to the logical and practical implications of the no-endorsement doctrine was already evident in the doctrine's first official appearance. Thus Justice O'Connor initially proposed the doctrine on the puzzling premise that the no-endorsement construction provided a cogent explanation of why a nativity scene in a Pawtucket, Rhode Island, municipal Christmas display was permissible. In its holiday context (which also included reindeer, Santa's sleigh, a Christmas tree, and other holiday symbols), the scene with figures of the baby Jesus with Mary, Joseph, angels, shepherds, and wise men sent no religious message. Or so argued O'Connor.[50] Critics reacted with indignant disbelief.[51] In fact, Pawtucket's nativity scene (which cost next to nothing and coerced no one) was objectionable to its critics only and precisely *because* it seemed to celebrate Christianity. Justices like O'Connor have resisted this sort of conclusion, though, especially when venerable or traditional expressions are at issue, and so they have tried to save revered expressions from invalidation by interpreting them as having primarily historical or cultural or ceremonial significance.

The interpretations often exhibit a strained quality. Thus, two decades after her attempted justification of the Pawtucket nativity scene, O'Connor's explanation of how the words "under God" in the Pledge of Allegiance do not send any religious message again left readers incredulous.[52] Cornell law professor Steven Shiffrin found O'Connor's rationalization "simply insulting."[53]

However erratic its application may be, though, the no-endorsement doctrine is a logical corollary of the Court's by now long-standing commitment to the idea that government is obligated to be religiously neutral and that this obligation entails confining government to the realm of the secular. So long as that commitment remains in force, the national motto and the Pledge of Allegiance—not to mention countless monuments and expressions and holiday displays and maybe even, if we stretch (as litigators and scholars sometimes will), the names of cities like Los Angeles or Corpus Christi[54]—remain on shaky constitutional ground, in principle if not in practice.

The (Selectively) Invisible Transformation

As we have seen, if there was a watershed or turning point in the dominant understanding and jurisprudence of American religious freedom, that point occurred not in 1947 with *Everson v. Board of Education,* as is commonly supposed, but rather with the school-prayer decisions of the early 1960s. It was perhaps fitting, therefore, that the decisions were immensely controversial at the time. Bruce Dierenfield reports that the first of these decisions, *Engel v. Vitale,* provoked "the greatest outcry against a U.S. Supreme Court decision in a century"[55] (a century that had included *Brown v. Board of Education*). At a conference of state governors, every governor except New York's Nelson Rockefeller denounced *Engel* and urged passage of a constitutional amendment to overturn it.[56]

And yet, revealingly, this reaction evidently came as a surprise to the justices themselves. Thus Dierenfield observes that "[i]n a rare moment of political tone-deafness, [Chief Justice Earl] Warren did not anticipate the fallout from the [*Engel*] case."[57] The justices who joined in the decisions, as well as many of their supporters, evidently viewed the decisions not only as continuous with long-

standing constitutional principles but as relatively narrow in their implications.[58] Professor Philip Kurland declared that *Engel* was "important but narrow
in breadth."[59] A *New Republic* essay found the outraged public reaction "remarkable," adding that "[m]ost authoritative observers believe that the practical consequences of *Engel v. Vitale* in our school system will be negligible."[60]

Conversely, impassioned critics, including many ordinary American citizens, saw the decisions as radical and transformative. Here the understandings of the cultural elite and less privileged Americans parted: thus John
Jeffries and James Ryan observe that "the controversy over school prayer
revealed a huge gap between the cultural elite and the rest of America."[61]

The enormous divergence in perceptions not only of the decisions' cor-
rectness but of their political and cultural significance, and the justices'
failure to anticipate the public reaction, are themselves important and revealing facts. Upon closer examination, we can understand how the prayer
decisions could have seemed at the same time of little moment to their cul-
tured supporters and radical to their less erudite critics. And we can see how
the critics' perception was ultimately more prescient than the supporters'.

As we saw in Chapter 2, the original purpose of the establishment clause
was not to constitutionalize any general principle, whether of no aid, secularism, or neutrality. Its purpose was simply to preclude the creation of a
national church and, a bit more broadly, to leave the support or regulation
(or lack of it) of churches to the states. Even so, the assumption that government is supposed to be secular can claim grounding, if not in the establishment clause itself, at least in the soft constitutionalism that prevailed throughout much of the nation's history and that constituted an essential component
of what we have called "the American settlement." Thus, as we saw in
Chapter 3, the idea that government should be secular had been (together
with a competing providentialist idea) one of two leading interpretations of
the Republic from the beginning. Devotees of the secularist view had long
regarded it (as they still do) as capturing something essential about the
Republic—as constitutive of the Republic, so to speak, and hence as "constitutional," at least in the lowercase sense of the term. For those who favored
this interpretation, the Court was doing nothing more in the prayer cases
than reaffirming what had been true from the beginning.

The revision could pass almost unnoticed (by its proponents, at least) in
part because of the changed understanding of constitutionalism, or the shift

from "soft" to "hard" constitutionalism discussed in Chapter 3. All the Court did, we might say, was to take a venerable proposition—that "the constitution requires government to be secular"—and capitalize the "c" in "constitution." (To be sure, a shift from lowercase to uppercase can be significant: think of the difference between being "catholic" and being "Catholic," or between being a "democrat" and being a "Democrat.")

The change was also less observable, to some, because of a gradual sociological shift that had occurred. In the early Republic, elite opinion if anything had tilted toward the providentialist conception: Washington, Adams, Story, and Lincoln were hardly negligible figures, and even the protosecularist Jefferson and Madison remained in central senses providentialist in their outlooks.[62] With the passage of the decades, however, elite opinion had gravitated decisively in the secular direction. Thus George Marsden chronicles the transformation of leading American private universities, most of which were founded by churches and began with a distinctly religious conception of their mission but became steadily more secularized during the course of the twentieth century.[63] Sociologist Christian Smith describes the "Secular Revolution" in which American educational, legal, media, and scientific institutions sloughed off their religious or theological dimensions during the late nineteenth and early twentieth centuries.[64]

Douglas Laycock observes that "nonbelievers are disproportionately in elite positions, where they have disproportionate influence on public discourse."[65] Thus Supreme Court justices are likely to come from, and to be formed by, this elite secular culture. So are legal scholars. So if, with the retreat of "soft" constitutionalism, one of the long-standing constitutional interpretations was now to be selected and elevated to hard Constitutional status, the victory of the secularist over the providentialist interpretation within the judiciary was pretty much foreordained. But from the perspective of those for whom the secularist view had already become virtually axiomatic, in elevating that view to Constitutional status, the Court was doing nothing more than clearly articulating what must always have been true—even if this truth had somehow been systematically overlooked and rampantly and unapologetically violated throughout much of American history. And this perspective is still pervasively manifest in legal scholarship, including the admirable but emphatically secularist recent histories by Steven Green and David Sehat.[66]

But in fact the elevation of the secularist interpretation was a change—and a momentous one at that. As discussed in Chapter 3, the distinctive American approach to religious freedom had been composed of a mix of hard and soft constitutional commitments. The hard commitments—to church-state separation and freedom of conscience—were important, and they set the structure within which the American approach operated. But they were limited in their reach. Most practical matters of "religion" fell within the region of soft constitutionalism. Here the American settlement had deftly avoided any definitive choice among competing views and interpretations by maintaining a principle of openness and contestation. Americans could believe and assert either secular or providential interpretations of the Republic, as seemed to them right, and they could elaborate and act on those interpretations with respect to whatever the local issues might be: school prayer, Sunday mail delivery, whatever. Both kinds of interpretations were *constitutional* (in the soft sense); neither was *Constitutional* (in the hard sense). The Constitution preserved the political and legal framework for such debates without itself taking sides in the debates. Indeed, a primary pacifying function of the Constitution was to assure citizens who might be on the losing side of a local or lower-level decision that there was something above and beyond the currently dominant view—namely, the (agnostic) Constitution—that did not confirm or embody that view, and hence that could still make a claim on their allegiance.[67]

The modern Supreme Court seemingly failed to understand this complex strategy; in any case, the Court tacitly repudiated it. In effect, by elevating the secularist interpretation to the status of hard Constitutional orthodoxy, the Court placed the Constitution itself squarely on the side of political secularism and relegated the providentialist interpretation to the status of a constitutional heresy. And the Court thereby tacitly but effectively repudiated the principle of open contestation under which over the decades Americans had negotiated their religious and secular differences.

In sum, in attempting to realize religious freedom, the Court's doctrines and decisions effectively reversed the distinctively American approach to the challenge of dealing with religious diversity. The Court thereby unlearned the lesson that Americans had taken from the religious strife that had afflicted post-Reformation Europe—namely, that if among competing faiths one is to be singled out as the officially preferred position, then the devotees of the various faiths will fight for that honor (and, perhaps more urgently, will fight not to be among the losers).[68] The wars of religion in early modern Europe had given bloody testimony of that dangerous propensity. Conversely, by forswearing any officially established religion, the United States had managed to avoid the sort of destructive political conflicts that had so often accompanied established religion elsewhere.[69]

In nineteenth- and twentieth-century America, however, the salient competing visions of the nation were no longer Catholic versus Protestant, as in the sixteenth century, but rather secularist versus providentialist. And by formally constitutionalizing one of the major competing visions and thus effectively establishing political secularism as an official and judicially enforceable constitutional orthodoxy, the Supreme Court repudiated the historic lesson and risked a renewal of the sort of destructive dynamic that had characterized life in early modern, post-Reformation Europe.

Embittered Discourse

In our kinder and gentler (or at least less heroic) times, fortunately, nothing comparable to the Thirty Years' War or the St. Bartholomew's Day Massacre has ensued. Even so, the divisive dynamic is visible, if not in physical violence, in an increasingly rancorous political discourse.

This deleterious effect on discourse is a natural consequence of the shift from a situation of open and legitimate contestation to a discourse structured in terms of constitutional orthodoxy (political secularism) versus constitutional heresy (political providentialism). In a regime of open contestation, it is possible to disagree respectfully. The party or position that happens to be out of power is not traitorous or heretical; it is rather the loyal opposition, to be respected as such, with its own contribution to make, and with a legitimate and constitutionally assured chance to become the prevailing party or position at some future time. Conversely, as religious conflicts over the centuries have demonstrated time and again, where disagreements are framed not in terms of legitimate contesting conceptions but rather in terms of an official position or orthodoxy versus heretical and illegitimate deviations, respectful disagreement becomes difficult; it is replaced by a discourse of accusation, anathematization, and abuse.

This dynamic became apparent promptly upon issuance of the transformative school prayer decisions. Sensing that their understanding of the nation had not merely lost out in the particular dispute but had effectively been ruled categorically heretical, partisans of a providentialist view reacted with angry denunciations. Senator Strom Thurmond thundered against *Engel* as a "major triumph for the forces of secularism and atheism which are bent on throwing God completely out of our national life."[70] On the other side of the issue, the normally moderate Philip Kurland perceived public criticism of the decisions as "violent and gross,"[71] and he responded in kind, calling the critics "religious zealots" and lumping them together with "racists" and John Birch Society extremists.[72]

This sort of bitter and divisive discourse continues today, surrounding not only establishment clause controversies per se but a host of related issues in which religion plays (or is thought to play) a part. Whether the issue is abortion, assisted suicide, same-sex marriage, or evolution in the classroom, a familiar rhetorical pattern repeats itself. Although citizens and advocates on the more traditional side of such issues may complain that secularists have foisted onto the Constitution an interpretation that "We the People" never put there,[73] for purposes of public debate they nonetheless frame secular-sounding rationales in support of their views and policies. Finding these secular rationales implausible, advocates on the secular side often respond by accusing their opponents of obscurantism and hypocrisy: the ostensibly secular rationales are dismissed as mere pretexts for religious reasons or motivations.[74] Justices themselves sometimes join in the demonizing and the mockery.[75]

Such dismissiveness has been apparent in recent judicial decisions invalidating laws prohibiting same-sex marriage. In one case, the Iowa Supreme Court considered a list of secular interests or goods that the state had invoked in support of the law: protecting the institution of marriage, promoting optimal conditions for the procreation and upbringing of children, and conserving state resources.[76] While acknowledging the importance of these interests, the court confidently concluded that the law favoring traditional marriage did not serve them, and the court went on to surmise that the opposition to same-sex marriage in reality was based not on these declared policies but rather on "deeply ingrained—even fundamental—religious belief." But this sort of belief, the court declared, could provide no legitimate basis of the law.[77]

In a similar vein, striking down California's Proposition 8, enacted by voters in support of traditional marriage, federal judge Vaughn Walker rejected the secular rationales offered by the law's supporters and concluded that the law lacked any rational basis. Citing data showing that an overwhelming majority of the California voters who attend church weekly (84 percent) had cast their ballots for Proposition 8, while a virtually identical proportion of citizens who never attend church (83 percent) had voted against it,[78] Walker implied that in reality the law had been enacted on the basis of religious motivations. But these motivations could provide no justification for the law, Walker declared, because the state has no legitimate interest in enforcing "private moral or religious beliefs."[79]

And indeed, it seems likely that religious citizens, at least when in litigating posture, are sometimes less than forthcoming about their deeper reasons. This reticence occurs under duress, however, because under current constitutional understandings, it is only by adopting a secularist vocabulary that these citizens are able to participate in the constitutional conversation at all. And even as they attempt to defend their positions in constitutionally admissible terms, believers in the providential conception often feel beleaguered and alienated. How can it be, they wonder, that the Constitution somehow forbids officials and citizens today to assert and act on the same sorts of openly religious rationales that are so evident on the face of the celebrated writings, speeches, and enactments of Jefferson, Madison, and Lincoln? Thus Harvard law professor Noah Feldman observes that "constitutional decisions marginalizing or banning religion from public places have managed to alienate millions of people who are also sincerely committed to an inclusive American project."[80]

To be sure, the alienation can run both ways. As we have seen, although the Supreme Court's doctrine officially condemns governmental expression endorsing religion, the courts have been erratic in implementing this prohibition. Much religious expression persists. (As Michael Newdow, the prominent atheist who litigated the Pledge of Allegiance case and many other cases, once pointed out to me over lunch, he could not even pay the tip without being confronted with "In God We Trust" on the currency.) Thus decisions condemning religious expression or excluding religious rationales from public justification alienate religious believers, but public religious expression and decisions upholding such expression (such as the Supreme Court decision rejecting Newdow's challenge to "under God" in the Pledge of Allegiance)[81] may cause secular citizens to feel like outsiders.

There is a difference, though, in the causal process. Proponents of the providentialist view are alienated by the establishment of political secularism as an official constitutional orthodoxy: they sense, correctly, that their understanding of what America essentially is has been officially declared to be heretical and inadmissible. Conversely, more secular citizens (like Newdow) who are alienated by governmental religious expressions are distressed by what they view as a failure to live up to the secularist orthodoxy—an orthodoxy that they embrace and that they believe (with the support of Supreme Court teachings since *Engel* and *Schempp*) the Constitution itself embraces. In short, one constituency is alienated by the official or de jure secular orthodoxy; another is aggrieved by what it perceives as an ongoing illicit but "*de facto* establishment"[82] of religion.

In this way, the elevation of secularism to an official constitutional position has managed to alienate both religious and secular citizens. And a dynamic of suspicion, resentment, and bewilderment has come to pervade the "escalating series of provocations and legal claims from both sides"[83] that constitute what is often called, in a description that becomes increasingly apt, the "culture wars."[84]

This much we can readily observe. Beyond these observations, to be sure, lie questions that will necessarily remain contestable, and speculative. How would our history have unfolded if the Supreme Court, instead of elevating the secularist interpretation to the status of official constitutional orthodoxy, had persisted in respecting and adhering to the "American settlement" that had developed over the first century and a half of the Republic? Would other forces and developments have produced the same kinds of cultural conflict we currently experience? Might the "open contestation" authorized by the traditional American approach have turned ugly, or violent? The 1950s of Eisenhower's "piety on the Potomac" seem to have been a relatively peaceful period in American history with respect to religion, as Will Herberg's *Protestant-Catholic-Jew* reflects.[85] But of course the following decade would be an era of conflict along various dimensions, and it would be implausible to attribute all of this conflict to the Supreme Court. Maybe religious and cultural conflict would have escalated in the country regardless of any path taken by the Supreme Court.

Maybe. For such historical counterfactuals there can be no confident answers. What we can say is this: The American settlement had worked (roughly and imperfectly, to be sure) to support an increase in religious freedom and diversity and interaction. But the Court set aside the American settlement (unwittingly, perhaps). And what has followed has not been the advent of civic peace and mutual respect. On the contrary.

Neutralizing Religious Pluralism

Our discussion thus far has suggested that by elevating the secularist interpretation from being one legitimate and respectable candidate to the sole and official constitutional dogma, the Supreme Court effectively undid the distinctive American settlement that had worked to domesticate the country's potentially divisive religious pluralism. Why would the Court take such a disruptive step? One possibility, suggested in the foregoing discussion, is that the justices simply did not understand what the American settlement had been. And the shift from soft constitutionalism (or what Larry Kramer calls "popular constitutionalism")[86] together with the sociological development of increasing secularization of American elites made the change seem at once inevitable and yet almost invisible.

But even judges or citizens who understood what the American settlement had been might have opted to exchange it for the new regime of secular neutrality. For all its ground-level success, after all, the American settlement was both theoretically uncouth and less than ideal in practice. While assuring citizens of differing faiths and differing interpretations of the Republic a continuing place at the constitutional table, the American settlement could not avoid the fact that some citizens would find themselves governed by policies and addressed by governmental expressions and practices that conflicted with their religious (or agnostic or atheistic) views. In that sense, some citizens would inevitably view themselves, as later cases put it, as religious "outsiders" in the political community.[87] Conversely, the neutrality principle promised to avoid this less than ideal state of affairs. Under religiously neutral government, it seemed, all citizens would be equals—with respect to religion anyway—and no citizen should ever need to feel like an outsider. So even if the more rough-hewn American settlement had been fully understood, the loftier promise of secular neutrality might well have proved irresistible.

We can appreciate the promise and the seemingly overpowering appeal of neutrality if we step back and consider the American experience against the backdrop of Western history. In Chapter 3, we saw that Western responses to the challenge of the religious pluralism let loose by the Reformation are sometimes seen as falling into three unfolding phases. In the first phase, typified by renewed inquisitions and persecutions and wars of religion, governments tried to restore unity through coercive enforcement of a religious orthodoxy. The bloodstained failures of this strategy generated a new phase or approach: toleration. Regimes continued to maintain some sort of orthodoxy, but dissent was permitted, or tolerated, at least within limits. But minorities and dissenters may find it galling to be merely "tolerated." Such discontent eventually led governments to embrace religious equality in place of toleration. And equality was taken to entail that governments should maintain a stance of secular neutrality.

We saw in Chapter 3 that the American settlement that prevailed from the time of the founding through the early twentieth century did not in fact embrace the ideal of secular neutrality. Conversely, modern constitutional jurisprudence arguably worked to bring the nation into line with this progressive logic. Under the new regime of secular neutrality, all citizens would be treated as equals; no one would be an insider or an outsider on the basis of religion. Or, at least, so ran a powerful current of progressive thinking.

So then, with the advent of secular neutrality, had the centuries-old problem of religious pluralism at last been solved? The escalating culture wars, noted earlier, suggest not. But why not?

For those who view particular governments or legal regimes as "neutral," a natural response is to blame the objectors. Secular government is fair to everyone, or at least it could be fair to everyone if people would just be "reasonable," as John Rawls would say.[88] The problem is that dissenters who oppose governmental secularism, or who decline to accept the conclusions of liberal theorizing, are being "unreasonable" (meaning, in Rawls's usage, not so much irrational as uncivil or uncooperative). We *could* "all just get along"—except that some people want to "impose their values on others," as the common expression goes, or to "lord it over" their fellow citizens, as Martha Nussbaum puts it.[89] Not surprisingly, modern political polemics are often cast in just these terms.

The accusations run both ways, of course. Secular liberals say their opponents are trying to impose their religious or moralistic values, while religious traditionalists think the liberals are trying to impose their secular or relativistic values on schools and businesses and culture generally.

As it happens, there is a less tendentious and self-serving explanation for the continued and seemingly intensifying cultural conflict. The fundamental difficulty is that the ostensible neutrality of the modern secular state turns out to be, on closer examination, little more than a sort of political optical illusion. That is because, to put the point crudely, genuine neutrality is impossible. So the seemingly irresistible appeal of neutrality turns out to rest on a spurious promise.

But why should neutrality be impossible? We can appreciate the difficulty from two different perspectives. First, the neutrality ideal is consistent with some religious positions but inconsistent with others. It is most obviously inconsistent with theocratic commitments. To be sure, full-throated theocrats are scarce in the United States today; their specters mainly haunt the darker alleys of the secular liberal imagination.[90] But there are evidently millions of citizens who believe government may and should support religion in mild ways, such as by sponsoring nativity scenes or maintaining the words "under God" in the Pledge of Allegiance or sponsoring a participation-optional National Day of Prayer. These citizens may believe as much on religious grounds. In rejecting such religious beliefs, neutrality itself is already not neutral in matters of religion.

Second, and perhaps more important, many or most or maybe all laws and governmental policies—including those self-described as "neutral"— will be consistent with some religious (and secular) views but inconsistent with others. So a law or policy will appear to be neutral only if we resolutely fail to notice—or, in other words, if we marginalize—those people and positions that the self-described neutrality rejects or contradicts.

The problem was already discernible when the "secular neutrality" position in the school-prayer cases was announced. The Supreme Court majority and Justice Brennan contended, as noted, that school prayer was not "neutral" because it was inconsistent with the beliefs of students, such as the plaintiffs in those cases, who were agnostic or who believed that prayer should be a purely private affair. This logic seems cogent enough: in a society composed of people of various religious views, as well as atheists and agnostics, an official practice of sponsoring school prayer can hardly be described as religiously "neutral." In a dissenting opinion, though, Justice Potter Stewart suggested that the Court had overlooked a different group of students and parents—namely, those who believed (perhaps as a matter of their own religious faith) that prayer is a public and collective obligation that should be performed in important public settings. Though not often encountered in elite secular circles, and thus perhaps foreign to most justices, this view has been common enough in American society, and as we saw in Chapter 3, it resonates with a providentialist tradition going back at least as far as George Washington's first inaugural address. In rejecting the beliefs of these citizens, Stewart reasoned, a ruling prohibiting school prayer offended neutrality: the ruling "is seen not as the realization of state neutrality, but rather as the establishment of a religion of secularism, or at the least, as government support of the beliefs of those who think that religious exercises should be conducted only in private."[91]

So who was right—Brennan or Stewart? But the question poses a false alternative. In reality, both justices were right (albeit from the perspectives of different constituencies), and both were wrong (because they ignored or marginalized other-minded constituencies). School prayer is *not* meaningfully neutral: it is inconsistent with the views of, among others, atheists. Neither is a prohibition on school prayer meaningfully neutral, because it rejects the views of citizens who believe on religious grounds that school prayer is desirable or obligatory. Given such a conflict in views, no neutral position is available. There may, of course, be good prudential or constitutional or even philosophical or theological reasons for preferring one or the other position. But we can describe one of the positions as "neutral" only by neglecting to notice those citizens whose deeply held beliefs are thereby rejected.

Nor does it advance matters to cast the issue in terms of "imposing values." To be sure, proponents of school prayer do impose their values on students who oppose the practice. (Or at least they would if their position were to prevail.) By the same token, proponents of a prohibition on school prayer equally impose *their* views and values on those whose religious or other beliefs demand the practice. To make prayer public imposes on those who think it should be merely private, and vice versa.

The essential and intractable problem was noted at the time by Harvard law professor Ernest Brown. Commenting on *Schempp* in the *Supreme Court Review,* Brown discerned in the case a vexing "dilemma."[92] Schools inevitably teach moral values, he observed, and although a theistic approach to this task is plainly not neutral, a purely secular approach to values inculcation will likewise conflict with the views of students and parents who believe that moral values necessarily rest on a religious or theistic foundation.[93] Acknowledging "the impossibility of any substantive decision that was not non-neutral to a significant extent,"[94] Brown wished that the Court had avoided a decision on the merits, or else had addressed the controversy in free exercise terms.

The impossibility (and the internal incoherence) of neutrality were perhaps even more vividly conspicuous a few years later in a decision noted earlier, *Epperson v. Arkansas,*[95] in which the Court's insistence on neutrality was especially imperious. The Court believed that an Arkansas law forbidding the teaching of evolution in public schools had been adopted in order to insulate biblical literalist religion against contrary views; that presumed motivation made the law less than neutral toward religion. and hence constitutionally invalid.[96] As Justice Hugo Black noted in a concurring opinion, though, on the Court's own declared premises—namely, that evolution directly contradicts the teachings of some religions and that the Constitution imposes an "absolute" prohibition against public school teachings that "'aid or oppose' any religion"—it would follow at least as inexorably that the teaching of evolution in the public schools is constitutionally prohibited. Thus, without going beyond the Court's own assertions, one could logically conclude (a) that neutrality is violated by a prohibition on the teaching of evolution and (b) that neutrality is violated by the teaching of evolution.[97]

But at least as a practical matter, those possibilities pretty much exhaust the alternatives.[98] So it seems, once again, that there is no neutral space or position. The ostensibly "absolute" command of the Constitution is one that, try as we might, we simply cannot obey.

Proponents of secular neutrality sometimes respond that secular government could be neutral if everyone would simply see the wisdom of forgoing the beliefs or commitments that conflict with it. In this spirit, Douglas Laycock pleads that "*if we could all agree* on the principle of government neutrality toward religion, we could all abandon our efforts to influence government on religious matters, and devote all that energy to religious practice and proselytizing in the private sector."[99] Laycock's plea seems at the same time sound and silly. It is true that if everyone could agree on some version of neutrality (such as Laycock's), or on governmental secularism, then one set of conflicts could be avoided. But of course the proponents of *any* position can say exactly the same thing. "If only we could all agree on [Catholicism, Protestantism, scientific naturalism, agnosticism, or whatever], we could avoid these disagreements." Moreover, this plea is likely to seem entirely sensible to anyone making it, because the position around which consensus is being proposed will seem true, right, and reasonable; that, after all, is why its proponents embrace it. But of course the position does *not* seem true, right, and reasonable to others: that is the nature of pluralism. For all of its sophisticated exponents, therefore, the admonition to "try to see it my way" does not go far in resolving conflicts among people's sincere beliefs and commitments; it amounts not so much to a remedy for pluralism as to an effort to wish pluralism away.

The Sophistication of Neutrality

In suggesting that the dominant modern strategy for addressing pluralism is fundamentally flawed, the argument that neutrality is impossible and thus illusory can be deeply unsettling and, for some, flatly inadmissible. Not surprisingly, therefore, judges doggedly continue to profess their commitment to neutrality,[100] while theorists shore up the ideal by devising seemingly endless refinements to their accounts.[101]

The issue has been debated at length; we can hardly consider all the variations and responses here.[102] But we should notice one frequent and especially pertinent refinement that contends that neutrality does not exist in the abstract and on its own; it exists only relative to what is sometimes called a "baseline."[103] Here is an analogy:[104] In a baseball game, the umpires are expected to be neutral. That seems like a perfectly sound and reasonable expectation. But of course this expectation does not stop umpires from ruling for or against teams or players in particular situations: some pitches will be called "strikes," some "balls"; some runners will be "out" and some "safe," and so forth. What neutrality means in this context is that the umpires will enforce the rules of the game, whatever they are, evenly and consistently against both teams. Those rules constitute the baseline against which an umpire's neutrality is measured, and possible.

Similarly, given some constitutional baseline about how government is supposed to act in matters affecting religion, a government can be neutral by complying consistently with that baseline, or by enforcing it evenly against all citizens and institutions, whatever their religious beliefs or dispositions. If the baseline prescribes that government must be secular, for example, as modern Supreme Court decisions suppose, then government will be neutral by forgoing public prayer (which is religious) and by teaching evolution (which is secular) but not creationism (which is deemed to be religious)—even if these policies effectively reject some citizens' religious views.

The baseline account of neutrality fits nicely with the school prayer decisions and subsequent cases: the Supreme Court's assumption, evidently, is that government can be neutral relative to a secular baseline. Unfortunately, this refinement simply pushes the impossibility objection down to a deeper level—to the problem of nonneutral baselines.[105] True, we can declare a policy of teaching evolution but not creationism "neutral" by reference to, say, a baseline of governmental secularity. In similar fashion, it could logically (if ludicrously) be said that a law requiring all citizens to recite the "Hail Mary" ten times daily is religiously neutral—relative to a baseline of Roman Catholicism, that is—so long as the law is enforced consistently against all citizens, whether they are Catholic, Protestant, Hindu, agnostic, or whatever. But the obvious objection in each instance is that although a decision, law, or practice may be neutral relative to the baseline, *the baseline itself* is manifestly not neutral. The Catholic baseline is obviously not neutral, but then neither is the secular baseline: it is not neutral with respect to whatever religious views conflict with it. More specifically, the secular baseline is not neutral toward views that do not accept the claim that religion is purely private in nature or that government must or should be strictly secular. And these views are held, it seems, by millions and millions of Americans—by all those Americans who think that the Pledge of Allegiance ought to contain the words "under God" and that it is perfectly okay and even fitting to celebrate a National Day of Prayer.

Nor is this merely an academic or theoretical criticism. On a very practical level, a nonneutral baseline is at least as destructive of the egalitarian and inclusive aspirations associated with the ideal of neutrality as a nonneutral decision, law, or policy is. If government alienates citizens or treats them unequally (or as "outsiders") by supporting religious views they do not accept, or by contradicting views they do accept, the problem is not cured by adding that government is consistently following a baseline that happens to be incompatible with those religious views. If anything, the invocation of the baseline exacerbates the problem; it amounts to telling the citizen who complains that the government has rejected or disparaged her religion, "But that's our consistent policy. We always do things that way." Or, in other words: "You didn't just happen to lose this time; we're consistent, so in these sorts of matters you can expect to lose *every* time." Perceptions of inequality, and of "outsider" status, are thereby confirmed and aggravated.

Andrew Koppelman attempts to escape these difficulties by interpreting neutrality as a "fluid" concept governed not by a single foreordained and universal baseline but rather by multiple and flexible baselines that may vary from time to time and context to context.[106] There are "many possible neutralities,"[107] and we have to choose the one that best suits the particular context. But complicating and subdividing neutrality in this way does nothing to remedy the fundamental problem. Within each more local context, all the difficulties just discussed simply repeat themselves on a smaller scale. Thus, whether we are contemplating a uniform, overarching principle or a shifting or "fluid" set of local resolutions to a shifting set of problems, so long as there is real substantive conflict, any outcome or resolution that sides with one view or family of views and rejects others cannot be described as neutral in any meaningful or helpful sense.

Indeed, in conceding that we must select from a large menu of possible neutralities to suit the particular context, Koppelman effectively acknowledges that the notion of neutrality itself—neutrality as a regulative ideal—cannot do any real work. All the work, rather, is done by the various desiderata (and Koppelman helpfully discusses a number of them)[108] that influence the choice of a baseline against which to measure neutrality for a particular context or problem. In essence, it all becomes a matter of figuring out what the best or most just position is for a given context, and then (using that position as a baseline) labeling whatever the position prescribes "neutral."

Indeed, Koppelman comes very close to admitting that "neutrality," in his sophisticated treatment, is not so much a principle or premise from which conclusions can be drawn as a label to be pasted on to specific conclusions reached on other grounds.[109] Thus Koppelman salvages neutrality by elevating it—or perhaps reducing it—to an honorific, useful more for rhetorical than for analytic or evaluative purposes.

Denial

Our reflection on the simultaneous irresistibility and impossibility of neutrality suggests a possible redescription of the progression of Western responses to pluralism. Consistent with more familiar depictions, we previously described that progression as evolving from strategies of coercively maintained religious orthodoxies to policies of religious toleration and thence to the dominant modern position of secular neutrality. This third phase is standardly understood as a decisive and welcome departure from earlier phases: in phases one and two, governments maintained some sort of religious orthodoxy, even if deviations from that orthodoxy were tolerated, while in the third phase more enlightened and inclusive governments forswear any orthodoxy in favor of a position of neutrality. But it now appears that this neutrality is an illusion. So it might be more accurate to say simply that the dominant orthodoxies (a perhaps off-putting term that simply means "right opinion" or "right teaching") have changed: earlier religious orthodoxies have been replaced by secular liberal orthodoxies. The secular orthodoxies, of course, are not necessarily any more static or cohesive than were earlier Christian orthodoxies (with their "almost riotous diversity"),[110] and they may be maintained in more or less rigorous or tolerant fashion, just as earlier Christian orthodoxies could be.

This redescription, however, leaves out one crucial feature of the modern posture. Earlier religious orthodoxies could be candid about their character *as orthodoxies*, or as beliefs that were publicly articulated and commended and that served as bases for public discourse and decisions. Pre-Henry VIII, English monarchs did not deny or apologize for their official Catholicism; post-Mary, they did not pretend that their governments were anything other than an Anglican variety of Protestantism. (Some monarchs—the Jameses and Charleses—were sometimes suspected of an opposite proclivity—of only pretending to support Protestantism.) Under the constraint of professed commitments to neutrality, by contrast, modern secular orthodoxies typically refuse to acknowledge their character as orthodoxies.

The classic, even legendary manifestation of this tendency is the Supreme Court's declaration in *West Virginia State Board of Education v. Barnette* that "[i]f there is any fixed star in our constitutional constellation, it is that no official, high or petty, can prescribe what shall be orthodox in politics, nationalism, religion, or other matters of opinion, or force citizens to confess by word or act their faith therein."[111] In addition to being "eloquent and epochal," "among the great paeans to human liberty," "a ringing endorsement of religious freedom," "haunting," and "among the most eloquent pronouncements ever on First Amendment freedoms,"[112] as admiring commentators have gushed, *Barnette*'s majestic declaration also has the less fortunate feature of being flatly false, not to mention incoherent. True, citizens may not be forced to "confess" their faith in favored beliefs; carved off from the overall declaration, that part of the *Barnette* statement may deserve our approval. But government officials both "high" (such as Supreme Court justices, including the justices in *Barnette*) and "petty" (such as teachers in public schools) every day prescribe what shall be orthodox (or, in other words, correct opinion or teaching) in the sorts of matters *Barnette* enumerates. Indeed, the Court's statement itself presents itself as a correct and judicially enforceable (and perhaps even unalterable, as the metaphor of a "fixed star" suggests) declaration of a correct teaching about the nature of government and law in the United States.[113]

In these respects, *Barnette* is typical. Even as they aggressively assert themselves, modern liberal secular orthodoxies typically hold themselves out not as orthodoxies, but rather as being opposed to orthodoxy. As merely "neutral."

In short, modern professions of secular neutrality typically deny their own character: in this respect, and not only in their secular content, they differ from earlier religious orthodoxies. This feature—denial, and self-denial—is perhaps the real innovation and core of the modern strategy for addressing pluralism. The practitioners of that strategy have to be, as Frank Ravitch puts it, "masters of illusion,"[114] usually even with respect to themselves. Yale law professor Paul Kahn describes this tendency in more general and portentous terms: "[W]hen we put the modern state on the couch, we find a social organism that is simultaneously deeply in fear of its own death (the existential crisis) and in deep denial of the fact that it is willing to do anything at all to put off that death (liberal theory)."[115]

Maybe the denial and self-denial have been necessary, or at least excusable. It might be that there is no truly satisfactory way to reconcile modern hyperpluralism with an ambitious egalitarianism, or hyperegalitarianism, that seeks not only to provide equal basic rights to all—rights to vote, to speak, and so forth—but to avoid causing any citizen to "feel like an outsider" on the basis of his or her sincere beliefs. Inevitably, governments will make decisions, and will express themselves, and those decisions and expressions will of necessity accept some and reject others among the welter of competing beliefs. So unless governments are willing to relinquish the commitment to treating citizens as equal in that strong (and, in reality, unattainable) sense, there perhaps is no remedy except a resort to denial and (collective) self-deception. We cannot actually *be* neutral. But we can *pretend*—even or especially to ourselves—that we are.

The problem, though, is that the pretense seems not to be working anymore, as the intensifying culture wars suggest—or at least not well. As with a magic trick that has been performed often and ineptly, the illusory nature of neutrality becomes more conspicuous. And so we may come to perceive more acutely and appreciatively the rough-hewn practical virtues of the less elegant and less pretentious American settlement, with its central principle *not* of neutrality, or secularism, but rather of open contestation within a framework committed to church-state separation and freedom of conscience. We may even come to regret the loss that was incurred when judges and theorists opted, perhaps without quite knowing what they were doing, to set aside that workaday settlement in favor of . . . what? A more comprehensive and ambitious neutrality that might well be attractive except for the inconvenient fact that it is little more than a cherished, beguiling illusion.

5

The Last Chapter?

In November 2011, Stanford law professor (and former federal judge) Michael McConnell debated Harvard law professor Noah Feldman at Georgetown University on the topic "What's So Special about Religious Freedom?"[1] McConnell reminded the audience that the First Amendment singles out religion for special protection, and he argued that this treatment continues to be appropriate today. For his part, Feldman conceded the first half of McConnell's argument: the First Amendment provides, and framers like Madison supposed, that religious freedom is deserving of special protection. But that supposition is no longer justified, Feldman argued. The Constitution's special treatment of religion was based on historical conditions and theological commitments that happened to prevail at the founding. But conditions are different now, and in a modern liberal state it is unacceptable for government to act on theological rationales.

Feldman's position did not appear to be driven by any animosity toward religion. Nor is any such animosity evident in his other work.[2] Religious belief and expression should still be protected under other constitutional provisions, he insisted, such as freedom of speech. But there is no longer any warrant for singling out *religious* freedom as a special constitutional commitment.

Ordinary citizens might suppose that Feldman's position was radical, perhaps calculated to provoke (as academic positions sometimes are). Is it really plausible that we would repudiate what many have long regarded as "the first freedom"—one that by Feldman's own admission the framers favored and gave pride of place in the Bill of Rights? Far from being audacious, though, in an academic environment Feldman's argument might more accurately be characterized as ho-hum. In recent years, scholars and theorists have increasingly gravitated to this conclusion in one form or another.[3] A few of these scholars are pretty plainly disdainful of religion,[4] but others (including Feldman) are not; indeed, some think they are acting and arguing in the interest of religion.[5]

Thus Douglas Laycock, himself a leading scholar and litigator of religious freedom, reports that "scholars from all points on the spectrum now question whether there is any modern justification for religious liberty."[6] Nor is it only academics who are skeptical of special protection for religious freedom. The Obama administration's positions in the much-discussed "contraception-mandate" controversy[7] and in the less prominent but (for present purposes) more pointed "ministerial-exception" case[8] strongly suggest that the administration is similarly disinclined to favor special legal protection for religion. In general, the administration argued in the ministerial-exception case, churches and religious associations should enjoy the same freedom of association that nonreligious associations have—no less, but also no more. There should be no special constitutional protection covering the right of churches to select ministers according to their own faith-based criteria and judgments. (We will look more closely at the ministerial-exception case in due course.)

Professor Laycock, himself a vigorous proponent of religious liberty, worries that "[f]or the first time in nearly 300 years, important forces in American society are questioning the free exercise of religion in principle—suggesting that free exercise of religion may be a bad idea, or at least, a right to be minimized."[9] Once again, though, the argument usually is not that religion or religious freedom should be suppressed—as they were in, say, the Soviet Union, or in the Mexico depicted in Graham Greene's *The Power and the Glory*—but only that there is no justification for singling out freedom of religion for special recognition. Think of it this way: In the American constitutional tradition, we sometimes talk generically about "freedom" or "liberty"—and this generic liberty receives minimal constitutional protection—but we also have a list of particular and especially cherished freedoms that enjoy special judicial and political solicitude: freedom of speech, freedom of the press, freedom of assembly,[10] and others. Traditionally, freedom of religion has been on that list—even at the top of the list. Challenging this tradition, Feldman and like-minded thinkers want to take freedom of religion off the VIP list, so to speak, while allowing that religious people and groups should receive the same protection that others receive under the other freedoms.

If this proposal comes to be accepted, the outcome would be in one sense the last chapter in the story of American religious freedom. The story would then tell how, building on themes that had developed over the past two millennia, founding-era Americans conceived of religious freedom as deserving of respect and legal protection, how this commitment informed commitments to other rights, such as freedom of speech, and how those other rights eventually displaced the ancestral commitment to freedom of religion. It is not self-evident that this denouement would be tragic: after all, ancestors are pretty much progenitors who are remembered, even revered, but who are not around anymore. So it would be in this case. Religious freedom RIP.

And yet there are those, like McConnell and Laycock (and also—full disclosure—myself), who are not enthused about ending the story now or in this way, and who would view such an ending as premature and deeply unfortunate. Those who are not ready for the story to end seemingly include (for now, in alternate terms anyway) the justices of the Supreme Court. Thus the Court rejected the Obama administration's Feldman-like position in the ministerial-exception case[11]—and not in a 5–4 conservative/liberal split, but unanimously, and emphatically. So it seems that the story is not necessarily winding down.

And indeed, one might ask: If the founders favored a special commitment to religious freedom, expressly writing it into the Constitution, and if many Americans still favor that position, why amend constitutional jurisprudence to strike freedom of religion from the list of specially preferred liberties? It is a formidable question, I think, and it will reappear from time to time in this chapter. But it is also a real question, not a rhetorical one: it is not a question calculated to intimidate opponents (like Feldman) into embarrassed submission. On the contrary.

So in this chapter we will look at two large-scale historic developments that have combined to make religious freedom a vulnerable constitutional commitment. Edward Gibbon famously argued that the Roman Empire fell as a result of one internal development (the rise of Christianity) and one more external development (the incursions of the so-called "barbarians"). In an analogous way, the regime of religious freedom is currently in jeopardy through the convergence of one development that is partly internal to the tradition of religious freedom and a different development that is mostly independent of that tradition. The internal development is the erosion of the rationales for religious freedom by a secularism that, ironically, can be seen as an implication or at least an offshoot of religious freedom itself. The mostly independent development is the impressive advance of a formidable political and cultural movement that marches under the banner of "equality" and that bids to become a new national orthodoxy with features reminiscent of those that characterized state-supported orthodoxies during the centuries of Christendom.

Religious Inversion, Secular Subversion

The undermining of the justifications for religious freedom has resulted from developments already discussed at some length in Chapters 1 and 4. In Chapter 1, we saw how the distinctive components of the American version of religious freedom—namely, separation of church and state and freedom of conscience—descended from historic Christian commitments. More specifically, Christianity, in stark contrast to Roman religion and political practice, taught that humans are subject to dual legitimate authorities. We should render unto Caesar what is Caesar's and unto God what is God's.[12] This "render unto" dualism persisted over the centuries in Christian thought: thence Augustine's two cities and, later, Luther's and Calvin's two kingdoms. The Christian division of temporal and spiritual jurisdictions animated the papal campaign for "freedom of the church"—a remote progenitor of American "separation of church and state"—and also, in a post-Reformation and more Protestant development, the movement for freedom of the "internal church" of conscience.

These achievements were powerfully reinforced by another Christian theme—namely, the emphasis on sincere and voluntary faith as the only path to eternal salvation. This distinctively Christian rationale was powerfully deployed by the modern champions of religious toleration and religious freedom—Roger Williams, John Locke, James Madison, Thomas Jefferson. In conjunction with the dual-jurisdictions theme, the voluntary-faith rationale led to the conclusion that, as Madison put it, religion is "wholly exempt from [the state's] cognizance."[13]

So far, so good. But this Madisonian conclusion produced a potentially vitiating paradox. If religion is wholly outside the state's cognizance, wouldn't it follow that the state is precluded from acting on religious rationales? So, did religious freedom mean that governments could no longer rely on the historic rationales for religious freedom? Would religious freedom cancel itself out by vetoing its own supporting premises?

The possibility was rendered more probable by another familiar modern strand of logic that we considered in Chapter 4 and that goes basically like this: religious freedom means that the state must treat people of all religions (or none) *equally,* . . . which in turn entails that the state must remain *neutral* in matters of religion, . . . which in turn entails that the state must remain *secular,* . . . which entails that the state cannot act on or endorse religious views or rationales. We saw in Chapter 4 how this logic of secular neutrality has dominated the modern discourse and jurisprudence of religious freedom. But again, if the state cannot act on or endorse any religious views, then it would seem to follow that the state cannot act on the religious rationales—the dual-jurisdiction rationale and the voluntary-faith rationale—that produced the commitment to religious freedom in the first place. In this way, religious freedom turns on and negates its own supporting rationales.[14] It is like the snake that circles around and swallows itself by the tail.

This self-subverting logic is hardly inexorable, but it is seductive, and intriguing to secular thinkers. Professor Feldman's position in the Georgetown debate may be viewed as the culmination of this logic.

So, if religious freedom can no longer be justified on the basis of the historic rationales that generated the commitment to religious freedom in the first place, what follows? Should we renounce our commitment to religious freedom as a specially protected right, as Feldman (along with other scholars and, arguably, the Obama administration) have concluded, leaving religious people and groups to fend for themselves on grounds of freedom of speech, freedom of association, and the like? That is one possibility, but hardly the only one. It might be, for example, that even if the historic and religious rationales are no longer available, more contemporary and secular rationales can step in to do the same work. At least until recently, this seemed to be the assumption of most modern scholars or thinkers who paid any attention to the issue[15] (or who *didn't* pay much attention to the issue).

Professor Douglas Laycock is a prominent and articulate representative of this point of view. Like Feldman, Laycock acknowledges that as a historical matter, religious freedom was to a significant extent the product of theological rationales;[16] also like Feldman, Laycock insists that it would be improper for government to rely on such rationales today.[17] But Laycock thinks that an adequate secular justification can still be offered for giving special protection to religious freedom.

Laycock's secular case for religious freedom rests on three propositions. First, because people care deeply about religion, attempts to impose or suppress religion have caused significant suffering and conflict. Second, religious beliefs matter immensely to the believers, sometimes leading them to fight, kill, revolt, or suffer martyrdom. Conversely, and third, religious beliefs are of little importance to civil government.[18] From these nontheological propositions, Laycock believes we can extract a solid commitment to religious liberty.

So, how strong is this defense? Laycock's first two propositions, basically empirical in nature, would be difficult to dispute. Attempts to suppress religion surely have led to conflict, and suffering: think of the attempts in England to suppress Protestantism (under "Bloody Mary") and then Catholicism (under Elizabeth and James I). And religion plainly is very important to some people, who will sometimes take strong or even desperate action on the basis of their religious commitments: think of the Maccabean insurgents remembered at Hanukkah, or the Catholic conspirators who gave us Guy Fawkes Day, or the perpetrators of 9/11. Both friends and foes of religion will likely concede, and even insist on, this point.

Laycock's third proposition—that religious beliefs are of little importance to government—is more normative, and more contestable. Indeed, a critic might suggest that the proposition is blatantly question-begging: haven't debates about religious freedom basically reflected underlying disagreements precisely about the relevance of religion to government? Still, there is a sense in which the proposition might be acceptable to constituencies of both secularist and providentialist interpretations of the Republic. As we saw in Chapter 3, secularists contend that government should stay clear of religion; for their part, American providentialists have typically insisted that government has no interest in the particularities of different religious beliefs. Remember Eisenhower's oft-mocked providentialist statement: "[O]ur form of government has no sense unless it is founded in a deeply felt religious faith[,] and I don't care what it is."[19]

There is surely much that could be debated here; for now, though, let us just say that all of Laycock's propositions, charitably regarded, have a decent claim to being at least broadly plausible. So then is the commitment to religious freedom secure after all?

One objection would assert that Laycock's rationale is fatally overbroad. Even if his contentions are true with respect to religious beliefs, they are not true *only* of religious beliefs: there are other kinds of deeply held or intense personal beliefs—philosophical or moral or aesthetic beliefs of various kinds, perhaps—about which we could say that their suppression would cause suffering and conflict, that the beliefs are of extraordinary importance to some people, and that they are or should be of little importance to government. Laycock acknowledges that under his rationale, critics "may argue that other strong personal commitments should have been protected as well."[20]

Laycock responds to this objection in two ways. First, he suggests that "religion" be defined broadly to include many deeply held beliefs that might not conventionally be thought of as religious.[21] Even so, he acknowledges that his rationale may cover some beliefs that just cannot be considered "religion," and at this point he appeals to constitutional text and history. We protect religion and not other beliefs or concerns to which his secular rationale might also extend, he says,

> for the sufficient reason that other strong personal commitments have not produced the same history. The [constitutionally] protected liberty is religious liberty, and although the word "religion" must be construed in light of continuing developments in beliefs about religion, we cannot rewrite the Constitution to say that religious liberty should not receive special protection.[22]

This is a lawyerly answer, and although it may leave theoretical purists feeling a bit queasy, the answer may also be good enough for government work. Laycock is right: the Constitution does refer to "religion" and not to "sincere and deeply held beliefs." Why isn't that stark fact enough to settle the debate? Indeed, one might push the point even further and ask, why do we need any extratextual rationale at all for religious freedom? The fact is that the Constitution expressly says, in the First Amendment, that religious freedom gets special protection. So if someone (like Professor Feldman) asks why religious freedom should be protected, why isn't "Because the Constitution says so" rationale enough?[23]

It is awkward, though, to have no better answer to give than this one, for at least two reasons. First, the meaning of constitutional provisions is frequently contested: this is conspicuously true of the First Amendment's establishment and free exercise clauses. And when controversies and competing interpretations arise, courts routinely and sensibly attempt to construe a law or constitutional provision so as to further its purpose or rationale. If there is no (admissible) rationale, however, or if the proffered rationale is overbroad or underinclusive relative to the provision, this enterprise of interpretation is frustrated.

Second, and perhaps even more important, it is not foreordained that even constitutional provisions will always remain in force. They can be repealed, as the Twenty-First Amendment repealed the Eighteenth (on prohibition). Much more commonly, a provision that no longer seems to resonate with the live commitments and values of a society is likely to become moribund in practice even though, technically, it is still "on the books"—or still in the Constitution. Constitutional provisions rise and fall in their importance and their "gravitational force."[24] A provision such as the contracts clause[25] can loom large in one period (the mid-nineteenth century)[26] and retreat into obscurity in a later period (the twentieth century);[27] conversely, a provision like the equal protection clause[28] can be "the last resort of constitutional arguments" (as Justice Holmes quipped)[29] and then somehow mature into one of the main movers and shakers of progressive constitutional jurisprudence. Hence if no cogent (and admissible) supporting rationale can be offered for the First Amendment religion clauses, they risk declining into relative inertness.

It is not entirely clear, though, how these general observations apply to religious freedom specifically. After all, it is not as if there is an entire absence of justification for protecting religious freedom as such. The classical theological rationales articulated by the likes of Jefferson and Madison have not so much been refuted as declared (by some jurists and theorists, like Feldman and Laycock) no longer admissible. But many Americans surely still find those rationales persuasive and admissible. In addition, secular rationales for religious freedom are not wanting: the problem seems to be that these are typically over- and underinclusive. They cover more than "religion" and less than everything we think of as "religion." We have already seen how this is true of Laycock's three-proposition rationale; and the same can be said of other familiar secular rationales, such as the claims that religion is divisive,[30] or that religion is central to people's sense of identity.[31] Not everything we call "religion" is *always* divisive—sometimes religion serves rather to unify[32]—nor is religion central to *everyone's* self-conception. Conversely, there are things other than religion that can be divisive, or central to some people's sense of identity.[33]

So the secular rationales tend to fit awkwardly with the particular constitutional commitments manifest in the religion clauses. Still, those rationales do provide reasons, even if imperfectly tailored reasons, in support of those commitments.

It might be that, together with constitutional text and history, these sorts of admittedly problematic rationales are solid enough to do the job. Even so, the situation hardly seems stable and secure. So long as there is no significant cost to religious freedom, or no major challenge to it, shaky rationales supplementing tradition and text and shored up by political inertia might be enough to sustain inherited constitutional commitments. Conversely, if a serious challenge arises, the edifice of religious freedom might well go the way of the proverbial house built upon the sand when the storms came along to batter it.[34]

And, as it happens, the storms are already beginning to beat on the constitutional edifice. There is currently a serious challenge, or set of challenges, to the long-standing commitments to religious freedom. This opposition presents itself under the irreproachable title of "equality."

The Challenge of Modern Equality

Equality, like religious freedom, is a venerable American ideal. That "all men are created equal" was one of the ostensibly self-evident truths invoked to justify the Declaration of Independence from England; in Lincoln's revered Gettysburg formulation, this was *"the* proposition" to which the nation was "dedicated" from the beginning. Gordon Wood explains that "[e]quality was in fact the most radical and most powerful ideological force let loose in the Revolution."[35] At the same time, a long line of critics and detractors discerned a disturbing measure of inconsistency and hypocrisy in the nation's simultaneous professions of equality and its treatment of blacks, Native Americans, women, and minorities of various sorts (racial, ethnic, religious, linguistic, and so forth). The second half of the twentieth century thus witnessed an intensification of efforts to realize equality—through judicial decisions, statutes and regulations, and education—and also to broaden the scope of what equality is thought to entail. Beginning with religion and race, the campaign for equality expanded its efforts to include women, and later—this seems to be the current front line—gays and lesbians.

The relationship between equality and religious freedom has been complicated. Often the notions have seemed to be intimate allies—identical twins, almost. We have already seen how the most common modern conception of religious freedom—one strongly hinted at by Madison and ascendant (for better or worse) in modern religion clause jurisprudence—understands this freedom in terms of religious equality.[36] The state must be neutral as among religions, thereby treating them all as equals, and must not discriminate among citizens, even in its expressions, on the basis of their religion (or lack thereof).

In addition, the claim is often made that religion provided the justification—and still provides the best or even only plausible justification—for the proposition that all people are in some sense morally equal. After all, it is hardly obvious (if I may be permitted a gross understatement) that humans are of equal worth, moral or otherwise: we differ dramatically in our abilities, qualities, and virtues. Even so, we are in some important sense of equal worth—so goes the argument—because we are all made "in the image of God" (as the Bible says)[37] or because we are "created equal" (as the Declaration of Independence says) by being "endowed by [our] Creator" with inalienable rights or dignity. Commenting on the Declaration's assertion, Columbia law professor George Fletcher explains that "[b]ehind those created equal stands a Creator, who is the source of our inalienable rights 'to life, liberty, and the pursuit of happiness.' "[38] Without these religious presuppositions, some argue, substantive claims about equality or equal moral worth make little sense.[39] On this view, equality is not only compatible with religion but dependent on religion for its plausibility.

In recent decades, though, the formerly cozy connection between equality and religion has become, if not severed, at least severely strained. For one thing, modern theorists of equality usually do not invoke religious justifications for the claim of "equal worth." They may not offer any justifications at all, but may instead treat the claim as politically or epistemically axiomatic and hence in no need of extraneous justification. Examining the positions of leading theorists including Ronald Dworkin, John Rawls, Kai Nielsen, Joel Feinberg, Thomas Nagel, and Alan Gewirth, Louis Pojman finds that none of these theorists offers any cogent justification for egalitarian commitments; usually the theorists simply assert or assume equality, or else posit that in the absence of any persuasive objection, we should adopt a "presumption" of equal worth.[40]

Pojman finds this strategy unsatisfactory. He conjectures that egalitarian commitments are "simply a leftover from a religious world view now rejected by all of the philosophers discussed in this essay,"[41] and he wonders whether "perhaps we should abandon egalitarianism and devise political philosophies that reflect naturalistic assumptions, theories which are forthright in viewing humans as differentially talented animals who must get on together."[42] But secular liberal theorists seem to draw an opposite inference. If compelling justifications for our commitments to equal worth are lacking, the proper inference is not that we should abandon those commitments, but rather that the commitments do not need any external justification: we should instead accept them as basic and axiomatic (at least in a liberal democracy).

Critics like Pojman may find this assuming away of the question of justification intellectually irresponsible. Irresponsible or not, though, such assuming is by now common, and commonly accepted. Thus contemporary theorists routinely treat equality as axiomatic. Equality is "a foundational value," Martha Minow and Joseph Singer explain. "It is a fundamental principle in our society that all people are . . . entitled to be treated with equal concern and respect."[43] Ronald Dworkin agrees: "A political community has no moral power to create and enforce obligations against its members," Dworkin declares, "unless it treats them with equal concern and respect."[44] Or theorists talk about "equal regard,"[45] or "equal citizenship,"[46] or "the equal importance of all human lives."[47]

In this equality-oriented framework, traditional virtues and vices get reordered. Previously "deadly sins" like pride, lust, and sloth are displaced on the list of evils by more currently loathsome traits—bigotry and intolerance—that are thought to violate the "equal respect" axiom. Consequently, a good deal of political polemics (and, for that matter, of constitutional jurisprudence)[48] consists of efforts to show that one's opponents are acting from bigotry or prejudice,[49] or are failing to accord "equal respect" to some disadvantaged but deserving group.

Equality has moved away from religion not only in its justifications (or disavowal thereof, or indifference thereto) but also in the substantive content that it is thought to carry. Theorists usually understand that just in itself, the concept of equality has no universal or intrinsic substantive content or implications. Equality surely does not entail the absurd notion that all persons, situations, and cases must always be treated in exactly the same way, so that if people who can see are permitted to drive, blind people must be given the same privilege. Rather, equality implies that *like cases* (or, as the common phrase goes, "similarly situated" instances or classes) should be treated in the same way. But the substantive criteria for determining which cases or classes are relevantly alike or "similarly situated" cannot simply be deduced from the abstract concept of equality; they must be supplied from other sources.[50] For political and legal purposes, the substantive content assigned to equality is likely to come from the surrounding political culture. If it is widely supposed that people of different races or genders are relevantly different, then equality will not require that they be treated in the same way. Conversely, if we come to think that race or sex is irrelevant for legal or political purposes, then our commitment to equality will condemn any discrimination on these grounds.

Professor Laycock suggests that in recent decades, two cultural developments have loaded equality with substantive content that often places it in conflict with religious freedom. One has been the increase in the number and visibility within American society of nonbelievers—atheists, agnostics, and even people who may have a religious affiliation but little actual belief or religious commitment.[51] Laycock explains how the more active presence of nonbelievers alters perceptions of religious freedom. When everyone or nearly everyone was a religious believer of one kind or another, religious freedom could be seen as "a sort of mutual non-aggression pact" that was beneficial to all. Today, by contrast, "[m]uch of the nonbelieving minority sees religious liberty as a protection only for believers. On that view, a universal natural right morphs into a special interest demand."[52] This development is apparent in the now-familiar claim that a practice that was once lauded as the fulfillment of religious freedom—namely, exempting religious believers (such as religious pacifists) from some laws that conflict with their faith—is actually a form of illiberal and unconstitutional discrimination.[53]

The other, probably even more important development, in Laycock's view, has been the growing momentum of the gay rights movement. Laycock observes that in 1993 the Religious Freedom Restoration Act passed with overwhelming support—a unanimous voice vote in the House of Representatives and a 97–3 approval in the Senate—but that five years later, after this act had been partially invalidated by the Supreme Court,[54] the more modest Religious Liberty Protection Act provoked such substantial opposition that it ultimately failed to pass. What had happened in the interim to produce such different political outcomes? Speaking not only as a scholar but also as an active participant in litigation and lobbying, Laycock explains that on the basis of several cases in which landlords had refused on religious grounds to rent to opposite-sex couples, gay rights groups had come to see religious liberty as an obstacle to their objectives.[55] He lays approximately equal blame on the gay rights movement and on religious conservatives who are loath to accept compromises. But however the responsibility is apportioned, the attitudes of opposition have hardened.

> The result of this history is that groups committed to sexual liberty naturally view traditional religion as their principal enemy. . . . If traditional religion is the enemy, then it might follow that religious liberty is a bad thing, because it empowers that enemy. No one says this straight out, at least in public. But it is a reasonable inference from things that *are* said, both in public and in private.[56]

Clashes between the gay rights movement and religious liberty are not confined to the United States. David Novak, a rabbi and scholar at the University of Toronto, discusses a case in Ontario—the Marc Hall case—in which a male homosexual student successfully sued his Catholic high school for discrimination because the school declined to let him bring his boyfriend as his date to the senior prom. Not only did the Catholic school lose the case, Novak reports, but the case provoked a good deal of public commentary that was hostile—hateful, Novak thinks—toward Catholicism because of its commitment to traditional Christian sexual morality.[57] In this rhetoric

Novak discerns an "antireligious agenda that makes Marc Hall a pawn in a much larger battle, of which he and his Catholic parents seem to be naively unaware."[58] Novak adds that "[t]he threat to religious liberty is by no means a uniquely Canadian problem. Indeed, it is a problem facing every religious community in every constitutional democracy."[59]

Gay rights, however, is hardly the only plank in the platform of secular egalitarianism that can come into conflict with religious freedom. Leslie Griffin emphasizes the conflicts between religious liberty and the equal treatment of women.[60] Laura Underkuffler, while conceding that "[r]eligious free exercise is important," argues that it should not be permitted to insulate what she calls "odious discrimination"—namely, discrimination based on "race, color, religion, national origin, sex, sexual orientation, or gender identity."[61] Although equality is a secondary theme in his analysis, James Dwyer argues that free exercise accommodation is bad for women and children.[62]

A New Orthodoxy?

Even so, it might seem that these conflicts should be readily negotiable. Why not simply pass legislation (or maintain legislation already in place) prohibiting discrimination based on sex or sexual orientation, for example, or recognizing same-sex marriage, while building in generous exemptions for religious objectors? Centrists like Laycock and Alan Brownstein who favor both religious freedom and gay rights propose such compromises,[63] and they appear not only disappointed but genuinely puzzled when the proffered compromises meet with suspicion and opposition from both the egalitarian and the religious activists.[64]

But the wariness about compromise is hardly surprising, and it is not merely a manifestation of arrogance or pigheadedness on the part of advocates on each side. Although centrists may view the more hard-line advocates as lamentably shortsighted,[65] it may in fact be the advocates who are taking the more realistic and long view. That is because the real conflict is not just a set of contingent skirmishes between, on the one hand, a small set of specific political proposals and, on the other, some peripheral teachings of a few religious faiths. The conflict is more fundamental than that.

Suppose that religious groups could set aside their specific objection to, say, same-sex marriage (as some religious groups can, and do). Even so, more essential conflicts would remain. Traditional faiths typically teach that some people's deeply held beliefs are true while others are false. Often they will teach that some people are saved and others are not, and that some ways of living are acceptable to God while others are abhorrent. In these ways, traditional religion in its very essence will often be a scandal and an offense against the whole ethos of contemporary liberal egalitarianism, with its commitment to "equal respect" for all persons and all ways of life or conceptions of "the good." To be sure, the traditionally faithful may insist that even as they condemn some kinds of *conduct* as immoral, they respect the equal moral worth of *people* who engage in such conduct—that they adhere to the injunction to "hate the sin but love the sinner." But secular egalitarians often find such professions close to incomprehensible,[66] and hence misguided or disingenuous. To say that someone's way of life is immoral, they argue, is necessarily to imply that the person is of lesser worth, even if the moralist explicitly denies this implication.

It seems, therefore, that traditional religion and contemporary secular egalitarianism are at some deep level fundamentally incompatible. This incompatibility is in some ways reminiscent of the differences we saw in Chapter 1 between classical paganism and the emerging Christian movement. Paganism, as we saw, was a this-worldly affair, and it took a relaxed attitude toward "truth." Christianity, by contrast, aimed for the eternal salvation of its adherents, and it linked this salvation to the adherence to truth (which was articulated with as much precision as theologians and church councils could muster) and to the rejection of error or heresy. These differences were fundamental, and so although pagan rulers alternated between persecuting Christians and putting up with them, Christianity could never be genuinely assimilated into pagan culture.[67] Centuries later, much of Christianity—and not only Christianity but what is sometimes called "strong religion" generally[68]—continues to have the features that Christianity exhibited in the Roman Empire. Conversely, in its this-worldly emphasis and its desire to separate culture and politics from larger questions of truth,[69] modern secular egalitarianism has some of the characteristics of classical paganism.

And yet (and this is a main reason that political compromise is so difficult today) in other respects, secular egalitarianism more closely resembles a secular version of Christendom, under which it was assumed that government should act on and impose a favored orthodoxy. We should note three similarities.

First, just as during the centuries from late antiquity through the Peace of Westphalia Christianity was thought to be the foundation of the social order, contemporary proponents of secular egalitarianism view equality as the foundation of our legal and political order.[70] True, there is room for debate about exactly what secular equality entails or requires (just as there were analogous debates within Christendom).[71] And secular egalitarianism allows for a range of choices and ways of life, so long as those choices and ways are not incompatible with egalitarianism. (Much in the way that Christendom supported an "almost riotous diversity"[72] of opinions,[73] vocations, and ways of life so long as they were not fundamentally incompatible with Christianity.) But the basic commitment—to equality or equal respect—is not merely one good thing among others (along with "domestic tranquility," economic prosperity, and other goods) that government tries to promote. The commitment is the very basis of political legitimacy in our constitutional order.

Second, just as the proponents of Christian orthodoxies often were (and are) inordinately certain of their views, the proponents of secular equalities often seem serenely untroubled by doubt. Such serenity may reflect the reclassification of equality, noted earlier, from being a proposition in need of justification (which, historically, was often religious) to a fundamental axiom for which no justification is required. In any case, just as the established proponents of Christian doctrines could not imagine that anyone could honestly and understandingly disagree, and therefore dismissed contrary views as the product of ignorance, willful error, or hypocrisy,[74] so the committed proponents of, say, same-sex marriage sometimes suggest that people who hold the contrary position can be acting only from hatred or irrational prejudice, or are in the grip of mindless tradition or religious authority.[75] And indeed, that is pretty much what federal judge Vaughn Walker concluded in the California Proposition 8 case.[76]

Third, and perhaps most portentously, secular egalitarianism is like Christianity and Christendom (and *unlike* classical paganism) in that it is not content to regulate outward conduct but instead seeks to penetrate into hearts and minds. After all, secular egalitarians favor "equal *concern* and *respect,"* and concern and respect are matters not just of external behavior but of internal attitudes, intentions, beliefs, and understandings. Naturally, therefore, the proponents of equal respect are concerned with purifying the beliefs and motives of government officials, and citizens, and also with assuring citizens not merely that they will be *justly treated* but that they are *equally respected.* Indeed, the whole purpose of central constitutional doctrines today is to avoid "dignitary" or "psychic" harms,[77] or to assure classes of people that they are not "outsiders" or "lesser members of the political community."[78]

In this spirit, in its decision declaring a right to same-sex marriage, the California Supreme Court noted that the state had already adopted domestic partnership laws that allowed same-sex couples to form unions enjoying virtually the same legal privileges and obligations that accompany marriage. So the difference between marriages and domestic partnerships had become mostly a matter of different labels. This material equivalency, however, did not satisfy the demands of equality and may even have aggravated the problem. That was because, in the court's view, the essential equivalency in the legal features of opposite-sex and same-sex unions made the assignment of different labels to those unions all the more conspicuous in conveying a sense of lesser respect, and thereby inflicting dignitary harm.[79]

From the perspective of this concern for beliefs and motives, a governmental act that might be perfectly acceptable if done with a proper secular purpose is unconstitutional if done with (or if perceived as having) an unapproved invidious purpose.[80] Similarly, a private act of violence performed with an inegalitarian motive—a racist or sexist or homophobic motive, for instance—is deemed more reprehensible than the same violent and illegal act done intentionally but with a different, less reprehensible motive: some such assumption apparently animates laws imposing heightened penalties on "hate crimes."[81] And minorities are thought to be harmed not just by discriminatory *actions,* or even by *words,* but by *beliefs.* Again, Judge Walker's decision in the California Proposition 8 case provides a nice illustration. Walker entered a "finding of fact" declaring that not only discriminatory law or conduct but "[r]eligious *beliefs* that gay and lesbian relationships are inferior to heterosexual relationships harm gays and lesbians." As examples of such harm, Walker quoted a series of Catholic, Protestant, and Orthodox teachings on the subject.[82]

THE RISE AND DECLINE OF AMERICAN RELIGIOUS FREEDOM

This conclusion—namely, that a set of religious beliefs in itself constitutes a harm to other citizens and a violation of their equality—demonstrates the fundamental conflict between traditional religion and the emerging egalitarian orthodoxy. Devout secularists and perceptive religionists alike sense or observe the deep and fundamental conflict between contemporary secular egalitarianism and traditional religion. So it is understandable that the proponents of the secular orthodoxies—secular proponents of same-sex marriage, for example, or of aggressive antidiscrimination legislation and policies—are not eager to accommodate religious deviations.[83] Why accommodate, and in a sense legitimate, views and practices that are archaic and vicious and subversive of the secular egalitarian order? It is likewise understandable that religious believers are wary about compromises, described in terms of "exceptions" or "exemptions," that effectively concede the dominant status of a secular orthodoxy that is fundamentally hostile to their beliefs and ways of life. Once secular egalitarianism is accepted and entrenched as the prevailing orthodoxy, how much sympathy or toleration can they expect to receive over the long run from their new and puritanically egalitarian secular masters?

A Negotiable Conflict?

To say that the conflict is irreconcilable is not necessarily to say that compromise is impossible. Indeed, compromise on seemingly uncompromisable matters has been an essential component in the American political tradition. Thus in the Philadelphia Convention that drafted the Constitution, the so-called Great Compromise negotiated the seemingly intractable issue of representation in the national legislature—an issue that implicated the fundamental and almost ontological question whether the new government was a union of states or of persons—by creating a legislature in which one branch would represent states and the other branch would represent the people. Also in the convention, and for almost three-quarters of a century afterward, Americans found ways to compromise on the issue of slavery. In retrospect, it is easy to look back with shame (and with self-ennobling condescension) on these compromises on a matter as fundamental as the enslavement of human beings. Without such compromises, however, the most likely result would not have been the liberation of slaves but rather the fragmentation of the Union.[84] More recently, although presented as an interpretation of the Constitution, the dividing up of abortion rights in *Roe v. Wade*[85] into an awkward trimester regime is hard to understand except as a judicially imposed truce on a matter as seemingly immune to compromise as the sanctity of life and the moral status of the fetus.[86]

Moreover, the constitutional system, with its separation of authority into a national government and fifty quasi-independent "sovereign" states, seems well designed to facilitate compromise. On contentious issues, it is possible for one position to prevail in one jurisdiction or on one level and for other positions to be adopted in other jurisdictions or on other levels. And indeed, the "American settlement," discussed in Chapter 3, took advantage of this system of federalism and division of jurisdictions to construct what might be viewed as a complex, ongoing compromise on the potentially incendiary subject of religion. Under that regime, more providentialist positions could prevail at one time or in one jurisdiction; more secularist positions could be adopted at other times and in other jurisdictions. School prayer could be (and *was*) forbidden in one state, permitted in another. Neither providentialist nor secularist interpretations or constituencies were permitted to triumph definitively; conversely, both were assured a continuing and legitimate place at the constitutional table.

As we saw in Chapter 4, however, the modern Supreme Court substantially undid the American settlement and reduced the possibilities of compromise by expanding the role of judge-enforced hard constitutional law in the domain of religion. As it came to be axiomatic that constitutional decisions must be "principled,"[87] opportunities for pragmatic compromise were reduced. And the "incorporation" of the religion clauses against the states, by mandating that the same constitutional constraints would apply to governments state, local, and national, significantly truncated the federalist space for reaching different accommodations in accordance with local circumstances.[88]

Even so, the Supreme Court may have unwittingly preserved, and indeed exemplified, the possibility of compromise in a different and less appealing way—namely, by being notoriously erratic (or, some might say, unprincipled) in its enforcement of ostensible constitutional commitments. The inconsistency of the Court's establishment clause jurisprudence has become legendary,[89] and critics generally view this erratic quality as something to deplore.[90] Occasionally, however, commentators take up the theme of the virtues of incoherence: the fact that the courts come out sometimes on the traditional or providentialist side of controversies and sometimes on the "progressive" or secularist side means that nobody and no side is losing all the time.

Thus, after noting the inconsistencies in religion clause decisions, Phillip Johnson suggested that "the fact that the constitutional doctrine is at times muddled and internally inconsistent does not necessarily mean that it is intolerable. On the contrary, the very fact that the holdings do not fit any abstract pattern may indicate that the Court is steering a careful path between undue preference for religion . . . and undue hostility to it."[91] William Marshall has argued in a similar vein. "I do not and cannot argue," Marshall says, "that the Court has embarked on anything remotely approaching a consistent course. Yet there may well be a potential benefit created by this wavering. Because there have been no clear winners, there also have been no clear losers, and it may be that it is the elimination of winners and losers that the religion clauses are ultimately about."[92]

It is hard to admire this kind of compromise—namely, one that results from flagrant inconsistency in adhering to announced doctrines.[93] I suggested in the preceding chapter that the Court's unsteady approach, far from pacifying competing constituencies, has left everyone deeply unhappy: adherents of the providentialist interpretation are resentful because their view has been officially declared heretical (and also, of course, because they often lose particular battles), while the secularist side is embittered because of what it perceives as a continuing de facto establishment of religion that is inconsistent with declared constitutional doctrine. In the end, though, the courts' inconsistent course has meant that, for better or worse, the conflict reflected in the debate between Professors McConnell and Feldman remains unsettled. And recent decisions, in which the Supreme Court has decisively straddled the divide, suggest that this irresolution is likely to continue.

The Supreme Court on the Fence

Consider how in close succession, the Supreme Court appeared to embrace, first, the position favored by Professor Feldman and, not long afterward, the position favored by Professor McConnell. It would be easy to become mired in the doctrinal labyrinths that justices and commentators attempted to negotiate in these cases. For our purpose, we will try to avoid those lawyerly quagmires and instead observe how the Court first rejected and then accepted the basic "religion is special" position.

Christian Legal Society v. Martinez[94] arose when Hastings Law School, a public law school in San Francisco, denied official recognition to the Christian Legal Society (CLS) because the group accepted as members only students who could endorse its "Statement of Faith" and who agreed to follow prescribed principles, one of which forbade sex outside heterosexual marriage. Because this restriction effectively excluded sexually active homosexuals from being members of the society, the law school ruled that CLS violated the school's nondiscrimination policy. CLS (represented in the Supreme Court, as it happened, by Professor McConnell) responded that the denial of official recognition, evidently the first of its kind in the school's history, violated the group's rights of freedom of speech, freedom of association, and freedom of religion.

The controversy presented a host of disputed questions, both factual (What was the law school's policy, exactly? Was the law school's decision a pretext for excluding a Christian group?) and legal (What sort of "public forum" is a public law school?). For present purposes, the crucial point is that the Supreme Court majority treated the case almost entirely under current free speech doctrine, according to which the law school's policy was presumptively constitutional as long as it was not intended to suppress the expression of ideas on a viewpoint-discriminatory basis.[95] Because the purpose of the nondiscrimination policy was presumably to prevent discrimination, not to suppress views, the Court found no free speech violation.

But what about freedom of association and freedom of religion—seemingly the rights most directly implicated? After all, the Hastings policy was not directly about speech at all. But it did exclude from the law-school forum particular kinds of associations—in particular, associations formed on the basis of an operative commitment to a familiar kind of religious faith. So one might have thought that association and religious freedom would be the decision's dominant themes. In fact, they received barely any notice in the Court's opinion. Because the right of "expressive association" has been viewed as a corollary of free speech, the Court tersely observed, it would be "anomalous" to find a violation of freedom of association where the requirements of free speech doctrine were satisfied.[96] As for the exercise of religion, the Court relegated its discussion of the issue to a brief footnote that merely stated that because the law school's policy treated student groups in the same way, there was no discrimination against religion, and hence no free exercise violation.[97]

By effectively melting freedom of association and freedom of religion into free speech, however, and by interpreting free speech to mean basically viewpoint neutrality in application—the Hastings policy was obviously not viewpoint neutral in its substance—the Court effectively eliminated protection for religious groups against nondiscrimination laws or policies (at least in a "limited public forum"). Focusing on the original Hastings policy under which certification had initially been denied,[98] Justice Samuel Alito pointed out the implications of this approach:

> [T]he policy singled out one category of expressive associations for disfavored treatment: groups formed to express a religious message. Only religious groups were required to admit students who did not share their views. An environmentalist group was not required to admit students who rejected global warming. An animal rights group was not obligated to accept students who supported the use of animals to test cosmetics. But CLS was required to admit avowed atheists.[99]

The *Martinez* decision seemed to evince the Supreme Court's acceptance of the sort of position favored by Professor Feldman: religious individuals and associations should enjoy the same protections that others enjoy under, for example, the free speech clause, but religion should not be singled out for special or differential protection. Moreover, this ostensibly equal treatment meant in reality that religion can be burdened in ways in which other sorts of commitments or interests will not be, because a rule prohibiting associations from conditioning membership on religious belief obviously will have a much more severe impact on churches or other religious associations than on other groups. An HMO or a country club can admit, say, Hindus or atheists without in any way altering its essential mission: a Christian church that admits Hindus and atheists as full members and officers will be compromising its character as a *Christian* church.

And yet it would be premature to conclude that Professor Feldman's "no special treatment for religion" position had triumphed decisively. In the following term, the Court unanimously came down in favor of special protection for religious institutions in a case called *Hosanna-Tabor Evangelical Lutheran Church v. EEOC*.[100]

The case raised the issue of the so-called "ministerial exception" to antidiscrimination laws and labor laws as applied to religious organizations. The underlying question presented by the case was basically this: Do antidiscrimination laws that forbid most employers to discriminate on the basis of sex apply as well to churches, or religious employers, that refuse, for example, to ordain women? Can the Catholic Church, for instance, decline to ordain women and thereby exclude women from a whole host of clerical positions? Or, as Richard Garnett puts the question, "[i]f it would be illegal for Wal-Mart to fire a store manager because of her gender, then why should a religiously affiliated university be permitted to fire a chaplain because of hers?"[101]

Although federal employment discrimination law expressly allows churches to discriminate in favor of hiring members of their own faith,[102] not all employment laws contain similar exceptions, and even federal law does not expressly permit churches to discriminate on grounds other than religion. In particular, the law does not explicitly permit churches to discriminate on grounds of sex. Just on the basis of the law as written, therefore, it would appear that a church that does not ordain and hire women for pastoral positions—the Catholic Church is the most conspicuous example—is in violation of federal law, and perhaps of state law as well. For decades, nonetheless, lower courts had ruled that churches have a constitutional right to employ otherwise forbidden criteria such as sex in hiring for "ministerial" positions. Litigation over the issue was common, but the typical dispute argued not over the existence of this ministerial exception but rather about whether a particular position was actually "ministerial." (For example, is the position of church organist "ministerial"?)[103]

Although uniformly accepted in the lower courts, however, the ministerial exception was much more controversial in academic discussions. Legal scholars pointed out that the constitutional basis of the doctrine was uncertain, that the exception fit awkwardly with current free exercise doctrine, and that it was in tension with prevailing egalitarian values.[104] Academic proposals to abandon the exception were (and are) common.[105] Surprisingly, none of the cases recognizing the exception had been reviewed in the Supreme Court. In *Hosanna-Tabor*, the Court finally had an opportunity to speak to the issue.

The case involved a "called" teacher, Cheryl Perich, who had been dismissed from a Lutheran school when, after a disagreement about the timing of her return to work following a medical leave of absence, Perich had hired a lawyer and threatened to sue the school. ("Called" teachers, as opposed to "lay" or "contract" teachers, were appointed by the congregation and given the title of "Minister of Religion, Commissioned.") The Equal Employment Opportunity Commission then proceeded to file a retaliation suit on behalf of Perich under the Americans with Disabilities Act. The Court of Appeals ruled for Perich, concluding that there was little difference between what the Lutheran school classified as "called" and "lay" teachers and that, despite its title, Perich's position was not truly ministerial in nature.

To the surprise of many, rather than focus on defending the position on which the Commission had already won in the Court of Appeals (namely, that the teacher's position was not "ministerial" in nature), the Commission, represented by the United States Solicitor General, primarily argued for the rejection of the ministerial exception altogether. For the most part, the Commission argued, religious employers should be treated like other employers.[106] So then was the Administration saying that if Wal-Mart cannot refuse to hire women as managers, the Catholic Church cannot refuse to ordain and employ women as priests? Not quite—not officially, at least. The Commission argued, as the Court put it, that if the Catholic Church or an Orthodox Jewish seminary were sued for its refusal to ordain women, "religious organizations could successfully defend against employment discrimination claims in those circumstances by invoking the constitutional right to freedom of association."[107] Given that this same "freedom of association" defense had been rejected by the Supreme Court[108] when asserted by organizations like the Jaycees, however, the Commission's position was puzzling at best. The bottom line, in any case, was that no special protection for religious associations or under the free exercise clause was warranted.

The Supreme Court rejected the Commission's position; moreover, it did so unanimously and emphatically, using terms like "untenable" and "remarkable"[109] (words that in the understated vocabulary of Supreme Court opinions typically mean something like "absurd" or "preposterous"). Reciting some of the long history (similar to what we reviewed in Chapter 1) of the church's struggle to achieve independence in its internal affairs from state regulation, the Court concluded that constitutional protection for church autonomy is *not* identical to or coextensive with the more generic freedom of association enjoyed by nonreligious groups. This conclusion was compelled, the Court thought, by the First Amendment itself, "which gives special solicitude to the rights of religious organizations."[110] The Court also ruled that the position of a "called" teacher in the Lutheran school was ministerial in nature, and hence was exempted from the coverage of the federal disabilities law. On its face, *Hosanna-Tabor* would appear to be a resounding victory for the "freedom of the church" and, more generally, for the idea that religious freedom is a special right.

But then of course just a year and a half earlier, in *Martinez*, the Court had appeared to come down on the other side of the "Is religion special?" question. So, are the two decisions simply and flatly inconsistent? Maybe, but it is difficult to say so with confidence, because both cases turned in part on doctrinal intricacies (like the amorphous "public forum" doctrine) that prevent a simple side-by-side comparison. And of course future cases will likewise turn on such doctrinal intricacies (as well as on others, such as the amorphous doctrine of "standing").

At this point, consequently, it would be rash to predict with confidence that either *Hosanna-Tabor* or *Martinez* presages how the Court will come down in future cases. The fundamental debate in which Professors McConnell and Feldman skirmished, and in which Americans generally are knowingly or unknowingly engaged, looks to continue for some time to come.

Freedom of Religion and the Future of the Church

I might conclude this chapter, however, with one tentative and conditional prediction: the fate of religious freedom will likely depend to a large extent on the fortunes of "the church." As we have seen in the course of this book, religious freedom has historically been connected, in close if complicated ways, to the church. And this connection is likely to continue. So ultimately, if the church continues to be a vigorous and vital institution in society, religious freedom will probably be okay. Conversely, if the church declines, religious freedom (and, perhaps, much else) is likely to go down with it.

This may seem to be a gloomy observation, because the church may seem to be in poor shape these days. For one thing, it may seem that "the church" (in the singular) doesn't exist anymore; instead, we have a sprawling multiplicity of independent and sometimes mutually antagonistic churches and faiths. For another, some of the major churches have been conspicuously afflicted with scandal and internal dissension. And then there is the increase in the percentage of "nones"—people who on surveys indicate no religious belief or affiliation.[111] (Numbers can be deceptive, though: in one 2011 study, 10 percent of self-professed atheists said they pray at least once at week.)[112] Adding to these inconveniences is the perennial streak of anticlericalism—or suspicion of "organized religion"—that even religious believers often display. Richard Garnett observes that "[t]oday, churches . . . are often regarded as dangerous centers of potentially oppressive power, as in need of supervision and regulation by the state."[113]

So, if the fate of religious freedom is tied to that of the church, is decline inexorable? Not necessarily. In the first place, however lamentable the multiplicity of churches may seem from some theological standpoints, it is not necessarily a disability for the purpose of upholding religious freedom. A plurality of faiths makes religious freedom more necessary.[114] And scholars employing an economic analysis argue that religion, and churches, are actually stronger when there is competition in a sort of religious marketplace.[115]

Moreover, despite the obvious multitude of churches, in some contexts the practice of referring to "the church," in the singular, persists. Nor is that practice merely an anachronistic holdover; it captures something crucial in (many) Christians' self-understanding. Under the familiar view in which "the church" refers in part and perhaps most centrally to something like "the invisible church" and the various observable "churches" are understood to be instantiations or manifestations of that more mystical entity,[116] it is still meaningful to refer to "the church," in the singular. Theologians have developed sophisticated ecclesiologies that emphasize the underlying or immanent unity in the midst of the conspicuous plurality.[117] In this vein, theological ethicist Gilbert Meilander writes:

> For my part, I believe that the Church's genuine oneness need not be translated into institutional unity. If this commits me to believing that the one holy catholic and apostolic church is "invisible," that's alright. Invisibility in this sense is not a way of escaping from time, place, and embodiment. On the contrary, it is a way of taking time, place, and embodiment seriously, a way of recognizing the multiform manner in which the one Church—under, surely, the governance of the Holy Spirit—has taken shape in human history.[118]

With respect to other negative indicators, it is good to recall that history usually doesn't unfold in linear ways. So if you take current trends and project very far forward, you'll nearly always be wrong. This is true in particular of the church (and, more generally, of religion). Who would have predicted in the year 100, or 200, or even 300 or 310 (in the midst of the Diocletianic persecution) that Christianity would become the official religion of the empire? Who would have predicted the eleventh-century papal revolution, with its campaign to liberate and purify the church, from the midst of the scandalous "dark century" that preceded it? In 1787, who could have foreseen the flourishing of faiths and churches in new American forms that would unfold in the nineteenth century? Through the nineteenth century and the first half of the twentieth, nearly all social scientists and prognosticators foresaw the inexorable decline of religion as modernization took hold.[119] Writing in 1968, the sociologist Peter Berger expressed a common view in predicting that "[b]y the 21st century, religious believers are likely to be found only in small sects, huddled together to resist a world-wide secular culture."[120] So much for predictions based on present trajectories or indicators.

One other observation seems necessary. At least in the view of believers, the church is not a merely human institution, and its fortunes will not be determined merely by human agency. Jacques Maritain explained that the church is, in the Christian view, "a supernatural mystery."

> [T]he Church is not only a visible and apparent reality but also an object of faith, not a system of administrative cog-wheels but the Body of Christ

whose living unity, incomparably more elevated and strong than in this world we describe as moral personality, is guaranteed by the action of the Holy Ghost.[121]

Maritain conceded that this idea would "scandalise unbelievers," and that "it would even be absurd for those who do not and those who do know what the Church is to form the same idea of what her rights are."[122] He was surely right about that much. Nonbelievers will likely find a hope for the church based on the "guarantee" of the Holy Ghost absurd, and quite likely unintelligible. They will think the believers are deluded. If that is so, then the church might well be destined to decline—and religious freedom, perhaps, along with it. We may be living in the last chapter of the story of American (and Western, and indeed global) religious freedom.

But then if the believers are deluded, ultimately, does the story really matter much anyway?

Whither (Religious) Freedom?

The standard story of American religious freedom tells how, under the influence of the Enlightenment, the American founders broke away from the intolerance and dogmatism of centuries of Christendom and courageously set out on a radical new experiment in religious liberty. More specifically, the founders adopted a Constitution that committed the nation to the separation of religion from government and thus to secular governance that would be neutral toward religion. These commitments were not immediately realized; on the contrary, the new nation suffered for a century and a half under a de facto Protestant establishment in which religious minorities or nonbelievers were persecuted, discriminated against, or marginalized. In the second half of the twentieth century, however, a more conscientious Supreme Court finally undertook to realize the promise of the First Amendment's commitment to religious freedom and religious equality. Even now the achievement is under threat, however, mainly from religious conservatives or traditionalists who are hostile to the constitutional commitments.

In this book, we have considered a revised version of this story. In the revised version, the story begins in late antiquity with the emergence of a new religion—Christianity—with distinctive commitments to a separation of spiritual and temporal authorities and to an inner, saving religiosity that was of necessity sincere and voluntary. Over the centuries, Christians sometimes neglected and betrayed these commitments—but sometimes expounded them, and struggled to uphold them. So the American embrace of church-state separation and freedom of conscience is best understood not as a radical innovation but rather as a retrieval and consolidation of these classic commitments (with a measure of easygoing pagan toleration mixed in) under the conditions of the American Republic. These themes, together with a commitment to openness and contestation between perennial providentialist and secularist interpretations of the nation, constituted the distinctive American settlement of the problem of religious pluralism.

This settlement, though theoretically inelegant and practically imperfect, was more successful than previous strategies had been in promoting civic peace and freedom in a religiously diverse world. Nonetheless, the modern Supreme Court rejected the settlement—or perhaps forgot it, or simply failed to understand it. The result has been a notoriously chaotic jurisprudence and a nation increasingly polarized along religious lines. Moreover, by rendering the classic theological rationales inadmissible, modern constitutional doctrine and political philosophy leave the commitment to religious freedom weakly defended and vulnerable. This vulnerability is reflected in the increasingly common academic position (arguably influential within the Obama administration) that a special constitutional commitment to religious freedom is unjustifiable and probably unjust.

Both the standard and revised stories depict religious freedom as presently embattled. But the challenge to religious freedom is arguably less severe in the standard story than in the revised version. If the threat to religious freedom comes from religious conservatives who reject the proverbial "wall of separation," the response, it would seem, is simply to hold steady and resist this challenge. Religious conservatives may have considerable political power, but they are far from being able to dictate what national law or policy should be. They have, after all, been on the losing side in the last two presidential elections (thereby making Bush-era predictions of an imminent "theocracy"[1] seem just a bit silly).

In the revised story, by contrast, religious freedom is being subverted by . . . religious freedom itself (as currently understood), which through its commitments to equality and neutrality and secular government has effectively deprived itself of its historical reasons for being. Thus enfeebled, and faced with being flattened by the juggernaut of "equality," religious freedom's long-term chances do not look promising.

Nor is it self-evident that this possible ending of the story is anything to lament. Even if a special commitment to religious freedom becomes merely a memory, after all, we would still have freedom of speech, freedom of association, and a host of other rights. With all these rights and protections in place, who needs freedom of religion (as the title of an article by legal philosopher James Nickel asks)?[2]

It is understandable, of course, that the churches and the profoundly devout might want to retain a constitutional right specially designed for themselves and their life commitments. In the same way, golfers might like a constitution honoring a special "right to golf," and gardeners might be pleased to support a constitutional amendment singling out a "freedom to garden." But in each case, the rest of us might naturally ask why these people shouldn't be content to have the same freedoms to speak and assemble and associate—and vote, and procreate, and so forth—that everyone else has. And if this conclusion means that the story of American religious freedom has reached "The End" and is now into the credits and acknowledgments . . . , well, so be it. Religious freedom had a good run. Nothing lasts forever.

And yet there may be reason, even for the profoundly undevout, to regret the loss of the classical commitment to freedom of the church (including the "inner church" of conscience). Reflect for a moment on a pithy declaration by that eloquent, truculent malcontent Thomas Paine: "My own mind is my own church."[3] Paine, of course, was hardly a pious Christian. In the same paragraph, he proudly proclaimed his view that "[a]ll national institutions or churches, whether Jewish, Christian, or Turkish, appear to me to be no other than human inventions, set up to terrify and enslave mankind." And his statement itself—"My own mind is my own church"—sounding in the frequently professed modern predilection for "thinking for yourself," expresses his characteristic posture of skepticism toward and independence from any sort of institutional authority.[4] Even so, Paine found it useful to his freedom-favoring purpose to invoke the heritage of the church's struggle to establish a *jurisdiction* beyond the regulatory reach of this-worldly officials or authorities. His mind was his church, and thus was beyond the reach of mundane powers.

As we saw in Chapter 1, James Madison drew on that same religious tradition in defending religious freedom as a "right." By this Madison did not mean (as we might today) merely a privilege or immunity that governments may (or may not) choose to confer, or an "interest" that should be assigned significant "weight" in political or judicial "balancing." Religion was free, rather, in the sense that it was a domain "wholly exempt from [government's] cognizance." And if the right to religious freedom in this jurisdictional sense is not secure, Madison warned, then all other rights will be likewise imperiled.[5] Claims about so-called rights will become mere appeals to the benevolence and good grace of the government. And it is dangerous, Madison suggested, to trust governments to be benevolent and gracious.

In this respect, as in others, Madison seems to have been prescient. Thus, with the benefit of more than two centuries of additional experience, Rajeev Barghava reports that "states that fail to protect religious freedom usually trample on other freedoms too."[6]

Today, to be sure, the jurisdictional-style claims made by Madison and Paine—and Roger Williams, and Pope Gregory VII—are difficult to advance, or even to grasp. Instead, those resisting governmental power are more likely to speak the language of justice, or political morality. The state, we say, ought to treat its subjects fairly. It ought not to disrespect their human dignity. A government that transgresses these constraints is to that extent unjust.

So, are these different idioms—*of jurisdiction,* and *of justice*—merely different vocabularies for making the same kinds of claims and objections? Maybe—but maybe not. To say that the government *ought not* to do something is not strictly equivalent to—is in a crucial sense weaker than—saying that government has *no jurisdiction* to do something.

Cognizant of this distinction, perhaps, John Stuart Mill proposed his famous "harm principle" not merely as a sort of guiding exhortation but rather as an attempt to draw a *jurisdictional* line restricting governmental authority.[7] That line, it might be hoped, could serve to replace the jurisdictional boundaries once associated with freedom of the church and, later, of the inner church of conscience. But as we saw in Chapter 1, the harm principle is (to put the point gently) spectacularly supple in its applications.[8] The principle can bend or extend to suit the preferences and intuitions of theorist, or ruler. Moreover, unlike in Mill's day, the harm principle today has to contend with (or be interpreted and applied in accordance with) an emerging egalitarian orthodoxy seemingly regarded as axiomatically true and just by its proponents.

So, how confident should we be in the capacity of Mill's principle, or something like it, to contain the aspirations and pretensions of rulers, and electorates, devoted to achieving equality (as they understand it) and comfortable in the knowledge of their own righteous purposes? In childlike fashion, perhaps, let us indulge the assumption that unlike so many rulers throughout history, our contemporary governors are true men (and women) and good, genuinely motivated by a desire to govern justly. Even so, we might recall Justice Louis Brandeis's observation that "[e]xperience should teach us to be most on guard to protect liberty when the Government's purposes are beneficent. . . . The greatest dangers to liberty lurk in insidious encroachments by men of zeal, well-meaning but without understanding."[9]

So it is just possible that the forgetting or forgoing of the logic of jurisdiction that animated the commitment to freedom of church and conscience, and thereby set and underscored bounds to the jurisdiction of the state, might turn out to be a loss to be sorely lamented. Even, perhaps, by those feistily independent and fiercely irreverent souls (like Paine) who are, as they suppose, beholden to no faith or external authority, and whose "own mind is [their] own church."

Notes

Book Epigraph

Jacob Burckhardt, The Civilization of the Renaissance in Italy 5 (S. G. C. Middlemore trans., New York: Barnes & Noble, 2001) (first published 1878).

Prologue

1. Sidney E. Mead, The Lively Experiment 60 (1960).
2. Holy Trinity Church v. United States, 143 U.S. 457, 471 (1892).
3. See, e.g., Frank Lambert, Religion in American Politics 184–217 (2008); Susan Jacoby, The Age of American Unreason 183–209 (2008); and Isaac Kramnick & L. Laurence Moore, The Godless Constitution: A Moral Defense of the Secular State 150–206 (2005).
4. Stephen G. Gey, Life after the Establishment Clause, 110 W. Va. L. Rev. 1, 2 (2007).
5. See, e.g., Kevin Phillips, American Theocracy (2006).
6. Ronald Dworkin, Is Democracy Possible Here? 79 (2006).
7. See generally David Sehat, The Myth of American Religious Freedom (2011). Although Sehat's engaging book is explicitly offered as a challenge to American myths about religious freedom, it seems to me more an instance of the standard story, albeit a dark version that doggedly debunks more cheerful or idealistic tellings of that story.
8. See, e.g., No Establishment of Religion: America's Original Contribution to Religious Liberty (T. Jeremy Gunn & John Witte Jr. eds., 2012).
9. See, e.g., Henry Steele Commager, The Empire of Reason 40 (1977) (Enlightenment thinkers believed that "with Reason as their guide they could penetrate to the truth about the Universe and about Man, and thus solve all of those problems that pressed upon them so insistently").
10. See Christian Smith, Moral, Believing Animals 63–94 (2003); and Jerome Brunner, Making Stories: Law, Literature, Life (2002).
11. H. Richard Niebuhr, The Kingdom of God in America (1937).

1. American Religious Freedom as Christian-Pagan Retrieval

1. Christopher Hitchens, God Is Not Great: How Religion Poisons Everything (2007).
2. Everson v. Board of Education, 330 U.S. 1, 8–9 (1947).
3. Thomas Paine, The Age of Reason, in The Theological Works of Thomas Paine (1794).
4. 1 & 2 Edward Gibbon, The History of the Decline and Fall of the Roman Empire 57, 447 (David Womersley ed., 1994) (first published 1776, 1781).
5. David Hume, The Natural History of Religion 134, 162–163; David Hume, Dialogues and Natural History of Religion (J. C. A. Gaskin ed., 1993) (first published 1757).
6. See Peter Gay, The Enlightenment: An Interpretation; The Rise of Modern Paganism 169–170 (1966); Jonathan Israel, A Revolution of the Mind: Radical Enlightenment and the Intellectual Origins of Modern Democracy 199–220 (2010).
7. Ramsay MacMullen, Christianity and Paganism in the Fourth to Eighth Centuries 2, 14 (1997). For a contrasting view, see David Bentley Hart's oddly titled Atheist Delusions: The Christian Revolution and Its Fashionable Enemies (2009). In truculent but immensely learned fashion, Hart contends that in their zeal to depict paganism favorably and Christianity unfavorably, some historians—MacMullen in particular—have treated the historical evidence with a crafted carelessness sometimes arising almost to mendacity. Id. at 53–54, 147–158.
8. Robin Lane Fox, Pagans and Christians (1986).
9. Jonathan Kirsch, God against the Gods: The History of the War between Monotheism and Polytheism (2004).
10. J. A. North, Roman Religion 9, 76–77 (2000). The historian Polybius remarked on this distinctive religiosity in the second century BCE. Polybius, The Rise of the Roman Empire 349 (Ian Scott-Kilvert trans., Penguin Classics 1979). See also Fox, Pagans and Christians, at 82 (describing "the gods' role on every level of social life and their pervasive presence").
11. See David Stockton, The Founding of the Empire, in The Oxford History of the Roman World 146, 161–163 (John Boardman et al. eds., 1986).
12. But see Hart, Atheist Delusions, at 119–120 (arguing that "[t]he very notion that polytheism is inherently more tolerant of religious differences than is 'monotheism' is, as a historical claim, utterly incredible").
13. 1 Gibbon, History of the Decline and Fall, at 57.
14. Paul Veyne, When Our World Became Christian, 312–394, at 35 (Janet Lloyd trans., 2010).
15. Kirsch, God against the Gods, at 10.

16. Charles Freeman, AD 381: Heretics, Pagans, and the Dawn of the Monotheistic State 18 (2008).

17. 1 Gibbon, History of the Decline and Fall, at 57.

18. See Nicholas Purcell, The Arts of Government, in The Oxford History of the Roman World 180, 186–189 (John Boardman et al. eds., 1986). Cf. Martin Goodman, Rome and Jerusalem 148 (2007) (discussing "[t]he tolerance of the [Roman] state in allowing provincials to retain non-Roman lifestyles").

19. 1 Gibbon, History of the Decline and Fall, at 56.

20. North, Roman Religion, at 63.

21. See Hart, Atheist Delusions, at 118–119:

> The polytheism of the Roman Empire may have had enormous patience for a remarkable diversity of cults, but it certainly had none for any great diversity of religions. . . . In this sense, and in this sense only, was the greater Roman world religiously "tolerant": it was tolerant of creeds that were simply different expressions of its own religious temper and that were, in consequence, easily absorbed. It was tolerant, that is to say, of what it found tolerable. When, however, it encountered beliefs and practices contrary to its own pieties, alien to its own religious sensibilities, or apparently subversive of its own sacral premises, it could respond with extravagant violence.

22. See Goodman, Rome and Jerusalem, at 150 (Druids), 379–487 (Jews); North, Roman Delusions, at 63–66 (followers of Bacchus), 67–68 (Chaldeans, Isis worshippers); Fox, Pagans and Christians, at 594–595 (Manichees).

23. Tacitus, Annales XV.43, at 354 (Michael Grant trans., 1959).

24. Eusebius, The Church History 289–320 (Paul L. Maier ed. & trans., 1999).

25. Id. at 293. More generally, Adrian Goldsworthy explains that

> [p]ublic executions [of Christians] were also often included in public entertainments. Not all Christians were killed. Men might be sent to labour in the appalling conditions of imperial mines, while women were sometimes sent to work in brothels. On other occasions fines or imprisonment were used, again in the hope of persuading the accused to recant. When the death sentence was imposed, it was often inflicted in extremely savage ways, even by Roman standards. Usually the crowd reveled in the slaughter.

Adrian Goldsworthy, How Rome Fell 98–99 (2009).

26. See 1 Gibbon, History of the Decline and Fall, at 57.

27. Luke 20:21–26.

28. See Brian Tierney, The Crisis of Church and State, 1050–1300, at 8 (1964).

29. Augustine, The City of God (written 413–426).

30. See John Witte Jr., Law and Protestantism: The Legal Teachings of the Lutheran Reformation 87–117 (2002).

31. Luke 22:38.

32. See Tierney, Crisis of Church and State, at 8.

33. For example, Hebrew scripture records that the first king of Israel, Saul, was condemned by the prophet Samuel for wrongfully assuming the authority to perform a ritual sacrifice under exigent circumstances before a major battle. 1 Sam. 13. However, early modern interpreters tended to emphasize the unity of religious and civil authority in Jewish history, although, paradoxically, they derived a lesson of religious toleration from that unity. See Eric Nelson, The Hebrew Republic: Jewish Sources and the Transformation of European Political Thought (2010). Nelson argues that seventeenth-century thinkers like Erastus, Grotius, Hooker, Harrington, Selden, and Hobbes derived from their interpretation of the Hebrew constitution an Erastianism in which all law, including religious law, came from the civil sovereign, but because the civil sovereign should act only to promote public objectives and civil peace, the conclusion was that internal opinion and religious belief should not be enjoined by civil law. In this way, Erastianism led to religious toleration. Id. at 88–137. In fact, it is not so clear that the thinkers discussed by Nelson eschewed a divided sovereignty. They evidently did affirm an "internal" realm that was subject to God but beyond the jurisdiction of the civil sovereign (except, significantly, in the time of Moses, when, they thought, God himself was the civil sovereign). Id. at 94, 96, 126–127, 133.

34. Hans-Joseph Klauck, The Religious Context of Early Christianity 32 (2003).

35. North, Roman Religion, at 22–34. See also Robert Louis Wilken, The Christians as the Romans Saw Them 6 (2d ed. 2003).

36. Quoted in North, Roman Religion, at 22.

37. Bernard Lewis, The Crisis of Islam 20 (2003).

38. Lewis continues: "In pagan Rome, Caesar was God. For Christians, there is a choice between God and Caesar, and endless generations of Christians have been ensnared in that choice. In Islam there was no such painful choice. In the universal Islamic policy as conceived by Muslims, there is no Caesar but only God, who is the sole sovereign and the sole source of law." Id. at 6–7.

39. See Hugo Rahner, Church and State in Early Christianity 39–183 (Leo Donald Davis, S.J., tr. 1992).

40. See Tierney, Crisis of Church and State, at 49–50, 182–189.

41. See Rahner, supra note at 113, 136–137, 157, 171–172, 174, 236–237.

42. Some scholars have recently argued that it is a mistake to treat Christianity, paganism, and other faiths as different members of a common category of "religion"—or even that the very category of "religion" is misconceived. See,

e.g., William T. Cavanaugh, The Myth of Religious Violence (2009). By now, though, and for our purposes, it seems unnecessary and virtually impossible to abjure the term.

43. Veyne, When Our World Became Christian, at 6.

44. These contrasts are not intended to be exhaustive. For example, David Bentley Hart argues that Christianity was also distinctive in teaching a conception of the person that was markedly different from anything in the pagan world and might be seen as animating the idea of human dignity that is pervasive in modern thinking about religious freedom and human rights. Hart, Atheist Delusions, at 166–182, 213.

45. On the widespread belief in demons in late antiquity, see Peter Brown, The World of Late Antiquity 53–55 (1971); and E. R. Dodds, Pagan and Christian in an Age of Anxiety 117–118 (1965).

46. Hume, Natural History of Religion, at 176.

47. 1 Gibbon, History of the Decline and Fall, at 59. For criticism of this common "cynical" interpretation, see North, Roman Religion, at 31–32.

48. Veyne, When Our World Became Christian, at 33.

49. Id. at 35.

50. Id. at 43–44.

51. Paul Veyne, Did the Greeks Believe in Their Myths? xi (1983).

52. North, Roman Religion, at 78, 84.

53. Wilken, Christians, at 58. See also Fox, Pagans and Christians, at 31 ("[Romans] did pay detailed acts of cult, especially by offering animal victims to their gods, but they were not committed to revealed beliefs in the strong Christian sense of the term.").

54. Guy G. Strousma, The End of Sacrifice: Religious Transformations in Late Antiquity 9 (Susan Emanuel trans., 2009).

55. See Phillip Jenkins, Jesus Wars (2010).

56. The Athanasian Creed thus concludes with the pronouncement that "[t]his is the Catholic Faith, which except a man believe faithfully, he . . . can not be saved." The creed is reprinted in 2 Philip Schaff, The Creeds of Christendom 66, 70 (1931 ed.) Schaff, a nineteenth-century theologian, observed that the creed's "damnatory clauses, especially when sung or chanted in public worship, grate harshly on modern Protestant ears, and it may well be doubted whether they are consistent with true Christian charity and humility." 1 Philip Schaff, The Creeds of Christendom 40 (1931 ed.)]

57. Fox, Pagans and Christians, at 31.

58. John 8:32.

59. Fox, Pagans and Christians, at 39. Cf. Wilken, Christians, at 59 ("The gods were thought to preserve the city of Rome. . . . Through the providence of the gods

the earth came to life each spring, the wheat bloomed, the trees bore fruit, and the heavens opened to provide rain.").

60. Veyne, When Our World Became Christian, at 29, 28.

61. Wilken, Christians, at x. See also Pierre Chuvin, A Chronicle of the Last Pagans 9–10 (B. A. Archer trans., 1990).

62. Fox, Pagans and Christians, at 97.

63. See Wilken, Christians, at x (observing that for Judaism and Christianity, "religious faith . . . meant an interior transformation of the mind and heart").

64. Strousma, End of Sacrifice, at 15, 2 (emphasis in original). See also Wilken, Christians, at 63–65.

65. Matt. 5:21–30.

66. Luke 17:20–21.

67. Romans 4–5; Galatians 3–4.

68. See Veyne, When Our World Became Christian, at 23 ("The cardinal role that morality played in Christianity was largely alien to paganism."). See also Strousma, End of Sacrifice, at 21 (observing that "the ethical was not for the pagans an integral part of religion as it was for the Christians or for the Jews").

69. James 2:14–26.

70. See Heiko A. Oberman, Luther: Man between God and the Devil 204 (1989).

71. Dodds, Age of Anxiety, at 113–114.

72. Quoted in Paul Johnson, A History of Christianity 70 (1976).

73. Quoted in Brian Tierney, Religious Rights: A Historical Perspective, in Religious Liberty in Western Thought 32 (Noel B. Reynolds & W. Cole Durham Jr. eds., 1996). See also Veyne, When Our World Became Christian, at 90 ("Throughout the fourth century, it was repeated that it was not possible to compel consciences or to force people to believe.").

74. The Christian bishop and historian Eusebius lived through the persecution and described it in his history. Eusebius, Church History, at 289–320.

75. Robert Markus, Christianity and the Secular 21 (2006).

76. Adrian Murdoch, The Last Pagan 5 (2003).

77. Jacob Burckhardt, The Age of Constantine the Great 292 (Moses Hadas trans., 1949) (first published 1852).

78. For an overview of the debate and an argument that Constantine was genuinely Christian, see Peter J. Leithart, Defending Constantine 79–96 (2010). See also Diarmaid MacCulloch, A History of Christianity 191 (2010) ("There is no doubt that [Constantine] came to a deeply personal if rather capricious involvement in the Christian faith."). Cf. Veyne, When Our World Became Christian, at 121 ("All in all, the Christianization of the ancient world constituted a revolution set in motion by a single individual, Constantine, with motives that were exclusively religious.").

79. Veyne, When Our World Became Christian, at 8.
80. MacMullen, Christianity and Paganism, at 13; Peter Brown, Power and Persuasion in Late Antiquity 107–109 (1992).
81. See Hart, Atheist Delusions, at 3–44, 120.
82. See Wilken, Christians, at 165–166 ("Julian . . . initiated a frontal attack on the Christian movement, using the law to restrict Christian influence and the power and prestige of his office to promote the practice of the traditional pagan rites.").
83. H. A. Drake, Constantine and the Bishops: The Politics of Intolerance (2000).
84. Kirsch, God against the Gods, at 169–170.
85. Rodney Stark, Cities of God 196–199 (2007).
86. Id. at 200.
87. Brown, Power and Persuasion in Late Antiquity, at 129.
88. Brown, World of Late Antiquity, at 73.
89. See Rahner, supra note at 38–60.
90. See Peter Brown, The Rise of Western Christendom 80 (2d ed. 2003).
91. See MacCulloch, History of Christianity, at 299–301; Eamon Duffy, Saints and Sinners: A History of the Papacy 49–50 (1997).
92. See Peter Heather, The Fall of the Roman Empire: A New History of Rome and the Barbarians 125 (2006):

> [E]mperors were now intimately involved in both the settlement of Church disputes and the much more mundane business of the new religion's administration. To settle disputes, emperors called councils, giving bishops the right to use the privileged travel system, the *cursus publicus,* in order to attend. Even more impressively, emperors helped set the agendas to be discussed, their officials orchestrated the proceedings, and state machinery was used to enforce the decisions reached. More generally, they made religious law for the Church—Book 16 of the *Theodosian Code* is entirely concerned with such matters— and influenced appointments to top ecclesiastical positions.

93. See Duffy, Saints and Sinners, at 32–33.
94. See Rahner, supra note at 197–203, 233–235.
95. See id. at 235–237.
96. See generally Harold J. Berman, Law and Revolution: The Formation of the Western Legal Tradition 85–113 (1983).
97. William Placher observes that

> [i]n theory, everyone agreed that the church and the empire or kingdoms had separate tasks, both given by God. But in practice, when the church owned vast stretches of land and provided many governmental officials, it was hard to know where to draw

the line between the two. Gregory [VII] saw lay investiture as illegitimate interference in the church, but to Henry [IV] it seemed necessary to have some right to choose his own leading landowners and officials.

William C. Placher, A History of Christian Theology 136 (1983).

98. Duffy, Saints and Sinners, at 105.

99. Id. at 105–111.

100. The incident is recounted in Tierney, Crisis of Church and State, at 53–73. The quotations are from original documents reprinted in Tierney's account.

101. Id. at 58–60.

102. Id. at 61.

103. Id. at 63.

104. Id.

105. See generally Tierney, Crisis of Church and State.

106. See generally Frank Barlow, Thomas Becket (1986).

107. Tierney, Crisis of Church and State, at 141.

108. Duffy, Saints and Sinners, at 148.

109. Tierney, Crisis of Church and State, at 180–185.

110. Duffy, Saints and Sinners, at 164.

111. Charles Taylor, Modes of Secularism, in Secularism and Its Critics 32 (Rajeev Bhargava ed., 1998).

112. For a brief description, see Robert E. Rodes Jr., Ecclesiastical Administration in Medieval England 56–59 (1977).

113. See id. at 54.

114. See John Guy, Tudor England 258–264 (1988).

115. José Casanova, Public Religions in the Modern World 22 (1994).

116. See generally Nicholas P. Miller, The Religious Roots of the First Amendment: Dissenting Protestants and the Separation of Church and State (2012). The thinking of dissenting Protestants reflected a development about to be discussed—namely, a shift in emphasis from the outward church to conscience or "private judgment"—but the implications were similar in limiting the jurisdiction of the civil government. For example, with respect to one influential Protestant figure, Isaac Backus, Miller explains, "Backus ultimately rested his defense of full religious liberty on the three points common to Locke, Elisha Williams, and [William] Penn: (1) all spiritual knowledge is personal; (2) there is no ultimate earthly spiritual authority; and (3) therefore, the civil power has no jurisdiction in spiritual matters." Id. at 106. Similar themes appear in the other figures Miller discusses.

117. Thomas Curry explains that separation of the sort Americans contemplate today would have been "unthinkable" for the Puritans. Nonetheless,

the New England clergy limited themselves to religious affairs. They created no ecclesiastical courts to enforce marriage laws, probate wills, or assign fines for moral lapses. New England clerics, although on request they could and did give advice to the secular governments, could not hold civil offices, as the English bishops did. Nor did excommunication in New England deprive a person of secular rights.

Thomas J. Curry, The First Freedoms: Church and State in America to the Passage of the First Amendment 5 (1986).

118. Id.

119. Id. See also Timothy L. Hall, Separating Church and State 62 (1998) (footnotes omitted):

Although they viewed the destinies of ecclesiastical and civil power as linked in the sovereign plan of God, [Massachusetts Puritans] insisted that these two spheres of power held separate offices and exercised "distinct and due administrations." They desired to assure that the boundaries between church and state were maintained free from erosion "either by giving the spiritual power which is proper to the church into the hand of the civil magistrate . . . or by giving civil power to church officers. . . ."

120. See Philip Hamburger, Separation of Church and State 44–45 (2002). On Williams's fanaticism and on the religious basis of his separationism, see Hall, Church and State, and Steven D. Smith, Separation and the Fanatic, 85 Va. L. Rev. 213 (1999).

121. See generally Brian Moynahan, God's Bestseller: William Tyndale, Thomas More, and the Writing of the English Bible (2002).

122. For a brief account of the incident (which may not have involved the exact famous words passed down in the legend), see Martin Marty, Martin Luther 67–70 (2004).

123. For a helpful overview, see Alister E. McGrath, Reformation Thought: An Introduction 130–138 (1988). See also Carl E. Braaten, Principles of Lutheran Theology 54–57 (2d ed. 2007) (discussing "the tension between the Protestant principle and Catholic substance" in Lutheran ecclesiology).

124. John Witte Jr., God's Joust, God's Justice 16 (2006). Cf. Andrew R. Murphy, Conscience and Community 111 (2001) ("According to the orthodox view, conscience represented the voice of God within an individual.").

125. Cf. Tierney, Religious Rights, at 51.

126. Quoted in Timothy Hall, Separating Church and State: Roger Williams and Religious Liberty 87 (1998).

127. John Locke, A Letter Concerning Toleration, in John Locke, The Second Treatise of Government and A Letter Concerning Toleration 113, 119 (Dover 2002).

128. James Madison, A Memorial and Remonstrance against Religious Assessments, reprinted in The Sacred Rights of Conscience 309 (Daniel L. Dreisbach and Mark David Hall eds., 2009).

129. Virginia Act for Religious Freedom, reprinted in Church and State in the Modern Age: A Documentary History 63, 64 (J. F. MacClear 1995).

130. Elisha Williams, The Essential Rights and Liberties of Protestants: A Seasonable Plea for the Liberty of Conscience, and the Right of Private Judgment, in Matters of Religion, without Any Controul from Human Authority 12 (1744) (italics omitted).

131. Madison, Memorial and Remonstrance, at 309.

132. See Jonathan Israel, A Revolution of the Mind: Radical Enlightenment and the Intellectual Origins of Modern Democracy 199–220 (2010); David Sorkin, The Religious Enlightenment (2008); Henry F. May, The Enlightenment in America (1976).

133. See Nathan Chapman, Disentangling Conscience and Religion, __ U. Ill. L. Rev. __ (2012) ("For the most part, the founders embraced John Locke's theory of religion toleration.").

134. Locke, Letter Concerning Toleration, at 113, 115.

135. Id. at 118.

136. Id. at 118–119. For a detailed analysis showing how Locke's defense of religious toleration was grounded in and limited by his own religious assumptions, see Stanley Fish, The Trouble with Principle 163–175 (1999).

137. Virginia Act for Religious Freedom, reprinted in Maclear, Church and State, at 63, 64.

138. Henry F. May, The Divided Heart: Essays on Protestantism and the Enlightenment in America 169 (1991).

139. See Theodore K. Rabb, The Last Days of the Renaissance 75–78, 85–86 (2006).

140. Jacob Burckhardt, The Civilization of the Renaissance in Italy 156 (S. G. C. Middlemore trans., 2001) (first published 1878).

141. William Wordsworth, The World Is Too Much with Us, reprinted in Six Centuries of Great Poetry 364 (Robert Penn Warren & Albert Erskine eds., 1955).

142. See, e.g., Friedrich Nietzsche, The Birth of Tragedy; or, Hellenism and Pessimism (1886 ed.), in Basic Writings of Nietzsche 15 (Walter Kaufmann trans. & ed., 2000). Nietzsche reveals that in Christianity "I never failed to sense a *hostility to life*—a furious, vengeful antipathy to life itself." Id. at 23. The antidote was "a fundamentally opposite doctrine and valuation of life—purely artistic and *anti-Christian*" that he called "in the name of a Greek god: I called it Dionysian." Id. at 24.

143. 1 Gibbon, History of the Decline and Fall, at 103.

144. Gay, Enlightenment.

145. Thomas Jefferson, Notes on the State of Virginia, in Thomas Jefferson: Writings 285 (Merrill D. Peterson ed., 1984).

146. John Stuart Mill, On Liberty 13 (Stefan Collini ed., 1989).

147. See, e.g., State v. Parson, 447 S.W.2d 543, 546 (W. Va. Sup. Ct. App. 1994); United States v. Joseph, 37 M.J. 392, 397 (1993); and Boissonneault v. Mason, 221 N.W.2d 393, 393 (Mich. Sup. Ct. 1974).

148. Andrew Koppelman, Drug Policy and the Liberal Self, 100 Nw. U. L. Rev. 279, 279 (2006).

149. I develop this point at length in Steven D. Smith, The Disenchantment of Secular Discourse 70–106 (2010).

150. Joel Feinberg, Harm to Others (1984); Joel Feinberg, Offense to Others (1985); Joel Feinberg, Harm to Self (1986); Joel Feinberg, Harmless Wrongdoing (1990).

151. Feinberg, Harm to Others, at 12.

152. For a scathing criticism of the "new atheists," see Hart, Atheist Delusion, at 3–15, 219–223.

153. See, e.g., Hitchens, God Is Not Great; and Sam Harris, The End of Faith: Religion, Terror, and the Future of Reason (2004).

154. Ross Koppel, Public Policy in Pursuit of Private Happiness, 41 Contemporary Sociology 49, 49–52 (2012).

155. See Kirsch, God against the Gods, at 169–170.

156. See generally Jonathan Glover, Humanity: A Moral History of the Twentieth Century (1999).

157. I do not mean to suggest that the antecedents and influences were exclusively Christian. Consistent with the argument here, Eric Nelson challenges the standard view of religious toleration and freedom of conscience as the product of secularization, but he emphasizes the influence of Hebrew scripture—or of what Christians call the Old Testament—on modern thinkers in the development of toleration. Nelson, Hebrew Republic.

2. The Accidental First Amendment

1. Sidney E. Mead, The Lively Experiment 60 (1960).

2. The recorded discussion is reprinted in Creating the Bill of Rights: The Documentary Record from the First Federal Congress 150–151, 153, 157–159 (Helen E. Veit et al. eds., 1991) (hereinafter Documentary Record).

3. Leonard W. Levy, The Establishment Clause: Religion and the First Amendment 79 (1986).

4. For a more careful discussion of the point, see Steven D. Smith, The Constitution and the Pride of Reason 31–47 (1998).

5. U.S. Const. art. VI, sec. 3. For an insightful discussion of this provision, see Gerard V. Bradley, The No Religious Test Clause and the Constitution of Religious Liberty: A Machine That Has Gone of Itself, 37 Case W. Res. L. Rev. 674 (1987).

6. See David Sehat, The Myth of American Religious Freedom 29 (2011).

7. 3 Elliot's Debates, at 330.

8. 4 Elliot's Debates, at 208.

9. For a discussion of Madison's change of heart on the subject, see Paul Finkelman, The Ten Amendments as a Declaration of Rights, 16 S. Ill. L.J. 351, 382–385 (1992).

10. Documentary Record, at 64.

11. See Daniel A. Farber & Suzanna Sherry, A History of the American Constitution 32 (1990).

12. Documentary Record, at 66, 77.

13. Id. at 187.

14. See Thomas J. Curry, The First Freedoms: Church and State in America to the Passage of the First Amendment 140–148, 163–172 (1986).

15. Akhil Reed Amar, Anti-Federalists, *The Federalist Papers*, and the Big Argument for Union, 16 Harv. J.L. & Pub. Pol'y 111, 115 (1993) (footnotes omitted).

16. Quoted in Daniel L. Dreisbach, Thomas Jefferson and the Wall of Separation between Church and State 66 (2002).

17. Dwight argued that "[n]o free government has ever existed for any time without the support of religion. . . . But religion cannot exist, and has never existed for any length of time, without public worship." Timothy Dwight, Letter V: Vindication of the Establishment of the Public Worship of God by Law, in 4 Travels in New England and New York 283 (B. Solomon ed., 1969) (first published 1822).

18. Michael W. McConnell et al., Religion and the Constitution 50 (3d ed. 2011).

19. Michael W. McConnell, Establishment at the Founding, in No Establishment of Religion: America's Original Contribution to Religious Liberty 45, 64 (T. Jeremy Gunn & John Witte Jr. eds., 2012).

20. The argument is elaborated in Daniel O. Conkle, Toward a General Theory of the Establishment Clause, 82 Nw. U.L. Rev. 1113, 1133 (1988).

21. Steven Green misconstrues this interpretation and treats it as contending that the religion clauses were intended affirmatively to preserve state religious establishments; he then peremptorily dismisses this possibility. "[N]o one—in New England or elsewhere—would have been so bold as to argue that a primary purpose of the establishment clause was to preserve those crumbling, discredited institutions." Steven K. Green, The Second Disestablishment: Church and State in Nineteenth-Century America 68 (2010). Green is right. No one, then or today, would be so bold as to argue for that implausible interpretation: to protect an institution against federal interference is hardly the same as to preserve it. Green is attacking a straw person.

22. I have addressed these questions in more detail elsewhere. See Steven D. Smith, The Jurisdictional Establishment Clause: A Reappraisal, 81 Notre Dame

L. Rev. 1843 (2006); and Steven D. Smith, Foreordained Failure: The Quest for a Constitutional Principle of Religious Freedom 17–54 (1995).

23. Although Carl Esbeck agrees with what he calls a "general federalist" interpretation of the establishment clause, he sharply criticizes what he calls the "specific federalist" interpretation (of which, it seems, he takes me to be a proponent). This more specific interpretation, Esbeck says, "attributes to the Establishment Clause alone particular federalist intent, one not present in free exercise, free speech, free press, or other provisions in the first eight amendments." In addition, he says, "[d]evotees of specific federalism argue that the clause should not have been incorporated because the Court thereby ignored its unique federalist character." Carl Esbeck, The First Federal Congress, in No Establishment of Religion: America's Original Contribution to Religious Liberty 208, 212 (T. Jeremy Gunn & John Witte Jr. eds., 2012). I agree that those contentions would be untenable, but I at least have never advocated either of them.

24. Donald L. Drakeman, Church, State, and Original Intent 330 (2010).

25. Id. at ix (observing that "this no-national-religion interpretation is not the conclusion that I expected to reach when I began this project, nor is it necessarily in line with my personal views of how church and state should interact, but it appears to be compelled by an as-objective-as-possible analysis of the history").

26. Documentary Record, at 157–158.

27. For discussion, see Carl H. Esbeck, The Establishment Clause as a Structural Restraint on Governmental Power, 84 Iowa L. Rev. 1, 103 n.441 (1998).

28. See Curry, First Freedoms, at 216.

29. The veto message is reprinted in McConnell et al., Religion and the Constitution, at 317. I have added the italics.

30. Douglas G. Smith, The Establishment Clause: Corollary of Eighteenth-Century Corporate Law?, 98 Nw. U.L. Rev. 239, 271 (2003). For further supporting discussion, see Thomas C. Berg, Disestablishment from Blaine to Everson, in No Establishment of Religion: America's Original Contribution to Religious Liberty 307, 326–327 (T. Jeremy Gunn and John Witte Jr. eds., 2012).

31. Carl Esbeck suggests that the addition may have been made for stylistic purposes, and he offers a complicated explanation (which, I confess, I do not follow) of the asserted stylistic superiority of the wordier "respecting" language. Esbeck, First Congress, at 234.

32. Documentary Record, at 157–158. Steven Green acknowledges that Huntington's statement clearly expresses this concern, but he thinks that Sylvester's admittedly obscure statement more likely reflected a concern about eliminating federal expressions of religion such as days of prayer. And on the premise that only one congressman clearly expressed concerns about protecting state establishments from national interference, Green concludes that "[v]iewed in

its entirety, the House debate does not reveal an overriding interest in preserving state religious establishments under the federal establishment clause." Green, Second Disestablishment, at 69–71. Green's argument reflects several misconceptions. First, even if we accept that only one representative clearly made the point, the fact is that hardly any representatives spoke at all. It would be as accurate to turn the fact around and say that a significant percentage of the substantive concerns raised were federalist or jurisdictional in nature. Second, the jurisdictional interpretation does not claim either that the purpose of the establishment clause was to "preserve" state religious establishments, as noted earlier, or that the purpose of protecting such establishment clauses was an "overriding" purpose of the clause. Third, Green consistently trades on a false dichotomy: thus he poses the question "[w]hether Madison saw his new proposal as protecting the existing New England establishments or merely emphasizing the lack of national authority over religion." Id. at 70. But these supposed alternatives, far from being different or opposed, were in fact intimately connected. The reality was that the purpose of the clause was, as Green contends, to make explicit "the lack of national authority over religion"; and one consequence of this denial of authority (a consequence that at least some Americans, like Huntington, cared about, even if not as an "overriding purpose") was not to "preserve" the New England establishments but to insulate them against national interference.

33. Daniel Dreisbach suggests that the original Constitution's prohibition on religious tests for federal office may have reflected a similar concern. See Dreisbach, Defining and Testing the Prohibition on Religious Establishments in the Early Republic, in No Establishment of Religion: America's Original Contribution to Religious Liberty 252, 257 (T. Jeremy Gunn & John Witte Jr. eds., 2012) ("Some founders arguably supported a federal test ban because they valued religious tests required under state laws, and they feared a federal test might displace existing state test oaths and religious establishments.").

34. See Michael J. White, The First Amendment's Religion Clauses: "Freedom of Conscience" versus Institutional Accommodation, 47 U. San Diego L. Rev. 1075, 1075–1076, 1081 (2010).

35. See Noah Feldman, Divided by God 27–33 (2005); Steven K. Green, Federalism and the Establishment Clause: A Reassessment, 38 Creighton L. Rev. 761, 775 (2005) ("Moreover, Americans throughout the fourteen nascent states agreed that freedom of religious conscience was an essential right.").

36. See McConnell, Establishment, at 65.

37. For skeptical reflections on the possibility or ontological status of such principles, see Larry Alexander, Legal Objectivity and the Illusion of Legal Principles, in Institutionalized Reason 115 (Matthis Klatt ed., 2012).

38. See, e.g., John Witte Jr., Religion and the American Constitutional Experiment 37–55 (2000) (arguing that the Constitution contained six principles of religious freedom).

39. For more detailed discussion of the ubiquitous resort to "principles" in modern constitutional discourse, see Steven Smith, Constitution and the Pride of Reason, at 77–83.

40. Ronald Dworkin, Freedom's Law 74, 78, 73 (1996).

41. Ronald Dworkin, Law's Empire 53 (1986).

42. See Curry, First Freedoms, at 217–218.

43. See Green, Second Disestablishment, at 72.

44. Laura Underkuffler-Freund, The Separation of the Religious and the Secular, 36 Wm. & Mary L. Rev. 837, 954–955 (1995) (footnotes omitted).

45. Green, Second Disestablishment, at 72.

46. Id. at 73.

47. See Lee v. Weisman, 505 U.S. 577, 626 (1992) (Souter, J., concurring) (explaining away early invocations of religion by observing that "the Framers . . . , like other politicians, could raise constitutional ideals one day and turn their backs on them the next").

48. See, e.g., Douglas Laycock, Substantive Neutrality Revisited, 110 W. Va. L. Rev. 51 (2007).

49. See, e.g., Van Orden v. Perry, 545 U.S. 677 (2005) (permitting, by 5–4 vote, a Ten Commandments monument on Texas State Capitol grounds).

50. See Utah Highway Patrol Ass. v. American Atheists, Inc., 132 S. Ct. 12 (2011) (denying certiorari over strenuous dissent by Justice Thomas).

51. See, e.g., Freedom from Religion Foundation v. Obama, 641 F.3d 803 (7th Cir. 2011) (reversing, on standing grounds, lower-court decision ruling National Day of Prayer statute unconstitutional).

52. Douglas Laycock, "Nonpreferential" Aid to Religion: A False Claim about Original Intent, 27 Wm. & Mary L. Rev. 875, 919 (1985/1986).

53. Philip Hamburger argues that in the early Republic hardly anyone favored "separation of church and state," and that support for this idea came much later. Philip Hamburger, Separation of Church and State 287–334 (2002). But Hamburger acknowledges that many Americans in the early period favored religious disestablishment. At least in more contemporary terminology, these amount to much the same thing. For discussion of the point, see Douglas Laycock, The Many Meanings of Separation, 70 U. Chi. L. Rev. 1667 (2003).

54. Thus Steven Green criticizes the jurisdictional interpretation for "fail[ing] to acknowledge the dynamic change that was under way at the time," and he goes on to explain that at the time the First Amendment was adopted, state religious establishments were being abandoned in some states and were becoming more

controversial even in states that continued to maintain them. Green, Second Disestablishment, at 68. But cf. supra note 19 and accompanying text. But Green's argument is both mistaken and anachronistic. In fact, proponents of the jurisdictional interpretation need not "fail[] to acknowledge" this "dynamic change" that was in process. (I am explicitly acknowledging it here.) But the fact that a consensus would develop over the ensuing decades is no justification at all for reading that consensus back into the understanding of the enactors themselves.

55. See Kurt T. Lash, The Second Adoption of the Establishment Clause: The Rise of the Non-establishment Principle, 27 Ariz. St. L.J. 1085 (1995).

56. Id. at 1133. For further support, see Thomas C. Berg, Disestablishment from Blaine to *Everson,* in No Establishment of Religion: America's Original Contribution to Religious Liberty 307, 311–312 (T. Jeremy Gunn & John Witte, Jr. eds., 2012); and Steven G. Calabresi and Sarah E. Agudo, Individual Rights under the State Constitutions When the Fourteenth Amendment Was Ratified, 87 Tex. L. Rev. 7, 31–33 (2008).

57. Iowa Const. of 1857, art. I, sec. 3. For discussion, see Lash, Second Adoption, at 1133.

58. For an argument in the same vein, see Akhil Reed Amar, The Bill of Rights 246–257 (1998).

59. For Lash, the "second adoption" was reflected (though not explicitly acknowledged) in a new constitutional provision—namely, the Fourteenth Amendment. Lash, Second Adoption.

60. A particularly influential book in this respect has been Michael Kent Curtis, No State Shall Abridge: The Fourteenth Amendment and the Bill of Rights (1986).

61. See, e.g., Slaughterhouse Cases, 83 U.S. 36 (1872).

62. See Conkle, Toward a General Theory, at 1137–1140.

63. See, e.g., Amar, Bill of Rights, at 166–174.

64. Everson v. Board of Education, 330 U.S. 1 (1947).

65. See generally Thomas Hobbes, Leviathan (1660).

66. John Witte Jr., God's Joust, God's Justice 210–224 (2006).

67. For a helpful study, see Nathan Hatch, The Democratization of American Christianity (1991).

68. See Sarah Barringer Gordon, State vs. Church: Limits on State Power and Property from Disestablishment to the Civil War, 162 U. Pa. L. Rev. _ (forthcoming).

69. See, e.g., Serbian Eastern Orthodox Diocese v. Milivojevich, 426 U.S. 696, 708–709 (1976); Presbyterian Church v. Hull Church, 393 U.S. 440, 446 (1969); Gonzalez v. Roman Catholic Archbishop, 280 U.S. 1, 7–8 (1929); and Watson v. Jones, 80 U.S. 679, 727–729 (1871). For an insightful examination of one of these cases and its affirmation of the theme of the freedom of the church, see Richard W. Garnett,

"Things That Are Not Caesar's": The Story of Kedroff v. St. Nicholas Cathedral, in Richard W. Garnett & Andrew Koppelman, First Amendment Stories (2011).

70. See, e.g., NLRB v. Catholic Bishop, 440 U.S. 490 (1979).

71. Hosanna-Tabor Evangelical Lutheran Church v. EEOC, 132 S. Ct. 694 (2012).

72. See, e.g., Walz v. Tax Commission, 397 U.S. 664 (1970).

73. Lemon v. Kurtzman, 403 U.S. 602, 612–613 (1971).

74. See Nathan Chapman, Disentangling Conscience and Religion, __ U. Ill. L. Rev. __ (2012); White, First Amendment's Religion Clauses, at 1075–1076, 1081.

75. See Kurt T. Lash, The Second Adoption of the Free Exercise Clause: Religious Exemptions Under the Fourteenth Amendment, 88 Nw. U. L. Rev. 1106 (1994).

76. Cantwell v. Connecticut, 310 U.S. 296 (1940).

77. See Feldman, Divided by God, at 27–33.

78. This difference is reflected in modern scholars' treatment of the question of "incorporating" the free exercise clause. Various scholars have acknowledged the awkwardness of incorporating the establishment clause, which on its face looks like a structural or jurisdictional provision. See, e.g., Amar, Bill of Rights, at 33. For an analysis showing how this difficulty can be overcome, see Frederick Mark Gedicks, Establishment Clause Incorporation: A Logical, Textual, and Historical Defense, 88 Ind. L.J. 669 (2013). But they have perceived no similar difficulty with respect to free exercise. After all, the free exercise clause on its face seems to recognize a "right"; is it possible to read the clause any other way? So why should the free exercise clause not be incorporated into the Fourteenth Amendment? This reasoning oversimplifies. In fact, it is entirely possible to read the free exercise clause as a jurisdictional limitation on national powers; that, as we have seen, is in fact the most plausible interpretation of the enactors' purpose and understanding. Still, the fact that free exercise, or freedom of conscience, has enjoyed the support of a broad consensus since the founding period has made it natural to treat this provision as creating a "right" like others in later provisions of the Bill of Rights.

79. See, e.g., Simon's Executors v. Gratz, 2 Pen. & W. 412 (Pa. 1831) (rejecting Jewish executor's plea to be excused from Saturday appearance and rejecting contrary authority).

80. See Steven D. Smith, Religious Freedom and Its Enemies, 32 Cardozo L. Rev. 2033, 2036–2042 (2011).

81. Reynolds v. United States, 98 U.S. 145 (1878).

82. See, e.g., Sherbert v. Verner, 374 U.S. 398 (1963).

83. Employment Division v. Smith, 494 U.S. 872 (1990).

84. See Clark B. Lombardi, Nineteenth-Century Free Exercise Jurisprudence and the Challenge of Polygamy, 85 Ore. L. Rev. 369 (2006).

85. See, e.g., Fraternal Order of Police v. Newark, 170 F.3d 359 (3rd Cir. 1999) (ruling that Newark's regulation prohibiting wearing of beards by police officers violated Muslim police officers' free exercise rights).

86. On the federal level, the primary statutes are the Religious Freedom Restoration Act, 42 U.S.C. sec. 2000bb–2000bb-4, which remains in force with respect to the federal government, and the Religious Land Use and Institutionalized Persons Act, 42 U.S.C. sec. 2000cc–2000cc-5.

87. Marie Failinger remarks that freedom of conscience "began as an argument that government must ensure a free response by the individual called distinctively by the Divine within" but by now "has come to mean very little beyond the notion of personal existential decision-making." Marie Failinger, Wondering after Babel, in Law and Religion 94 (Rex J. Adhar ed., 2000).

88. See, e.g., 1 Kent Greenawalt, Religion and the Constitution: Free Exercise and Fairness 124–156 (2006).

89. Welsh v. United States, 398 U.S. 333 (1970); Seeger v. United States, 380 U.S. 163 (1965).

90. The point is developed in Steven Smith, Religion and Its Enemies, at 2037–2038.

3. The Religion Question and the American Settlement

1. See, e.g., Michael J. White, The First Amendment's Religion Clauses: "Freedom of Conscience" versus Institutional Accommodation, 47 San Diego L. Rev. 1075, 1075–1076, 1081 (2010).

2. See David Sehat, The Myth of American Religious Freedom 5–6 (2011).

3. Ran Hirschl, Constitutional Theocracy 21 (2010).

4. See William T. Cavanaugh, The Myth of Religious Violence 68 (2009).

5. See, e.g., id. at 57–122. Cavanaugh notes that the eminent scholar Wilfred Cantwell Smith "was compelled to conclude that, outside of the modern West, there is no significant concept equivalent to what we think of as religion." Id. at 61. See also Nicholas Lash, The Beginning and End of "Religion" 13–17 (1996) (describing "[t]he invention of 'religion'").

6. José Casanova, The Secular, Secularizations, Secularisms, in Rethinking Secularism 54, 62 (Craig Calhoun et al. eds., 2011).

7. Cavanaugh, Myth, at 81.

8. Id. at 83.

9. Jonathan Z. Smith, Relating Religion 179 (2004). For an insightful critical analysis of these claims, see Kevin Schilbrack, Religions: Are There Any?, 78 J. Amer. Acad. Relig. 1112 (2010).

10. See generally Walter Ullmann, Principles of Government and Politics in the Middle Ages 57–114 (1961).

11. See, e.g., John Rawls, Political Liberalism xxiv–xxviii (paperback ed. 1996).

12. Brad S. Gregory, The Unintended Reformation 84 (2012).

13. Gregory, Unintended Reformation, describes and explores this fragmentation at length.

14. Rawls, Political Liberalism, at xxiv.

15. See, e.g., Douglas Laycock, Sex, Atheism, and the Free Exercise of Religion, 88 Detroit-Mercy L. Rev. 407, 407–409 (2011). For further development of this three-stage understanding, see Steven D. Smith, Toleration and Liberal Commitments, in Nomos XLVIII: Toleration and Its Limits 243 (2008); Steven D. Smith, The Restoration of Tolerance, 78 Calif. L. Rev. 305 (1990).

16. See Diarmaid MacCulloch, A History of Christianity 663, 672 (2010).

17. But cf. David Bentley Hart, Atheist Delusions: The Christian Revolution and Its Fashionable Enemies 89 (2009) (arguing that "religious allegiances, anxieties, and hatreds were used by regional princes merely as pretexts for conflicts whose causes, effects, and alliances had very little to do with faith or confessional loyalties").

18. See Craig Calhoun, Secularism, Citizenship, and the Public Sphere, 75, 80, in Rethinking Secularism (Craig Calhoun et al. eds., 2011) ("What issued from the Peace of Westphalia was not a Europe without religion but a Europe of mostly confessional states.").

19. See Benjamin J. Kaplan, Divided by Faith: Religious Conflict and the Practice of Toleration in Early Modern Europe 144–234 (2007).

20. Thomas Paine, The Rights of Man, in Reflections on the Revolution in France and The Rights of Man 267, 324 (1973) (emphasis in original).

21. See John T. Noonan Jr., The Lustre of Our Country: The American Experience of Religious Freedom 69–70 (1998) (emphasis added).

22. Ralph Ketcham, James Madison, Thomas Jefferson, and the Meaning of "Establishment of Religion," in No Establishment of Religion: America's Original Contribution to Religious Liberty 158, 161 (T. Jeremy Gunn & John Witte Jr. eds., 2012).

23. See, e.g., Robert Audi, Religious Commitment and Secular Reason (2000). See also Rawls, Political Liberalism.

24. Jocelyn Maclure & Charles Taylor, Secularism and Freedom of Conscience 2 (Jane Marie Todd trans., 2011).

25. Steven K. Green, The Second Disestablishment: Church and State in Nineteenth-Century America 77 (2010).

26. Cf. id. at 388 (arguing that "events of the early nineteenth century temporarily arrested further disestablishment of the nation's institutions").

27. David Sehat describes this infusion as the "moral establishment." Sehat, Myth, at 51–69.

28. See Stephen M. Feldman, Please Don't Wish Me a Merry Christmas: A Critical History of the Separation of Church and State 185–187, 192–197 (1997).

29. See John T. McGreevy, Catholicism and American Freedom: A History 7–42 (2003).

30. Stuart Banner, When Christianity Was Part of the Common Law, 16 Law & Hist. Rev. 27, 43 (1998).

31. Holy Trinity Church v. United States, 143 U.S. 457, 471 (1892).

32. These documents are reprinted in The Sacred Rights of Conscience 597–614 (Daniel L. Dreisbach & Mark David Hall eds., 2009).

33. Id. at 600.

34. Id. at 598 (emphasis added).

35. Id. at 604–605.

36. Id. at 611.

37. Id.

38. James Madison, Memorial and Remonstrance Against Religious Assessments, reprinted in id. at 309–313.

39. Sacred Rights of Conscience, at 614.

40. See Daniel L. Dreisbach, Defining and Testing the Prohibition on Religious Establishments in the Early Republic, in No Establishment of Religion: America's Original Contribution to Religious Liberty 252, 271–272 (T. Jeremy Gunn & John Witte Jr. eds., 2012).

41. John Witte Jr., God's Joust, God's Justice 243–245 (2006).

42. Id. at 247.

43. Id. at 249–262.

44. James Davison Hunter, Culture Wars: The Struggle to Define America 71, 44 (1991) (emphasis omitted, added).

45. Id. at 44–45.

46. Id. at 51 (emphasis added).

47. Noah Feldman, Divided by God 7–8, 186–212 (2005).

48. Andrew Koppelman, Defending American Religious Neutrality 1 (2013).

49. Sacred Rights of Conscience, at 468.

50. Dreisbach, Defining and Testing, at 258.

51. Madison, Memorial and Remonstrance, at 311–312.

52. Reprinted in Sacred Rights of Conscience, at 446–447.

53. Derek H. Davis, The Continental Congress and Emerging Ideas of Church-State Separation, in No Establishment of Religion: America's Original Contribution to Religious Liberty 180, 190 (T. Jeremy Gunn & John Witte Jr. eds., 2012).

54. For an argument asserting the pervasiveness of this theme throughout American history, see Stephen H. Webb, American Providence 29–50 (2004).

55. Quoted in Green, Second Disestablishment: Church and State, at 23.

56. Quoted in Paul Horwitz, Religion and American Politics: Three Views of the Cathedral, 39 U. Memphis L. Rev. 973, 978 (2009).

57. For a discussion of this expanding inclusiveness, see Koppelman, Defending American Religious Neutrality, at 28–42.

58. See Noah Feldman, Divided by God, at 81.

59. See Kevin M. Schultz, Tri-faith America: How Catholics and Jews Held Postwar America to Its Protestant Promise (2011).

60. Will Herberg, Protestant-Catholic-Jew 87 (1983) (first published 1955). This "common faith," Herberg reported, "makes no pretensions to override or supplant the recognized religions, to which it assigns a place of great eminence and honor in the American scheme of things." Id. at 88–89.

61. See McCreary County v. ACLU, 545 U.S. 844, 893–898 (2005) (Scalia, J., dissenting).

62. Even more inclusive, perhaps, is Andrew Koppelman's recent claim that the Constitution requires a "neutrality" that permits government to regard "religion" as a good at a very high level of abstraction largely emptied of any theological content at all. See generally Koppelman, Defending American Religious Neutrality.

63. Noah Feldman, Divided by God, at 181.

64. Consider his second inaugural address:

> I shall need the favor of that Being in whose hands we are, who led our fathers, as Israel of old, from their native land and planted them in a country flowing with all the necessaries and comforts of life, who has covered our infancy with His providence and our riper years with His wisdom and power, and to whose goodness I ask you to join in supplications with me.

Reprinted in John T. Noonan Jr. & Edward McGlynn Gaffney Jr., Religious Freedom 206 (2d ed. 2001).

65. Daniel J. Boorstin, The Lost World of Thomas Jefferson (1993 ed.).

66. Id. at 30.

67. Henry F. May, The Enlightenment in America 295 (1976).

68. See Lee v. Weisman, 505 U.S. 577, 623–625 (1992) (Souter, J., concurring).

69. Sehat, Myth, at 65.

70. James Madison, Detached Memoranda, in Sacred Rights of Conscience, at 589, 591.

71. Sacred Rights of Conscience, at 614.

72. Sehat, Myth, at 39.

73. Green, Second Disestablishment: Church and State, at 104.

74. Cf. id. at 23 (asserting that "the founders viewed the authority for the new nation in secular Enlightenment terms").

75. McCollum v. Board of Education, 333 U.S. 203, 212 (1948).

76. See, e.g., Christopher Hitchens, God Is Not Great: How Religion Poisons Everything (2007); and Sam Harris, The End of Faith: Religion, Terror, and the Future of Reason (2004).

77. See Timothy L. Hall, Separating Church and State: Roger Williams and Religious Liberty 72–86 (1998).

78. See, e.g., Darryl Hart, A Secular Faith: Why Christianity Favors the Separation of Church and State (2006). Cf. Eric Nelson, The Hebrew Republic 137 (2010) ("Locke's politics is secular because, on his account, the Biblical God who sent us into the world 'by his order, and about his business' wants it that way.").

79. See Davis, Continental Congress, at 190.

80. Larry Kramer, The People Themselves 30–31 (2004) (emphasis added).

81. Id. at 30.

82. Cf. Steven K. Green, The Second Disestablishment, in No Establishment of Religion: America's Original Contribution to Religious Liberty 280, 286 (T. Jeremy Gunn & John Witte Jr. eds., 2012):

> [N]ineteenth century understandings of constitutionalism were not as formal or atomistic as they would become by the mid-twentieth century. When discussing a constitutional right or principle, nineteenth-century judges, lawyers, and public officials often would not identify a particular provision as its source. Instead, they took a more holistic and organic approach, commonly declaring the basis of a right or principle as resting in "our constitutional structure" or as inherent in the nation's "political institutions."

83. Kramer, People Themselves, at 24.

84. Elton Trueblood, Abraham Lincoln: Theologian of American Anguish 135–136 (1973).

85. See Green, Second Disestablishment: Church and State, at 61 (asserting that "[t]he no-religious-test clause . . . highlighted the secular nature of the Constitution and the new government's nonreliance on religious principles").

86. Reprinted in Sacred Rights of Conscience, at 475–476. See Noah Feldman, Divided by God, at 256 n.10.

87. See, e.g., Isaac Kramnick & R. Laurence Moore, The Godless Constitution: A Moral Defense of the Secular State 27–45 (2d ed. 2005); Susan Jacoby, Freethinkers: A History of American Secularism 28 (2004) (observing that "[w]ithout downgrading the importance of either the establishment clause or the constitutional ban on religious tests for officeholders, one can make a strong case that the omission of one word—God—played an even more important role in the construction of a secularist foundation for the new government").

88. See Donald L. Drakeman, Church, State, and Original Intent 283–305 (2010); and Richard R. John, Taking Sabbatarianism Seriously: The Postal System, the Sabbath, and the Transformation of America, 10 J. Early Republic 517 (1990).

89. See generally Steven K. Green, The Bible, the School, and the Constitution (2012). See also Green, Second Diestablishment: Church and State, at 303–325.

90. Vidal v. Girard's Executors, 43 U.S. 127 (1844).

91. Id. at 197–201.

92. Id. at 201 (decision based on "the constitution or laws of Pennsylvania" and "the judicial decisions of its tribunals").

93. Holy Trinity Church v. United States, 143 U.S. 457, 471 (1892).

94. For discussion, see Kramnick & Moore, Godless Constitution, at 26–44.

95. Sehat, Myth, at 42.

96. See Harry S. Stout, Upon the Altar of the Nation: A Moral History of the Civil War 273, 373 (2006).

97. For discussion of these movements, see Philip Hamburger, Separation of Church and State 287–334 (2002). See also Green, Second Disestablishment: Church and State, at 137–177.

98. Green, Second Disestablishment, at 298–299, 309.

99. Id. at 290, 304–311.

100. Rodney K. Smith, Public Prayer and the Constitution 187, 190 (1987).

101. The position receives perhaps its most sophisticated articulation in Ronald Dworkin, Law's Empire (1986).

102. See generally John Hart Ely, Democracy and Distrust (1980).

103. See generally Noah Feldman, Non-sectarianism Reconsidered, 18 J. L. & Pol. 65 (2002).

104. See McGreevy, Catholicism and American Freedom, at 7–42.

105. See id. at 90–105.

106. See Hamburger, Separation, at 449–454.

107. See Stephen Feldman, Please Don't Wish Me a Merry Christmas 185–187, 192–197 (1997).

108. See Douglas Laycock, Religious Liberty and Free Exercise: Back to the Future, in 1 Laycock, Religious Liberty 704–706 (2010).

109. See generally Jon Butler, Awash in a Sea of Faith (1992). See also Green, Second Disestablishment: Church and State, at 9 ("[T]he nineteenth century was also a time of accelerating religious diversity, from within Protestantism and from without.").

110. Cf. Sehat, Myth, at 27 (observing that "everyone purported to uphold the ideal of religious liberty," but that this ideal "became a rallying cry for those who wanted to create a Christian commonwealth, and for those who wanted to establish a secular state").

111. See, e.g., Kramnick & Moore, Godless Constitution.
112. Herberg, Protestant-Catholic-Jew, at 231.
113. These arguments are developed at much greater length in Steven D. Smith, Our Agnostic Constitution, 83 N.Y.U. L. Rev. 120 (2008).
114. Cf. Hunter, Culture Wars, at 128: "Each side of the cultural divide . . . speaks with a different moral vocabulary. Each side operates out of a different mode of debate and persuasion. Each side represents the tendencies of a separate competing moral galaxy. They are, indeed, 'worlds apart.'"
115. Bruce Ledewitz, Hallowed Secularism (2009).
116. Reprinted in Noonan & Gaffney, Religious Freedom, at 206.
117. See Banner, Christianity, at 43 ("From the United States Supreme Court to scattered local courts, from Kent and Story to dozens of writers no one remembers today, Christianity was generally accepted to be part of the common law. Yet in all these cases, from a lawyer's standpoint, the maxim made not the slightest bit of difference. Had Christianity *not* been understood as part of the common law, every single one of these cases would have come out the same.").
118. Green, Second Disestablishment: Church and State, at 364–377, 374, 376.
119. Mark A. Noll, The Contingencies of Christian Republicanism, in Protestantism and the American Founding 239, 238 (Thomas S. Engeman & Michael P. Zuckert eds., 2004).
120. Green, Second Disestablishment: Church and State, at 75.
121. 1 Alexis de Tocqueville, Democracy in America 392–393 (Henry Reeve trans., 1898). Mark Noll explains how the American merger of religion with the republican notion was an exceptional achievement, surprising to most Europeans. Mark A. Noll, America's God: From Jonathan Edwards to Abraham Lincoln (2005).
122. G. K. Chesterton, What I Saw in America, in 21 G. K. Chesterton, Collected Works 35, 45 (1990) (first published 1922).
123. John C. Jeffries Jr. & James E. Ryan, A Political History of the Establishment Clause, 100 Mich. L. Rev. 309–311 (2001).
124. Herberg, Protestant-Catholic-Jew, at 2.
125. Id. at 270.
126. See Sehat, Myth, at 27, 42, 68.
127. David Sehat's rich and informative recounting of the country's religious history is informed—handicapped, I would say—by his evident (and in my view question-begging) assumption that only the secular interpretation is consistent with religious freedom, and that a religiously influenced "moral establishment" is nothing more than a "religious establishment by proxy." Id. at 287. From a secularist perspective, this assumption may, of course, seem correct. But the

genius of the American settlement, as I have argued, is that it did not make this assumption but rather treated both the secularist and providentialist interpretations as legitimate contenders.

128. See especially id.

129. McGreevy, Catholicism and American Freedom, at 7–9.

130. Sehat, Myth, at 1–2.

131. See Leonard J. Arrington & Davis Bitton, The Mormon Experience 45 (paperback ed. 1992); and 3 Joseph Smith, History of the Church (rev. ed. 1978).

4. Dissolution and Denial

1. For a valuable discussion, see 1 Kent Greenawalt, Religion and the Constitution: Free Exercise and Fairness 124–156 (2006).

2. United States v. Seeger, 380 U.S. 163, 187 (1965).

3. See Christopher L. Eisgruber & Lawrence G. Sager, Religious Freedom and the Constitution 114 (2007).

4. Employment Division v. Smith, 494 U.S. 872 (1990). For further discussion, see Steven D. Smith, The Phases and Functions of Freedom of Conscience, in Religion and Human Rights: An Introduction (John Witte & M. Christian Green eds., 2012).

5. See, e.g., Hosanna-Tabor Evangelical Lutheran Church v. EEOC, 132 S. Ct. 694 (2012); Serbian Eastern Orthodox Diocese v. Milivojevich, 426 U.S. 696, 708–709 (1976); Presbyterian Church v. Hull Church, 393 U.S. 440, 446 (1969); Gonzalez v. Roman Catholic Archbishop, 280 U.S. 1, 7–8 (1929); and Watson v. Jones, 80 U.S. 679, 727–729 (1871).

6. Some commentators or scholars manage to slip from "church" to "religion" almost effortlessly without even noticing the crucial substantive change. See, e.g., T. Jeremy Gunn, The Separation of Church and State versus Religion in the Public Square, in No Establishment of Religion 15, 18 (T. Jeremy Gunn & John Witte Jr. eds., 2012) (advocating an interpretation that "favors the 'separation of church and state' (or more properly *religion* and the state)") (emphasis in original).

7. Everson v. Board of Education, 330 U.S. 1 (1947).

8. *Everson* declared:

> The "establishment of religion" clause of the First Amendment means at least this: Neither a state nor the Federal Government can *set up a church*. Neither can pass laws which aid one religion, aid all religions, or prefer one religion over another. Neither can force nor influence a person *to go to or to remain away from church* against his will or force him to profess a belief or disbelief

in any religion. No person can be punished for entertaining or professing religious beliefs or disbeliefs, for *church attendance or non-attendance*. No tax in any amount, large or small, can be levied to support any religious activities or institutions, whatever they may be called, or whatever form they may adopt to teach or practice religion. Neither a state nor the Federal Government can, *openly or secretly, participate in the affairs of any religious organizations or groups* and vice versa. In the words of Jefferson, the clause against establishment of religion by law was intended to erect *"a wall of separation between Church and State."*

330 U.S. at 15–16. The parts that I have italicized, and perhaps others as well, resonate with a classical commitment to freedom of the church.

9. See, e.g., *Everson* Revisited: Religion, Education, and Law and the Crossroads (Jo Renee Formicola & Hubert Morken eds., 1997).

10. John C. Jeffries Jr. & James E. Ryan, A Political History of the Establishment Clause, 100 Mich. L. Rev. 279, 287 (2001).

11. Douglas Laycock, A Survey of Religious Liberty in the United States, in Douglas Laycock, 1 Religious Liberty: Overviews and History 272, 289 (2010).

12. McCollum v. Board of Education, 333 U.S. 203 (1948) (invalidating release-time program); Zorach v. Clauson, 343 U.S. 306 (1952) (upholding release-time program).

13. This claim is elaborated at length in Steven D. Smith, Constitutional Divide: The Transformative Significance of the School Prayer Decisions, 38 Pepperdine L. Rev. 945 (2011).

14. Engel v. Vitale, 370 U.S. 421 (1962).

15. Abington School District v. Schempp, 374 U.S. 203 (1963).

16. See, e.g., Patrick M. Garry, The Institutional Side of Religious Liberty, 2004 Utah L. Rev. 1155, 1170 ("Under the First Amendment, schools should not be permitted to force children to adhere to a creed contrary to the moral or religious teaching of their family. For this reason, school prayer cases should only be analyzed under the Free Exercise Clause."); and Michael W. McConnell, Coercion: The Lost Element of Establishment, 27 Wm. & Mary L. Rev. 933, 934–936 (1985/1986) (arguing that the prayer invalidated in *Engel* was unconstitutional because it was coercive).

17. *Schempp, 374* U.S. at 246 (emphasis added).

18. Id. at 242 (emphasis added).

19. Id. at 222 (majority opinion). See also id. at 215. In a concurring opinion, Justice Douglas agreed that the Constitution requires governmental "neutrality" in matters of religion. Id. at 229 (Douglas, J., concurring). Justice Goldberg, joined by Justice Harlan, likewise endorsed the obligation of neutrality while empha-

sizing that this obligation permitted and even in some circumstances required governmental accommodation of religion lest neutrality devolve into "a brooding and pervasive devotion to the secular and a passive, or even active, hostility to the religious." Id. at 306 (Goldberg, J., concurring). Even Justice Potter Stewart, the lone dissenter in both prayer cases, agreed that the government was supposed to be neutral in matters of religion; he differed only with respect to whether a thoroughly secular school curriculum is in fact neutral toward religion. Id. at 313 (Stewart, J., dissenting).

20. Id. at 222.

21. Epperson v. Arkansas, 393 U.S. 97 (1968).

22. Id. at 103, 106 (emphasis added).

23. Board of Education v. Allen, 392 U.S. 236, 243 (1968).

24. Lemon v. Kurtzman, 403 U.S. 602, 612–613 (1971).

25. Occasionally the Court has not used the *Lemon* test. See Lee v. Weisman, 505 U.S. 577 (1992); Lynch v. Donnelly, 465 U.S. 668 (1984); and Marsh v. Chambers, 463 U.S. 783 (1983). Such decisions have sometimes led commentators to infer that the test was being abandoned; see, e.g., Michael Paulsen, Lemon Is Dead, 43 Case W. Res. L. Rev. 795 (1993), but such inferences have thus far proved to be premature.

26. Paul G. Kauper, Schempp and Sherbert, Studies in Neutrality and Accommodation, in Religion and the Public Order 3, 38 (Donald A. Gianella ed., 1963).

27. See, e.g., Committee for Public Education v. Nyquist, 413 U.S. 756 (1973); Roemer v. Maryland Public Works Board, 426 U.S. 736 (1976); Wolman v. Walter, 433 U.S. 229 (1977); Mueller v. Allen, 473 U.S. 388 (1983); Grand Rapids School District v. Ball, 473 U.S. 373 (1985); and Aguilar v. Felton, 473 U.S. 402 (1985).

28. Board of Education v. Allen, 392 U.S. 236 (1968) (books); Wolman v. Walter, 433 U.S. 229 (1977) (instructional materials).

29. Leonard Levy, The Establishment Clause: Religion and the First Amendment 128 (1986).

30. See, e.g., Grand Rapids School District v. Ball, 473 U.S. 373, 382, 394 (1985); Wolman v. Walter, 433 U.S. 229, 236 (1977); and Meek v. Pittenger, 421 U.S. 349, 363 (1975). Sometimes the effects prong proved insufficient, so that a decision to invalidate aid was forced to invoke the more obviously separationist "no excessive entanglement" prong. See, e.g., Aguilar v. Felton, 473 U.S. 402 (1985).

31. See, e.g., Lynch v. Donnelly, 465 U.S. 668, 683 (1984).

32. See Zelman v. Simmons-Harris, 536 U.S. 639 (2002); Mitchell v. Helms, 530 U.S. 793 (2000); and Zobrest v. Catalina Foothills School Dist., 509 U.S. 1 (1993).

33. See, e.g., Good News Club v. Milford Central School, 533 U.S. 98 (2001); Lamb's Chapel v. Central Moriches School Dist., 508 U.S. 384 (1993); and Widmar v. Vincent, 454 U.S. 263 (1981).

34. See Locke v. Davey, 540 U.S. 712 (2004).

35. See, e.g., Zelman v. Simmons-Harris, 536 U.S. 639, 663 (2002) (O'Connor, J., concurring); and Mitchell v. Helms, 530 U.S. 793, 841 (2000) (O'Connor, J., concurring in judgment).

36. Everson, 301 U.S. at 13.

37. Zorach v. Clauson, 343 U.S. 306, 312 (1952).

38. Douglas later sought to explain away the statement as a mere acknowledgment that Puritanism had "helped shape our constitutional law and our common law." McGowan v. Maryland, 366 U.S. 420, 563 (Douglas, J., dissenting).

39. For discussions of the varying and shifting meanings of "secular," see José Casanova, The Secular, Secularizations, Secularisms, in Rethinking Secularism 54, 62 (Craig Calhoun et al. eds., 2011); and Nomi Stolzenberg, The Profanity of Law, in Law and the Sacred 35 (Austin Sarat ed., 2007).

40. The argument was made but rejected in cases such as Citizens Concerned for Separation of Church and State v. Denver, 503 F. Supp. 823 (D. Colo. 1981), and Aronow v. United States, 432 F.2d 242 (9th Cir. 1970) (rejecting constitutional challenge to national motto In God We Trust).

41. Lynch v. Donnelly, 465 U.S. 668, 687–694 (1984) (O'Connor, J., concurring).

42. See, e.g., Zelman v. Simmons-Harris, 536 U.S. 639, 663 (2002) (O'Connor, J., concurring); Mitchell v. Helms, 530 U.S. 793, 841 (2000) (O'Connor, J., concurring in judgment).

43. Lynch v. Donnelly, 465 U.S. 668, 691–692 (1984) (O'Connor, J., concurring).

44. See, e.g., Allegheny County v. ACLU, 492 U.S. 573 (1989).

45. See, e.g., Salazar v. Buono, 139 S. Ct. 1803 (2010) (cross); McCreary County v. ACLU, 545 U.S. 844 (2005) (Ten Commandments plaques); Van Orden v. Perry, 545 U.S. 677 (2005) (Ten Commandments monuments); and Elk Grove School District v. Newdow, 542 U.S. 1 (2004) (Pledge of Allegiance).

46. For a forceful argument for this conclusion, see Steven B. Epstein, Rethinking the Constitutionality of Ceremonial Deism, 96 Colum. L. Rev. 2083 (1996).

47. Everson, 301 U.S. at 11–13.

48. Editorial, reprinted in Religious Liberty in the Supreme Court 138 (Terry Eastland ed., 1995).

49. Engel v. Vitale, 370 U.S. 421, 437 n.1, 440 n.5, 442 n.8 (1962).

50. Lynch v. Donnelly, 465 U.S. 668, 691–692 (1984) (O'Connor, J., concurring).

51. See, e.g., William Van Alstyne, Trends in the Supreme Court: Mr. Jefferson's Crumbling Wall; A Comment on Lynch v. Donnelly, 1984 Duke L.J. 770, 781; Norman Dorsen, The United States Supreme Court: Trends and Prospects, 21 Harv. C.R.-C.L. L. Rev. 1 (1986). Mark Tushnet remarked caustically that "Justice O'Connor's conclusion that the crèche did not endorse religion came as a surprise to most Jews." Mark Tushnet, The Constitution of Religion, 18 Conn. L. Rev. 701, 712 n.52 (1986).

NOTES TO PAGES 120–122

52. Elk Grove School District v. Newdow, 542 U.S. 1, 33–45 (2004) (O'Connor, J., concurring). Cf. Douglas Laycock, Comment: Theology Scholarships, the Pledge of Allegiance, and Religious Liberty; Avoiding the Extremes but Missing the Liberty, 118 Harv. L. Rev. 155, 235 (2004) (observing that "[t]his rationale is unconvincing both to serious nonbelievers and to serious believers").

53. Steven H. Shiffrin, The Pluralistic Foundations of the Religion Clauses, 90 Cornell L. Rev. 9, 70–71 (2004). Shiffrin adds, "I am sure that a pledge identifying the United States as subject to divine authority is asserting the existence and authority of the divine." Id.

54. See Douglas Laycock, Equal Access and Moments of Silence: The Equal Status of Religious Speech by Private Speakers, 81 Nw. U. L. Rev. 1, 8 (1986) (suggesting that, at least in principle, the names of cities such as Corpus Christi and Los Angeles are unconstitutional).

55. Bruce. C. Dierenfield, The Battle over School Prayer 72 (2007). Writing at the time, Philip Kurland observed that "[t]he immediate reaction to *Engel* was violent and gross." Philip B. Kurland, The School Prayer Cases, in The Wall between Church and State 142, 142 (Dallin H. Oaks ed., 1963). See also Robert S. Alley, Without a Prayer: Religious Expression in Public Schools 28, 230 (1996) (recalling that the school-prayer decisions "sent shock waves through large portions of the citizenry" and "caused an enormous uproar against the Supreme Court"); and Julia C. Loren, *Engel v. Vitale:* Prayer in the Public Schools 7, 61 (2001) (observing that "[t]he public outcry against the Court's ruling was swift and loud" and that "newspaper editorials across the country denounced the ruling"). Lucas Powe notes that *"Engel* produced more mail to the Court than any previous case (and few write to say what a good job the justices are doing)." Lucas A. Powe, The Supreme Court and the American Elite, 1789–2008, at 260 (2009). This opposition, though perhaps less strident today, has not disappeared; thus Kent Greenawalt reports that "[a] large segment of the American population persists in condemning the Supreme Court for taking religion out of schools and thus contributing to a secular, immoral, materialist cultural ethos." Kent Greenawalt, Does God Belong in Public Schools? 9 (2005).

56. Dierenfield, Battle, at 146.

57. See id. at 132.

58. See, e.g., Abington School District v. Schempp, 374 U.S. 203, 296–304 (1963) (Brennan, J., concurring) (emphasizing limited reach of the ruling).

59. Quoted in Dierenfield, Battle, at 136.

60. Reprinted in Religious Liberty in the Supreme Court, at 142.

61. Jeffries & Ryan, Political History, at 325.

62. See Chapter 3, notes 65–69 and accompanying text.

63. George M. Marsden, The Soul of the American University: From Protestant Establishment to Established Nonbelief (1994).

64. This change was accomplished through the efforts of "networks of activists who were largely skeptical, freethinking, agnostic, atheist, or theologically liberal; who were well educated and socially located mainly in knowledge production occupations." Christian Smith, Introduction: Rethinking the Secularization of American Public Life, in The Secular Revolution 1 (Christian Smith ed., 2003). The volume contains essays by a number of scholars chronicling the course of secularization in a variety of different institutions.

65. Douglas Laycock, Continuity and Change in the Threat to Religious Liberty, in Douglas Laycock, 1 Religious Liberty: Overviews and History 651, 679 (2010).

66. See David Sehat, The Myth of American Religious Liberty (2011); and Steven K. Green, The Second Disestablishment: Church and State in Nineteenth-Century America (2010).

67. See Steven D. Smith, Our Agnostic Constitution, 83 N.Y.U. L. Rev. 120 (2008).

68. Cf. Douglas Laycock, Religious Liberty as Liberty, in Douglas Laycock, Religious Liberty: Overviews and History 54, 70 (2010) ("If the government is allowed to take sides, the two sides will fight to control the government, and the government will disapprove of, discriminate against, or suppress the losers.").

69. Cf. Dierenfield, Battle, at 11 ("In short, the Founding Fathers created the world's first secular government as the best way to minimize the religious tensions that had perpetually plagued Europe.").

70. Kurland, School Prayer Cases, at 145 (quoting Thurmond).

71. Id. at 142.

72. Jeffries & Ryan, Political History, at 325–326.

73. This view is often articulated by Justice Scalia. See, e.g., McCreary County v. ACLU, 545 U.S. 844, 886–893 (2005) (Scalia, J., dissenting).

74. See, e.g., Laycock, Church and State in the United States: Competing Conceptions and Historic Changes, in Laycock, Religious Liberty, at 399, 425, 440.

75. See, e.g., McCreary County v. ACLU, 545 U.S. 844, 872–873 (2005); and Epperson v. Arkansas, 393 U.S. 97, 102 nn.9, 10 (1968).

76. Varnum v. Brien, 763 N.W.2d 862, 897–904 (Iowa 2009).

77. Id. at 904–906.

78. Id. at 952.

79. Id. at 930.

80. Noah Feldman, Divided by God 15 (2005).

81. Elk Grove School District v. Newdow, 542 U.S. 1 (2004).

82. The term is from Mark Dewolfe Howe's classic The Garden and the Wilderness 11–12 (1965).

83. Laycock, Church and State, at 422.

84. See James Davison Hunter, Culture Wars: The Struggle to Define America 71 (1991); and Laycock, Continuity and Change in the Threat to Religious Liberty, at 672–689.

85. Will Herberg, Protestant-Catholic-Jew 87 (1983) (first published 1955).

86. Larry Kramer, The People Themselves (2004).

87. Lynch v. Donnelly, 465 U.S. 668, 688 (1984) (O'Connor, J., concurring).

88. John Rawls, Political Liberalism 48–54 (paperback ed. 1996).

89. See, e.g., Martha C. Nussbaum, Liberty of Conscience: In Defense of America's Tradition of Religious Equality 8, 28 (2009).

90. In this vein, Ronald Dworkin reports that "[m]any Americans are horrified by the prospect of a new dark age imposed by militant superstition; they fear a black, know-nothing night of ignorance in which America becomes an intellectually backward and stagnant theocracy." Ronald Dworkin, Is Democracy Possible Here? 79 (2006).

91. Schempp, 374 U.S. at 313 (Stewart, J, dissenting).

92. Ernest J. Brown, *Quis Custodiet Ipsos Custodes?* The School Prayer Cases, 1963 Sup. Ct. Rev. 1, 13.

93. Id. at 12–15.

94. Id. at 14.

95. Epperson v. Arkansas, 393 U.S. 97 (1968).

96. Id. at 107–109.

97. Actually, these arguments are not equally inexorable. The Court's argument requires an additional premise—namely, that the Constitution prohibits laws or measures that might not themselves "aid or oppose" religion but that are motivated by a purpose of aiding or opposing religion—that might be contestable, and that the counterargument does not require.

98. Logically, there are other possibilities. States might not exactly prohibit the teaching of evolution but just not teach it. But hardly anyone favors that. Or states might prohibit the teaching of evolution for reasons unrelated to religion. But given the ease with which the *Epperson* court inferred illicit motivation from scanty evidence, this possibility seems more theoretical than real.

99. Laycock, Religious Liberty as Liberty, at 64 (emphasis added).

100. See, e.g., McCreary County v. ACLU, 545 U.S. 844, 860 (2005) ("The touchstone for our analysis is the principle that the 'First Amendment mandates governmental neutrality between religion and religion, and between religion and non-religion.'") (quoting Epperson v. Arkansas, 393 U.S. 97, 104 (1968)).

101. See Andrew Koppelman, Defending American Religious Neutrality (2013).

102. For consideration of some of the variations, see R. George Wright, Neutrality in Religion, 65 SMU L. Rev. 877 (2012); Steven D. Smith, The Paralyzing Paradox of

Religious Neutrality, in Religious Diversity, Politics, and Law (Kevin Schilbrack ed., forthcoming); and Steven D. Smith, Foreordained Failure: The Quest for a Constitutional Principle of Religious Freedom 77–98 (1995).

103. See, e.g., Koppelman, Defending American Religious Neutrality, at 17–18; Douglas Laycock, Formal, Substantive, and Disaggregated Neutrality toward Religion, in Douglas Laycock, 1 Religious Liberty: Overviews and History 17–19 (2010); and Larry Alexander, Liberalism, Religion, and the Unity of Epistemology, 30 U. San Diego L. Rev. 763, 793 (1993).

104. Koppelman, Defending American Religious Neutrality, at 17.

105. See Frank Ravitch, Masters of Illusion: The Supreme Court and the Religion Clauses 38 (2007).

106. Koppelman, Defending American Religious Neutrality, at 15–45.

107. Id. at 24.

108. See, e.g., id. at 46–64, 121–124.

109. See id. at 25 ("The invocation of neutrality in conversation is typically a short-hand gesture toward the generally understood value of removing some issues from political consideration, together with the arguments in favor of this removal.").

110. See Brad S. Gregory, The Unintended Reformation 84 (2012).

111. West Virginia State Board of Education v. Barnette, 319 U.S. 624, 642 (1943).

112. The quotations, from Leo Pfeffer, John Noonan, Glendon Schubert, Rodney Smolla, and Rodney Smolla again, are collected in Jay S. Bybee, Common Ground: Robert Jackson, Antonin Scalia, and a Power Theory of the First Amendment, 75 Tul. L. Rev. 251, 261 & n.15 (2000).

113. For a more detailed analysis, see Steven D. Smith, *Barnette*'s Big Blunder, 78 Chicago-Kent L. Rev. 625, 653–658 (2003).

114. Ravitch, Masters of Illusion.

115. Paul W. Kahn, Political Theology: Four New Chapters on the Concept of Sovereignty 27 (2011).

5. The Last Chapter?

1. The debate can be viewed at http://berkleycenter.georgetown.edu/rfp/events/what-s-so-special-about-religious-freedom.

2. See, e.g., Noah Feldman, Divided by God (2005).

3. Some explicitly question the justification for any special protection for religion. See, e.g., Micah Schwartzman, What If Religion Is Not Special?, 79 U. Chi. L. Rev. 1351 (2012); Christopher L. Eisgruber & Lawrence G. Sager, Religious Freedom and the Constitution (2007); Anthony Ellis, What Is Special about Religion?, 25 Law & Phil. 219 (2006); and James W. Nickel, Who Needs Freedom of

Religion?, 76 Colo. L. Rev. 941, 943 (2005). Others argue, in general or with respect to specific issues, for reinterpreting religious freedom to include nonreligious interests and beliefs and thus in effect to deny distinctive protection to religion or religious beliefs. In this vein, see Scott M. Noveck, The Promise and Problems of Treating Religious Freedom as Freedom of Association, 45 Gonz. L. Rev. 745 (2010); and Kathleen A. Brady, Religious Organizations and Free Exercise: The Surprising Lessons of Smith, 2004 BYU L. Rev. 1633.

4. See, e.g., Brian Leiter, Why Tolerate Religion? (2012).

5. See, e.g., Inazu, Religious Liberty without Religion; and Brady, Religious Organizations.

6. Douglas Laycock, Sex, Atheism, and the Free Exercise of Religion, 88 Detroit-Mercy L. Rev. 407, 423 (2011).

7. For an essay proposing that arguments defending application of the mandate to objecting religious employers are best understood as arguments against giving special protection to religious freedom, see Steven D. Smith, The Hard and Easy Case of the Contraception Mandate, U. Pa. L. Rev. Online 261 (2013).

8. Hosanna-Tabor Evangelical Lutheran Church v. EEOC, 132 S. Ct. 694 (2012).

9. Laycock, Sex, Atheism, at 407.

10. But see John D. Inazu, Liberty's Refuge: The Forgotten Freedom of Assembly (2012) (arguing that freedom of assembly has been devalued in modern constitutional jurisprudence).

11. Hosanna-Tabor Evangelical Lutheran Church v. EEOC, 132 S. Ct. 694 (2012).

12. Luke 20:21–26.

13. James Madison, A Memorial and Remonstrance against Religious Assessments, reprinted in The Sacred Rights of Conscience 309, 309 (Daniel L. Dreisbach and Mark David Hall eds. 2009).

14. For a more detailed elaboration of this argument, see Steven D. Smith, The Rise and Fall of Religious Freedom in Constitutional Discourse, 140 U. Penn. L. Rev. 1419 (1991).

15. See, e.g., 2 Kent Greenawalt, Religion and the Constitution: Establishment and Fairness 480–496 (2008).

16. Douglas Laycock, Religious Liberty as Liberty, in 1 Douglas Laycock, Religious Liberty: Overviews and History 54, 67 (2010).

17. Id. at 58.

18. Id. at 58–61.

19. Quoted in Paul Horwitz, Religion and American Politics: Three Views of the Cathedral, 39 U. Memphis L. Rev. 973, 978 (2009).

20. Laycock, Religious Liberty as Liberty, at 64.

21. Id. at 74–75.

22. Id. at 64–65.

23. Cf. Laycock, Sex, Atheism, at 430–431 ("I also think we should vigorously enforce free exercise simply because it is in the Constitution, and it is a fundamental error to pick and choose which constitutional rights we want to enforce. If we claim the right to enforce only the constitutional rights we like, then no constitutional right is safe from shifting public opinion.") (footnote omitted).

24. Cf. Ronald Dworkin, Taking Rights Seriously 113 (1977) (discussing the "gravitational force" of precedents).

25. U.S. Const. art. I, sec. 10 ("No State shall . . . pass any . . . Law impairing the Obligation of Contracts.").

26. See Bernard Schwartz, A History of the Supreme Court 75–77 (1993).

27. See Erwin Chemerinsky, Constitutional Law 602–603 (3d ed. 2009).

28. U.S. Const. amend. XIV, sec. 1 ("No State shall . . . deny to any person within its jurisdiction the equal protection of the laws.").

29. Buck v. Bell, 274 U.S. 200, 208 (1927).

30. Justice Stephen Breyer has sometimes stressed this rationale. See, e.g., Van Orden v. Perry, 125 Sup. Ct. 2854, 2868 (2005) (Breyer, J., concurring in the judgment). For a critical analysis, see Richard W. Garnett, Religion, Division, and the First Amendment, 94 Geo. L.J. 1667 (2006).

31. See, e.g., Eisgruber & Sager, Religious Freedom and the Constitution 124–128 (2007).

32. See, e.g., William P. Marshall, The Limits of Secularism: Public Religious Expression in Moments of National Crisis and Tragedy, 78 Notre Dame L. Rev. 11 (2002).

33. For elaboration of this point, see Steven D. Smith, Foreordained Failure 99–115 (1995).

34. Matt. 7:26–27.

35. Gordon S. Wood, The Radicalism of the American Revolution 232 (1992).

36. For a critical discussion of this development, see Noah Feldman, From Liberty to Equality: The Transformation of the Establishment Clause, 90 Cal. L. Rev. 673, 694–706, 723–730 (2002).

37. Genesis 1:26–27.

38. George Fletcher, In God's Image: The Religious Imperative of Equality under Law, 99 Colum. L. Rev. 1608, 1611 (1999).

39. See, e.g., Louis Pojman, On Equal Human Worth: A Critique of Contemporary Egalitarianism, in Equality: Selected Readings 282, 295 (Louis P. Pojman & Robert Westmoreland eds., 1997). Jeremy Waldron argues that John Locke's commitment to equality was grounded in religious assumptions, and that modern efforts to support the commitment have to this point proven unavailing. See generally Jeremy Waldron, God, Locke, and Equality (2002):

> [M]aybe the notion of humans as one another's equals will begin to fall apart, under pressure, without the presence of the

religious conception that shaped it. . . . Locke believed this general acceptance [of equality] was impossible apart from the principle's foundation in religious teaching. We believe otherwise. Locke, I suspect, would have thought we were taking a risk. And I am afraid it is not entirely clear, given our experience of a world and a century in which politics and public reason have cut loose from these foundations, that his cautions and suspicions were unjustified.

Id. at 243.

40. Pojman, On Equal Human Worth, at 283–294.

41. Id. at 283.

42. Id. at 296.

43. Martha Minow & Joseph William Singer, In Praise of Foxes: Pluralism as Fact and Aid to the Pursuit of Justice, 90 B.U. L. Rev. 903, 905 (2010).

44. Ronald Dworkin, Justice for Hedgehogs 330 (2011).

45. See, e.g., Eisgruber & Sager, Religious Freedom and the Constitution, at 75.

46. Id.

47. Dworkin, Justice for Hedgehogs, at 113.

48. Thus, citing "a substantial number of Supreme Court decisions, involving a range of legal subjects, that condemn public enactments as being expressions of prejudice or irrationality or invidiousness," Robert Nagel shows how "to a remarkable extent our courts have become places where the name-calling and exaggeration that mark the lower depths of our political debate are simply given a more acceptable, authoritative form." Robert F. Nagel, Name-Calling and the Clear Error Rule, 88 Nw. U. L. Rev. 193, 199 (1993).

49. For further discussion, see Steven D. Smith, Conciliating Hatred, First Things, June/July 2004.

50. The classic statement in legal literature is Peter Westen, The Empty Idea of Equality, 95 Harv. L. Rev. 537 (1982).

51. For a discussion of the increase in nonbelievers and an argument about the implications of this development, see Caroline Mala Corbin, Nonbelievers and Government Speech, 97 Iowa L. Rev. 347 (2012).

52. Laycock, Sex, Atheism, at 422.

53. See, e.g., Eisgruber & Sager, Religious Freedom and Constitution, at 78–120; William P. Marshall, In Defense of Smith and Free Exercise Revisionism, 58 U. Chi. L. Rev. 308 (1991).

54. City of Boerne v. Flores, 521 U.S. 507 (1997).

55. Laycock, Sex, Atheism, at 412–413.

56. Id. at 415.

57. David Novak, In Defense of Religious Liberty 88–99 (2009).

58. Id. at 99.

59. Id. at 86.

60. Leslie C. Griffin, *Smith* and Women's Equality, 32 Cardozo L. Rev. 1831 (2011).

61. Laura S. Underkuffler, Odious Discrimination and the Religious Exemption Question, 32 Cardozo L. Rev. 2069, 2090, 2072 (2011).

62. James G. Dwyer, The Good, the Bad, and the Ugly of Employment Division v. Smith for Family Law, 32 Cardozo L. Rev. 1781 (2011).

63. See Douglas Laycock, Afterword, in Same-Sex Marriage and Religious Liberty: Emerging Conflicts 189–190 (Douglas Laycock et al. eds., 2008); and Alan Brownstein, Gays, Jews, and Other Strangers in a Strange Land: The Case for Reciprocal Accommodation of Religious Liberty and the Right of Same-Sex Couples to Marry, 45 U.S.F. L. Rev. 1 (2010).

64. See, e.g., Laycock, Afterword, at 189, 191 (asserting that "[r]eligious minorities and sexual minorities could easily be on the same side" and that "[i]t is all very frustrating" that the groups cannot seem to cooperate).

65. See also Douglas Laycock, A Conscripted Prophet's Guesses about the Future of Religious Liberty in America, in 1 Douglas Laycock, Religious Liberty 445, 452–453 (2010):

> The leaders of the gay rights movement, and the leaders of the evangelical religious movement, both want a total win. They don't want to have to litigate over exceptions; they don't want to risk an occasional loss. It was the gay rights movement that rallied the broader civil rights movement to kill the proposed Religious Liberty Protection Act. There, religious groups offered far more in search of compromise than gay groups offered, but still the religious groups could not pass a bill guaranteeing religious liberty. That experience, and experience in state legislatures, leads me to predict with considerable confidence that there will be gay rights laws with absurdly narrow religious exemptions—perhaps eventually with no exemptions at all—and there will be conservative believers who oppose enactment, resist compliance, and seek exemptions.

66. See, e.g., Michael C. Dorf, Same-Sex Marriage, Second-Class Citizenship, and Law's Social Meanings, 97 Va. L. Rev. 1267, 1314 (2011); Michael Kent Curtis, Be Careful What You Wish For: Gays, Dueling High School T-Shirts, and the Perils of Suppression, 44 Wake Forest L. Rev. 431, 484 (2009); and Sharon E. Rush, Whither Sexual Orientation Analysis? The Proper Methodology When Due Process and Equal Protection Intersect, 16 Wm. & Mary Bill Rights J. 685, 720–721 (2008).

67. See Chapter 1, notes 43–74 and accompanying text.

68. Gabriel A. Almond et al., Strong Religion: The Rise of Fundamentalisms around the World (2003).

69. With reference to the secular liberalism of thinkers like Rawls, Jody Kraus thus explains that "[p]olitical liberalism's preferred strategy is to substitute the idea of reasonableness for truth." Jody S. Kraus, Political Liberalism and Truth, 5 Legal Theory 45, 55 (1999).

70. See supra notes 43–47 and accompanying text.

71. See, e.g., Philip Jenkins, Jesus Wars (2011).

72. See Brad S. Gregory, The Unintended Reformation 84 (2012) (describing the "almost riotous diversity" of beliefs and practices in Christendom on the eve of the Reformation).

73. See Alister McGrath, The Intellectual Origins of the European Reformation 69–121 (1987) (describing the rich diversity of views in late medieval theology).

74. See Michael W. McConnell, The Origins and Historical Understanding of Free Exercise of Religion, 103 Harv. L. Rev. 1409, 1422 (1990).

75. See, e.g., Andrew Koppelman, DOMA, Romer, and Rationality, 58 Drake L. Rev. 923, 942 (2010) (asserting that "[t]he case against same-sex marriage has become increasingly unintelligible, which obviously will have implications when courts go looking for a rational basis for laws that discriminate against gay people") (footnotes omitted).

76. Perry v. Schwarzenegger, 704 F. Supp. 2d 921 (N.D. Cal. 2010).

77. See, e.g., Nelson Tebbe & Deborah A. Widiss, Equal Access and the Right to Marry, 158 U. Penn. L. Rev. 1375, 1443–1449 (2010).

78. The assumption animating the no-endorsement doctrine is that if government endorses religion, it "sends a message to nonadherents that they are outsiders, not full members of the political community, and an accompanying message to adherents that they are insiders, favored members of the political community." Lynch v. Donnelly, 465 U.S. 668, 688 (1984) (O'Connor, J., concurring).

79. In re Marriage Cases, 183 P. 3d 384, 399–401 (Cal. Sup. Ct. 2008).

80. See, e.g., McCreary County v. ACLU, 545 U.S. 844 (2005). Equal protection doctrine makes discriminatory purpose decisive for invalidating facially neutral laws. See, e.g., Washington v. Davis, 426 U.S. 229 (1976).

81. For a careful critical analysis of this proposition, see Heidi M. Hurd & Michael S. Moore, Punishing Hatred and Prejudice, 56 Stan. L. Rev. 1081 (2004).

82. Perry v. Schwarzenegger, 704 F. Supp. 2d, 921, 985 (N.D. Cal. 2010) (Finding 77) (emphasis added).

83. See supra notes 63–65, and accompanying text. See also Chai R. Feldblum, Moral Conflict and Conflicting Liberties, in Same-Sex Marriage and Religious Liberty: Emerging Conflicts 123 (Douglas Laycock et al. eds., 2008).

84. See Sanford Levinson, Compromise and Constitutionalism, 38 Pepp. L. Rev. 821 (2011); Steven D. Smith, Lessons from Lincoln: A Comment on Levinson, 38 Pepp. L. Rev. 915 (2011).

85. Roe v. Wade, 410 U.S. 113 (1973).

86. The decision's attempt at reasoning has been found seriously wanting even by those who support the outcome. See, e.g., Mark Tushnet, Red, White, and Blue: A Critical Analysis of Constitutional Law 54 (1988) (describing the Court's opinion in *Roe* as "an innovation . . . the totally unreasoned judicial opinion").

87. The seminal statement is Herbert Wechsler, Toward Neutral Principles of Constitutional Law, 73 Harv. L. Rev. 1 (1959).

88. Several scholars have appreciated this loss and have proposed, in various ways, an expansion of that space. See Ira C. Lupu & Robert W. Tuttle, Federalism and Faith, 56 Emory L.J. 19 (2006); Mark D. Rosen, The Surprisingly Strong Case for Tailoring Constitutional Principles, 153 U. Pa. L. Rev. 1513 (2005); and Richard C. Schragger, The Role of Local in the Doctrine and Discourse of Religious Liberty, 117 Harv. L. Rev. 1810, 1888–1889 (2004).

89. See Gregory C. Sisk & Michael Heise, "Ideology All the Way Down": An Empirical Study of Establishment Clause Decisions in the Federal Courts, 110 Mich. L. Rev. 1201, 1244–1249 (2012).

90. See, e.g., id. at 1244, 1249–1257 (describing the subjectivity of current doctrine and decisions as "intolerable" and demanding greater formality and predictability).

91. Phillip E. Johnson, Concepts and Compromise in First Amendment Religion Doctrine, 72 Cal. L. Rev. 817, 839 (1984).

92. William P. Marshall, Unprecedential Analysis and Original Intent, 27 Wm. & Mary L. Rev. 925, 929 (1985/1986).

93. I have argued elsewhere that a better way of returning to a "softer" constitutionalism would be through tightening up standing requirements, as recent decisions have done (usually arousing the ire of constitutional scholars). See Steven D. Smith, Nonestablishment, Standing, and the Soft Constitution, 85 St. John's L. Rev. 407 (2011).

94. Christian Legal Society v. Martinez, 130 S. Ct. 2971 (2010).

95. *Martinez* was hardly the first case in which the Court treated a controversy over religion as a free speech case. Perhaps ironically, in an earlier important case, Professor McConnell had prevailed in obtaining funding for a campus Christian newspaper precisely by arguing that given the eligibility of other student publications, the denial of such funding by the University of Virginia was an instance of viewpoint discrimination in violation of the free speech clause. Rosenberger v. Rector, 515 U.S. 819 (1995). Of course, insofar as religion is expressive, there is nothing to prevent it from being regarded under both the free speech clause and the religion clauses.

96. *Martinez*, 130 S. Ct. at 2975.

97. Id. at 2995 n. 27.

98. In the course of the litigation, Hastings interpreted what on its face appeared to be a standard nondiscrimination policy as an "all-comers" policy, such that all groups had to accept all applicants for membership (subject to a few constraints of uncertain scope and meaning).

99. *Martinez*, 130 S. Ct. at 3010 (Alito, J., dissenting).

100. Hosanna-Tabor Evangelical Lutheran Church v. EEOC, 132 S. Ct. 694 (2012).

101. Richard W. Garnett, Do Churches Matter? Toward an Institutional Understanding of the Religion Clauses, 53 Vill. L. Rev. 273, 287 (2008).

102. This exception was upheld against a constitutional challenge in Presiding Bishop v. Amos, 483 U.S. 327 (1987).

103. Tomic v. Catholic Diocese, 442 F.3d 1036 (7th Cir. 2006).

104. See, e.g., Caroline Mala Corbin, Above the Law? The Constitutionality of the Ministerial Exemption from Antidiscrimination Law, 75 Fordham L. Rev. 1965 (2007).

105. See id.; and Ian Bartrum, Religion and Race: The Ministerial Exception Reexamined, 106 Nw. U. L. Rev. Colloquy. 191 (2011) (arguing that the exception should not shield churches against claims of race discrimination). For a list of articles calling for curtailment of the exception, see Christopher C. Lund, In Defense of the Ministerial Exception, 90 N.C. L. Rev. 1, 4 n.6 (2011). As his title suggests, Lund carefully defends the exception.

106. The government acknowledged that religious employers are permitted under federal law to discriminate in employment on the basis of religion. The government also acknowledged that courts should avoid deciding religious questions or excessively entangling themselves in religious matters. Brief for the Federal Respondent.

107. Hosanna-Tabor Evangelical Lutheran Church v. EEOC, 132 S. Ct. 694, 706 (2012).

108. See, e.g., New York State Club Ass. v. City of New York, 487 U.S. 1 (1988); Board of Directors of Rotary International v. Rotary Club, 481 U.S. 537 (1987); Roberts v. United States Jaycees, 468 U.S. 609 (1984). To be sure, the Boy Scouts had prevailed on a freedom of association claim in upholding their right not to employ a gay scoutmaster. Boy Scouts of America v. Dale, 530 U.S. 640 (2000). The relevance of *Dale* was dubious, however, because the Court had not ruled that discrimination based on sexual orientation should prompt "heightened scrutiny" by the courts in the way in which discrimination based on race or sex does.

109. *Hosanna-Tabor Evangelical Lutheran Church*, 132 S. Ct. at 706.

110. Id.

111. For discussion, see Laycock, Sex, Atheism, at 419–422.

112. Id. at 420.

113. Richard W. Garnett, "Things That Are Not Caesar's": The Story of Kedroff v. St. Nicholas Cathedral, in First Amendment Stories (Richard W. Garnett & Andrew Koppelman eds., 2011). Cf. Veli-Matti Karkkainen, An Introduction to Ecclesiology 7 (2002) (observing that "the term *church* for better or worse reasons has been loaded with so many unfortunate connotations from authoritarianism to coercion to antiquarianism").

114. Cf. John Neville Figgis, Churches in the Modern State 101 (1913) ("It was the competing claims of religious bodies, and the inability of any single one to destroy the others, which finally secured liberty.").

115. See Rodney Stark & Roger Finke, Acts of Faith: Explaining the Human Side of Religion (2000).

116. See, e.g., Karkkainen, Introduction to Ecclesiology, at 51–53, 168–169. Cf. Brigham Young, Discourses of Brigham Young 441 (John A. Widtsoe ed., 1976) ("When this Kingdom is organized in any age, the Spirit of it dwells in the hearts of the faithful, while the visible department exists among the people, with laws, ordinances, helps, governments, officers, administrators, and every other appendage necessary for its complete operation to the attainment of the end in view.").

117. See, e.g., 3 Roger Haight, Ecclesial Existence (2008).

118. Gilbert Meilander, The Catholic I Am, First Things, Feb. 2011, 27, 28. For reservations about this position, see Henri de Lubac, The Splendor of the Church 84–102 (Michael Mason trans., 1953).

119. José Casanova explains:

> In one form or another, with the possible exception of Alexis de Tocqueville, Vilfredo Pareto, and William James, the thesis of secularization was shared by all the founding fathers: from Karl Marx to John Stuart Mill, from Auguste Comte to Herbert Spencer, from E. B. Tylor to James Frazer, from Ferdinand Toennies to Georg Simmel, from Emile Durkheim to Max Weber, from Wilhelm Wundt to Sigmund Freud, from Lester Ward to William G. Sumner, from Robert Park to George H. Mead. Indeed, the consensus was such that not only did the theory remain uncontested but apparently it was not even necessary to test it, since everybody took it for granted.

José Casanova, Public Religion in the Modern World 17 (1994).

120. Peter Berger, A Bleak Outlook Is Seen for Religion, New York Times, Feb. 25, 1968, 3.

121. Jacques Maritain, The Things That Are Not Caesar's 31 (J. F. Scanlan trans., 1930).

122. Id. at 24.

Epilogue

1. See, e.g., Ronald Dworkin, Is Democracy Possible Here? 79 (2006); and Kevin Phillips, American Theocracy (2006).
2. James W. Nickel, Who Needs Freedom of Religion?, 76 Colo. L. Rev. 941, 943 (2005).
3. Thomas Paine, The Age of Reason 6, in The Theological Works of Thomas Paine (1794).
4. Id.
5. The right to religious freedom, Madison argued,

   is held by the same tenure with all our other rights. . . . Either, then, we must say that the will of the Legislature is the only measure of their authority, and that in the plenitude of this authority, they may sweep away all our fundamental rights; or, that they are bound to leave this particular right untouched and sacred.

   James Madison, Memorial and Remonstrance against Religious Assessments, reprinted in The Sacred Rights of Conscience 309, 313 (Daniel L. Dreisbach & Mark David Hall eds., 2009).
6. Rajeev Bhargava, Rehabilitating Secularism, in Rethinking Secularism 99 (Craig Calhoun et al. eds., 2011).
7. John Stuart Mill, On Liberty 13, 76 (Stefan Collini ed., 1989) (emphasis added).
8. For discussion, see Steven D. Smith, The Disenchantment of Secular Discourse 70–106 (2010).
9. Quoted in Robert Nisbet, The Twilight of Authority 178 (1975).

Acknowledgments

This book distills themes that I have been writing about for many years now, and there would be no way to list the countless friends, colleagues, and critics who have generously (or sometimes indignantly) helped (or provoked) my thinking through discussion or through comments on previously published work. To all of them, I apologetically offer a general "thank you." However, some names need to be mentioned. Two good friends and colleagues at the University of San Diego, Larry Alexander and Maimon Schwarzschild, have for more than a decade been constant interlocutors on these and countless other subjects. I am indebted as well to Mike Newdow, whose views are in some respects almost the opposite of my own, and who over the years, in a challenging but civil and constructive way, has regularly given me detailed critical reactions to my work on religious freedom. In addition, I should thank the people who specifically commented on all or part of the current book, including Don Drakeman, Chris Eberle, Rick Garnett, Andy Koppelman, Michael Perry, Frank Ravitch, David Sehat, Merina Smith, and George Wright. The first several chapters of the book were presented at the 2012 Annual Law and Religion Roundtable, held at Harvard Law School, and Chapter 5 was presented in a workshop at Brigham Young University and in the 2013 Brandeis lecture at Pepperdine; I am indebted to the various interlocutors who offered suggestions and criticisms in these fora. Erika Oliver helped prepare the index under a short deadline. Thanks and more to all.

Index